A CRITICAL HISTORY OF
THE NEW AMERICAN STUDIES,
1970–1990

RE-MAPPING THE TRANSNATIONAL
A Dartmouth Series in American Studies

SERIES EDITOR
Donald E. Pease
Avalon Foundation Chair of Humanities
Founding Director of the Futures of American Studies Institute
Dartmouth College

The emergence of Transnational American Studies in the wake of the Cold War marks the most significant reconfiguration of American Studies since its inception. The shock waves generated by a newly globalized world order demanded an understanding of America's embeddedness within global and local processes rather than scholarly reaffirmations of its splendid isolation. The series Re-Mapping the Transnational seeks to foster the cross-national dialogues needed to sustain the vitality of this emergent field. To advance a truly comparativist understanding of this scholarly endeavor, Dartmouth College Press welcomes monographs from scholars both inside and outside the United States.

For a complete list of books available in this series, see www.upne.com.

Günter H. Lenz, edited by Reinhard Isensee, Klaus J. Milich, Donald E. Pease, and John Carlos Rowe, *A Critical History of the New American Studies, 1970–1990*

Helmbrecht Breinig, *Hemispheric Imaginations: North American Fictions of Latin America*

Jimmy Fazzino, *World Beats: Beat Generation Writing and the Worlding of U.S. Literature*

Zachary McCleod Hutchins, editor, *Community without Consent: New Perspectives on the Stamp Act*

Kate A. Baldwin, *The Racial Imaginary of the Cold War Kitchen: From Sokol'niki Park to Chicago's South Side*

Yuan Shu and Donald E. Pease, *American Studies as Transnational Practice: Turning toward the Transpacific*

Melissa M. Adams-Campbell, *New World Courtships: Transatlantic Alternatives to Companionate Marriage*

David LaRocca and Ricardo Miguel-Alfonso, editors, *A Power to Translate the World: New Essays on Emerson and International Culture*

Elèna Mortara, *Writing for Justice: Victor Séjour, the Mortara Case, and the Age of Transatlantic Emancipations*

Rob Kroes, *Prison Area, Independence Valley: American Paradoxes in Political Life and Popular Culture*

GÜNTER H. LENZ

A CRITICAL HISTORY OF THE NEW AMERICAN STUDIES, 1970–1990

Edited by Reinhard Isensee,
Klaus J. Milich, Donald E. Pease,
and John Carlos Rowe

DARTMOUTH COLLEGE PRESS
HANOVER, NEW HAMPSHIRE

Dartmouth College Press
An imprint of University Press of New England
www.upne.com

Manufactured in the United States of America
Typeset in Sabon and Scala Sans by Integrated Publishing Solutions

Publication of this book was made possible in part by a generous gift from The Friedrich Ulfers Foundation.

Hardcover ISBN: 978-1-5126-0002-5
Paperback ISBN: 978-1-5126-0003-2
Ebook ISBN: 978-1-5126-0004-9

Library of Congress Cataloging-in-Publication Data available on request
5 4 3 2 1

For Ruth, Christopher,
and Katharina Lenz

CONTENTS

DONALD E. PEASE

SERIES EDITOR'S PREFACE: GÜNTER LENZ'S TRANSCULTURATION OF U.S. AMERICAN STUDIES

FROM ITS BEGINNING, the overarching aim of Günter Lenz's scholarly project was to foster transnational reframings of U.S. American Studies. To realize that aim Lenz devised complex strategies—transculturation, hybridization, and dialogics—that challenged U.S. Americanist scholars in particular to relinquish their privileged positions and take up concepts and strategies that would interconnect the transnational, intercultural process already at work in the United States with networks whose complexity and diversity exceeded the grasp of nationalist discourse.[1]

A tireless advocate of cross-cultural dialogues, Günter Lenz was adept at posing challenging questions to Americanist scholars on both sides of the Atlantic. Lenz asked U.S. Americanists whether they could break the habit of interpreting the work of international scholars as mere paraphrases of their own propositions. He asked German Americanist scholars to consider whether they could mount responsible critiques of U.S. cultural imperialism without asking whether and how their own American Studies programs collaborated with such exploitation.

I first met Günter Lenz in 1989 at Harvard's Center for Literary Studies at a discussion led by Philip Fisher of his introduction to a special issue of *Representations* devoted to the New American Studies.[2] At that seminar, Fisher described the political culture of the United States as unlike that of Europe, because "we have no ideology, and we have no ideology because we lack the apparatus of ideology: a national religion, a unitary system of education under the control of the state, a cultural life and media monopolized by the state by means of ownership and subsidy."[3]

Lenz initiated the conversation that followed Fisher's presentation with a question that he addressed to everyone at the meeting: whether, in the wake of the Cold War, U.S. Americanist scholars might consider abandoning exceptionalist standpoints and begin recognizing a world of multiple and incompatible modernities. Lenz then recommended (to Fisher and everyone else at the Center for Literary Studies Seminar) that our modes of analysis be rethought so as to produce a transcultural and transnational model of American Studies.

Our paths crossed on several subsequent occasions—at meetings of the American Studies Association and the Modern Language Association, and at scholarly conferences in Berlin and Dartmouth. I invited Günter Lenz to publish papers that he had delivered at three of the Dartmouth conferences in works I edited, entitled "Americas Abroad," *The Futures of American Studies*, and *Re-Framing the Transnational Turn in American Studies*.[4] In the remarks that follow I attempt to explain the abiding significance of Günter Lenz's project of transculturation and address what critics of transnational American Studies have singled out for critique: current transnationalism reproduces an exceptionalist logic that runs counter to the initial impetus of undoing it.

From Anti-Americanism to Günter Lenz's Reinvention of Americanization

Fernando Ortiz coined the term "transculturation" to describe the transformative, self-altering processes whereby colonized peoples drew selectively from and imaginatively reinvented cultural materials transported from the metropole. Transculturation differed from practices of acculturation in that it subverted essentialism in all of its forms.[5] To explain the epistemological effects of processes of transculturation, Lenz described the forms of knowledge produced by peripheralized, diasporic, and migrant groups as capable of altering the negative meanings that the metropole had assigned them and subverting the discursive frames of reference to which those meanings had been anchored.

Lenz typically began his account of transculturation with the observation that almost all Western nation-states had drawn and redrawn their territorial boundaries through warfare, the slave trade, imperial expansion, and colonialism. Since the United States and Europe were constructed from the outside in as well as from the inside out, neither European nor U.S. culture could be understood without recognition of the external pressures exerted upon them by processes of decolonization and opposition to imperialism.

To foster such recognition, Lenz constructed a chronotope that brought together two utterly distinct historical moments—the European "discovery" of America at the beginning of the modern era and European antagonism to America at the outset of the "era of globalization." The structure of feeling suffusing Lenz's chronotope was informed by contradictory affective dispositions toward America—as fifteenth-century Europeans' utopian dream and as contemporary Europeans' phobic object. Lenz strategically deployed this structure of feeling and this *longue durée* to diagnose European anti-Americanism as a defense against the processes of cultural creolization accompanying globalization.[6]

According to Lenz, European anti-Americanism was but a recent chapter in the European invention of America as utopian or dystopian. By inventing and reinventing America, Europe was also inventing and reinventing itself. Through the displacement of unwanted economic and cultural initiatives onto U.S. imperialism, Western Europeans attempted to hold onto an imagined cultural heritage that would enable them to avoid recognition of intercultural interactions that exceeded their national boundaries. In an effort to change Europeans' prevailing attitude, Lenz affirmed the state of affairs that some of his fellow Europeans found difficult to acknowledge, that in the era of globalization, European national cultures had become inherently intercultural, multicultural, and transnational.[7]

In "Transnational American Studies: Negotiating Cultures of Difference, Multicultural Identities, Communities, and Border Discourses," Günter Lenz underscored the need to persuade Western nation-states to stop representing "their 'own' culture in clear contradistinction to 'other' cultures. . . . allowing only for selective acculturation by individuals and granting of citizenship" by showing them how to "conceive of their culture as always having been constituted in a 'multicultural' and 'intercultural' manner."[8]

Cultural fields normally achieve self-identity through reference to their positive Other, and they are normally unified through the exclusion of persons and processes associated with a negative Other. But Lenz's transcultural initiatives questioned this transferential model whereby cultures would obtain self-consistency through the dual process of identification with a positive ego-ideal and disidentification from negative Others. According to Lenz, an Americanist field identity is not a fixed position; it is a critical positionality that lives in and through the consciousness of heterogeneity and diversity.

In arguing that American Studies should be understood as a relational field comprising different and intrinsically fluid social formations, Lenz stipulated that the expulsion of the negative Other should not play a role in the facilitation of such transcultural exchanges. Lenz's project deployed a dialogical apparatus that would simultaneously connect and transform German and U.S. multicultural formations through the process Lenz termed "transculturation." In place of validating either U.S. liberal pluralism or German ethno-nationalism, Lenz fostered processes of transculturation that affiliated German with Americanist multicultural anxieties. Lenz held up a German mirror for U.S. Americanists and a U.S. mirror for German Americanists so as to reflect the crises taking place in both national cultures. Lenz then linked these cross-cultural crises with transnational dialogics—what Lenz called "radical recontextualizations"—whose transactions exceeded the appropriative powers of both German and U.S. nationalisms.[9]

Although Lenz described anti-Americanism as a structure of feeling that he wanted brought to an end, Lenz's essays are nevertheless informed by a profound resistance to the processes of Americanization propagated by U.S. American Studies scholars. The transcultural processes Lenz put to work in his scholarship unsettled the concept of Americanness itself. They also suspended the workings of Americanization. Lenz derived the epistemological authority for his project from the production of forms of knowledge that were incompatible with every existing iteration of U.S. American Studies.

Lenz's affective disposition may have originated from entrenched historical memories of postwar "democratic re-education programs" that played an important part in the control that the United States exercised over the processes of political and economic modernization in postwar Germany. Germans who were trained as Americanist scholars through the "Americanization" at work in postwar "democratic re-education" underwent a form of epistemic violence requiring them to identify as the "negative Other" out of whose exclusion the U.S. Americanists who instructed them consolidated their field identities. Lenz's strategies of transculturation subverted the asymmetrical pedagogical structures and dismantled the identificatory structures through which German re-education was putatively achieved.[10] Lenz intended the knowledges that he thereby produced to effect changes in the "culture" of U.S. American Studies. Lenz designated the locus of his revisionary scholarship "American Culture Studies."

Does Lenz's American Culture Studies Have a Method?

As should be clear from this brief account, Lenz's project is informed by a decorum of dual referentialities. Lenz positioned his work at a site in between cultures where he called for dialogical transactions that would necessitate acts of mutual translation to activate meanings and potentialities latent in each of the cultures in dialogue.

Lenz assigned the efficacy of these processes to their capacity to render the participants open to unforeseeable transformations. The agents of these processes subjectivized contradictory and at times antagonistic iterations of formerly subjugated knowledge. Lenz proposed that Americanist scholars regard themselves as nomads who travel physically and mentally across borders so that they might reflect critically upon the ways in which their conceptual paradigms, literary artifacts, and cultural theories continually undergo deterritorializing metamorphoses.

Lenz invented the notion of American Culture Studies to demonstrate the impact of a wide range of discursive formations—British Cultural Studies, the discourse of the borderlands, the critique of U.S. imperialism—on the field of U.S. American Studies. Individually and collectively these discourses produced multicultural and intercultural communities able to redefine the United States from the outside in and to resituate its territories within a global as opposed to strictly hemispheric space.

But the knowledges of the global processes at work in Lenz's American Cultural Studies could not be aligned to any school of American Studies practiced in the United States. Indeed, American Cultural Studies facilitated transcultural relations that posed radical alternatives to three of the core elements of U.S. American Studies: it deterritorialized U.S. American Studies' geographic center, it relativized its interpretive agent, and it pluralized its perspective.[11]

What Lenz calls "American Culture Studies" does not describe a new disciplinary field. The "American Culture" referenced is not reducible to the territorial landmass of the United States; it names the intersemiotic process of global interconnectivity itself.[12] The "studies" of this inherently creolized and creolizing process require a multidimensional methodology that turns the representation of the United States as an imperializing power inside out.[13]

The locus of enunciation for American Culture Studies underwent relocation each time Lenz performed a transcultural transaction. Neither a stable institutional site nor the designation of an area of study, "American Culture Studies" was a placeholder for the cumulative effect of Lenz's transcultural practices.

Rather then subsuming events and processes under an encompassing interpretive framework, Lenz's dialogical method acquired its authority by generating innovative sites of intercultural collaboration and collision.

Because he refused descriptions of the field of American Studies as the research correlative of an imperializing or globalizing state, Lenz also undermined the construction of a nationalistic metadiscourse. The value of American Culture Studies lies precisely in its repudiation of the us against them, here rather than there, at home and abroad dualisms through which the discourse of American exceptionalism had secured U.S. hegemony.[14]

The transcultural processes at work in American Culture Studies inspired Lenz to proffer the following definition of the transformed hegemon: "American culture is not the homogeneous, powerful globalizing Other, but it is in itself multiplicitous, inherently differentiated and conflicted, and always changing in active response to alternative multicultural and intercultural experiences and discourses."[15]

Günter Lenz's theories of transculturation called for Americanists everywhere to become involved in open-ended, critical, multifocal dialogues. Because Lenz's dialogical imagination constitutes the precondition for formations of transnational American Studies that do not replicate versions of American exceptionalism, we need Günter Lenz's vision now more than ever.

JOHN CARLOS ROWE

INTRODUCTION

GÜNTER H. LENZ (1940–2012) was one of the leading scholars of American Studies in Germany. He was born in Braunschweig on February 7, 1940, grew up in Frankfurt, and completed his undergraduate studies in English and American Literature and Culture, German Literature, Philosophy, and Sociology at Johann Wolfgang Goethe University in Frankfurt am Main, where he also completed his PhD (1968) with a dissertation titled *S. T. Coleridge's Theory of Poetry: The Paradigmatic Role of the Concept of the Imagination in Romantic Poetics.* For more than two decades (1972–93), he was Professor of American and English Studies at Johann Wolfgang Goethe University. In 1993, he accepted the position of Professor of American Literary and Cultural Studies at the Humboldt University in Berlin, a position he held until his retirement from the university in 2005. During his career, he received many distinctions, notably the American Studies Association's Bode-Pearson Award for Lifetime Achievement in 1999. Lenz was the first foreign recipient of this award.

In addition to his doctoral dissertation (published in 1970), Lenz published sixty-four scholarly essays between 1972 and 2011 and edited or coedited twelve volumes between 1977 and 2006.[1] He was an active participant in the transformation of American Studies as a discipline from the predominant myth-and-symbol school approach of the 1960s and 1970s to the New American Studies of the 1980s and 1990s. Johann Wolfgang Goethe University is famous for its Institute for Social Research, whose faculty in the interwar years constituted the core of the Frankfurt school of critical theorists. Their leftist critiques of social, cultural, economic, and political phenomena had a profound influence on Lenz, who was also committed to continuing the legacy of the 1930s U.S. Left. Lenz's own work follows a clear genealogy from both the German and U.S. leftist traditions and looks for their complementarities in the most influential critical theories of his own generation: structuralism, poststructuralism, postcolonial studies, ethnic studies, minority discourse, and feminism.

Like such leading figures of the Frankfurt school as Theodor Adorno, Walter Benjamin, and Max Horkheimer, Lenz understood cultural work to be a crucial index of social, economic, and political conditions. Rejecting a conventional Marxian distinction between the economic base and social superstructure, Lenz followed the revisionary Marxist ideas that today we identify with post- or neo-Marxian theory and that are usually distinguished from political communism and affiliated with Western socialism. Lenz's radical criticism followed no specific orthodoxy, in part because he understood the new, postmodern conditions manifest in First World nations in the postwar era. Culture is a productive "industry," as Horkheimer and Adorno had argued persuasively in *The Dialectic of Enlightenment* (1947), alarmed and fascinated by what they witnessed in the United States after fleeing Nazi terror in Germany.[2] These new social, economic, and global conditions required new theories and methods to understand phenomena that did not fit the traditional Marxist interpretations of industrial economies and their social formations.

Lenz brought to this work an extraordinary transnational perspective, influenced by the cosmopolitanism of Frankfurt school theory, his own wide reading in European theory and American Studies, and his frequent studies abroad: as a university student at the University of Bristol in England (1964–65), Research Fellow of the American Council of Learned Societies at Yale University (1974–75), Visiting Professor of English at the University of Wisconsin, Milwaukee (Fall 1984), Research Resident at the Humanities Research Institute of the University of California, Irvine (Fall 1989 and Winter 1990), Visiting Professor at the University of California, Santa Cruz (Winter 1995), Harris Professor of German at Dartmouth College (2010–11), and a frequent visiting professor at other European universities, especially through the Erasmus Program. Active in the American Studies Association and the German Association for American Studies, in both of which organizations he held numerous administrative positions, Lenz was a transnational scholar in theory and practice.

Lenz's transnational perspective is not unique among his generation of postwar German Americanists. Along with Heinz Ickstadt, Winfried Fluck, Helmbrecht Breinig, Berndt Ostendorf, Hartmut Isernhagen, the late Lothar Bredella, and many others, Lenz transformed American Studies in Germany from a field shaped by U.S. intellectual and political agendas to a discipline with its own distinctive understanding of U.S. and

Western Hemispheric relations. Although still focused primarily on the United States, German American Studies is often situated in "North American Studies" institutes that consider Canada central to their work. Many of us who were committed to comparative American Studies learned intellectual and institutional lessons from our German colleagues. Unlike the immediate postwar situation in Germany in which U.S. Information Service "German-American Houses" sponsored U.S. visitors and cultural events, many of which were difficult to distinguish from U.S. state propaganda, German American Studies in the 1970s sought its own institutional and intellectual agenda.

Like many of his colleagues in American Studies on both sides of the Atlantic, Lenz was shaped profoundly by the historical events of the late 1960s and early 1970s. In this period, "New Left" activism developed around the world as a consequence of continuing social injustice, the growing disparity of First World wealth and Third World poverty, and the endless "little wars," especially in Southeast Asia, during the Cold War. Caught between the neoimperialism of the capitalist U.S. and communist Soviet Union, civil, anticolonial, feminist, gay, indigenous, and ethnic rights movements coalesced as alternatives to the state and its governmentality. Such groups gained public attention not only through massive public demonstrations but also by means of strategic uses of cultural media. In Germany, these issues revolved around the promise of postwar social democracy and greater opportunity for all in the face of new capitalist inequities blamed by many on Germany's dependence on the United States. The Cold War was a daily reality for Germans living in a divided nation, which many thought would never be reunited, and the threat of nuclear annihilation was equally tangible for people living in heavily militarized West and East Germany. Both West Germany and East Germany were effectively colonized nations, proving grounds for U.S. and Soviet imperial aggression.

Lenz's scholarly career is defined by his effort to define a leftist intellectual position that would be responsive to the new, changing relations of postwar Europe and the United States. For him and other German intellectuals on the left, transnational coalitions were possible with ethnic minorities, women, the working class, and colonized subalterns, not with the state powers that for so long had trumpeted their successful political alliances and economic ties. As class divisions, women's rights, and immigrant communities, especially composed of Turkish *Gastarbeiter*, became central political issues in West Germany and as East Germany's socialism failed politically and economically, a leftist counterculture to Marxist orthodoxy and laissez-faire capitalism offered options to many people inside and outside the academy.

Within the increasingly globalized academy, however, Left-intellectual positions were not so easily articulated and defended. European structuralism's theoretical authority overlapped with modernization projects that included the rise of fascism in Germany, Italy, and Spain. German Communists and Frankfurt school neo-Marxists had been targets of the Nazis, many murdered in the Holocaust or driven out of Germany. In the immediate postwar years, anti-Communism in the United States caused the Frankfurt school to survive primarily in the works of individual scholars, not as a coherent movement. "Red scares" in the 1920s in the United States, news of the Stalinist purges in the 1930s in the Soviet Union, and McCarthyism in the Cold War had caused the Communist Party of the USA (CPUSA) to lose all political authority.[3] The "New Left" movements of the late 1960s in the United States were often characterized by their rejection of "Old Left" ideology. In the same period, new intellectual movements, including poststructuralism, challenged the fundamental economic, social, and political categories of the traditional Left.

Günter Lenz was one of the few intellectuals in American Studies to insist upon the continuing relevance of the Old Left to New Left activist and scholarly work. Whereas second-wave feminists insisted on the marginalization of gender issues and African American activists complained that race had been ignored by the CPUSA, Lenz recognized that the radical work of the 1930s Left in the United States had treated issues of race and gender as integral with class. Long before Michael Denning's pioneering work, *The Cultural Front* (1996), Lenz recognized the multiple ways Left intellectuals in the 1930s had challenged the dominant values of the U.S. capitalist economy and political state.[4] Denning interprets the radicalism of the 1930s Left not only in terms of its efforts to organize labor and shape electoral politics, but also in the broader contexts of cultural work that would transform U.S. attitudes toward issues of race, class, and gender. What survives from the U.S. Left of the 1930s is what we still find relevant in the Frankfurt school's writings from the 1930s to 1960s: an anticipation of the postindustrial, postmodern social and economic conditions shaping our daily lives in inescapable ways from roughly 1970 to the present.

Poststructuralism relies on the claim that there is nothing outside the text, that everything of human significance is irreducibly a representation, whose system of signification, or semiotics, relies on a language whose grammar has only the appearance of "naturalness" and "reality."

Everything is socially and thus linguistically constructed. Because both society and language change historically, our access to the meanings of such representations is irreducibly historical. The consequences of this theoretical insight for the large issues of human existence are by no means self-evident, but one result is ineluctable: political change must take into account such conditions of human representation. Lenz worked to reconcile the basic claims of poststructuralism with the radical critiques of the 1930s in the United States and the Frankfurt school in Germany, as well as with the traditional aims of American Studies to "understand" the United States.

As Lenz recognizes, American Studies grew out of critiques by scholars like F. O. Matthiessen and Caroline Ware in the 1930s and 1940s of the failure of the United States to achieve its democratic promise, but the discipline remained bound to the consensus model of studying the nation. Unprepared for the radical critiques of the 1960s and 1970s, American Studies relied on the myth-and-symbol school to study the coherence of the United States rather than its emerging characteristics as a multiculture. Although Lenz is always careful to defend the best scholars of the myth-and-symbol school from the accusation that this approach merely reinforced U.S. ideology, he understands the inherent problem of the method as its inability to account for categorical differences. Insofar as poststructuralism theorized "difference," following Ferdinand de Saussure's pioneering claim that "in language there are only differences *without positive terms*," deconstruction and other procedures identified with poststructuralism seemed to Lenz to be crucial means of theorizing the social differences fundamental to the United States.[5] Today Lenz's move from the "consensus" history to what we now recognize as "dissensus," to borrow Sacvan Bercovitch's term, or "multiculturalism" seems self-evident, necessary, and fully motivated by the changing social realities of the United States.[6] But American Studies scholars resisted deeply and powerfully challenges to the consensus history that by the 1970s was institutionally fundamental to the discipline.

We should not forget how antitheoretical myth-and-symbol school scholars were to the revolutionary ideas that influenced both U.S. intellectuals and political activists between 1970 and 1990. Poststructuralism and the Frankfurt school were not the only "imported" approaches that were often met by American Studies scholars with arguments in defense of their own "native" and "exceptionalist" approaches. American feminism in the 1970s was deeply divided over the value of the Continental feminisms of such poststructuralists as Luce Irigaray, Hélène Cixous, and

Julia Kristeva. African American scholars argued about the validity of Afrocentrist theories introduced in the early 1960s, and Chicano activists insisted on the relevance of postcolonial and "Third World" revolutionary theories for their own national agendas.[7] This antitheoretical bias is particularly evident in Henry Nash Smith, Leo Marx, and Richard Slotkin's reassessments of their work in Bercovitch and Jehlen's 1986 collection, *Ideology and Classic American Literature.*[8]

Lenz typically avoids the most adversarial aspects of the arguments for and against the myth-and-symbol school, stressing instead the continuities he can trace from the 1930s radical critique through the social protest of the 1960s New Left to the multicultural debates of the 1980s. He is interested in the genealogy of leftist theory and practice that have adapted to new historical circumstances and have revised key concepts to meet new social conditions. Rather than position himself as a disciple of any theoretical position or advocate of traditional American Studies, Lenz draws on the best of each tradition to find an appropriate method of interpretation and to identify the most appropriate hermeneutic objects. It seems to me this merely describes the work of sensible scholarship, especially in historically evolving contexts. And that is precisely what distinguishes the scholarly work of Günter Lenz as a practical cultural critic and theorist.

After he retired from the Humboldt University in 2005, Lenz was preparing a book-length study of the transformation of the field of American Studies in the crucial decades from 1970 to 1990. As a commentator on, contributor to, and participant in these intellectual and institutional changes in his field, he was well situated to offer other scholars a comprehensive and balanced interpretation of that crucial era. Building on essays he wrote in the midst of these changes, he intended to show how the revolution in theory, the emergence of postmodern socioeconomic conditions, the increasing globalization of everyday life, and postcolonial responses to continuing and new forms of colonial domination had transformed American Studies as a discipline focused on the distinctive qualities of the United States to a field encompassing the many different "Americas" and Canada in the Western Hemisphere, as well as how this complex region influenced and was interpreted by the rest of the world. In tracking the shift of American Studies from its exceptionalist bias to its unmanageable global responsibilities, Lenz wanted to show the crucial roles played by different, still foundational theories developed first by the U.S. Left in the 1930s, the Frankfurt school in Germany and elsewhere between 1930 and 1960, Continental poststructuralism, neo-Marxism, and postcolonialism.

The present volume consists of edited chapters of Lenz's proposed book. In addition to an introduction, Lenz planned six chapters and a conclusion. He had drafted five of the six chapters at the time of his death in 2012. Although the sixth, "Minority Discourses: Feminist Criticism and African-American Criticism," was never written, the subjects that were to be addressed are widely represented in Lenz's published essays. The unfinished manuscript posed a number of editorial problems, including Lenz's different plans for the contents. Two of the editors, Donald Pease and Klaus Milich, had encouraged Lenz to decide on the best contents, begin revisions, and write the missing sections and chapters. Unfortunately, Lenz never decided which contents would be best. Lenz's former doctoral student, Klaus Milich, was instrumental in collecting manuscripts for all of the planned contents, digitizing those manuscripts surviving only in print format, and sharing these materials with the four editors.

Such editorial projects are time-consuming and difficult to accomplish in the midst of other responsibilities, especially when four people are involved. In 2014, I assumed responsibility for the textual editing of the manuscript, subject to the approval of my colleagues in this project. Therefore, as textual editor of this volume I decided to include in place of the proposed sixth chapter an essay that Lenz had published earlier. This essay, which appears as chapter 6 in this volume, "Cultural Hybridity and Diaspora in African American Literature and Criticism: Fictions of a Postmodern Multiculturalism," first published in 2000 in Utz Riese, ed., *Kontaktzone Amerika: Literarische Verkehrsformen kultureller Übersetzung* (Heidelberg: Carl Winter), 73–108, well represents Lenz's interpretation of minority discourse and African American feminism in the 1980s and 1990s. In the other drafted chapters, Lenz had left sections to be completed later. In chapter 2, "New Historicism, New American Exceptionalism, and New American Studies: Versions of a New Synthesis," Lenz had planned a section on the work of Richard Poirier's *The Renewal of Literature: Emersonian Reflections* (1987) to complement his discussions of George Kateb's and Stanley Cavell's uses of the Transcendentalists to redefine American Studies.[9] He had also planned a conclusion for this chapter. In chapter 3, "American Studies and Literary and Cultural Critique: The Question of Radical Traditions," Lenz had planned sections on F. O. Matthiessen, Caroline Ware, Henry Nash Smith, and Leo Marx, as well as a section on Sacvan Bercovitch's *The Rites of Assent* (1993). In chapter 4, "American Cultural Critique: Toward a Politics of Postmodernism and Postcolonial Discourse," he had planned a concluding section entitled "Postcolonial Discourse, African-American Postmodernism, and Subaltern Studies: Cornel West and Gayatri Spivak." In chapter 5, "Postmodern Anthropology, Multicultural Critique, and American Culture Studies," he intended to conclude with a section entitled "American Culture Studies: Institutionalizing and Teaching Multicultural Critique." Lenz's list of publications provides a variety of essays that address all of these topics, and I speculate that it was his intention to gather these published essays, edit and revise them, and add new material to complete the missing sections mentioned in this paragraph. Rather than make an educated guess about how to fill these missing sections in the book, I decided simply to edit what has survived as part of the planned book, with the exception of my editorial decision to substitute a single published essay for the missing chapter 6.

Had he completed his book, Lenz would have told his version of the scholarly transformation of American Studies from a discipline committed to the unique qualities of the "American experience" into a transnational field committed to the study of the United States in its Western Hemispheric and global relations. Such a narrative would have carried us from the 1930s U.S. Left to the second decade of the twenty-first century, and it would have required new work Lenz had not yet written when he completed the plan for this book. What we have in the book I have edited is a fascinating account of the emergence of the new American Studies between 1970 and 1990, two of the three decades in which Lenz was an active participant in the metamorphosis of a field from the provincial study of U.S. nationalism to the comparative, transnational field that we have today. Lenz did not suggest a title for his proposed book, so I have offered "A Critical History of the New American Studies, 1970–1990" as a descriptive placeholder. Presumptuous as it is for me to offer any title, I think this one well serves Lenz's purposes in this book. To be sure, this unfinished manuscript does not offer us a conventional or comprehensive history of the new American Studies, even in this period. Nevertheless, it reads effectively as an account of how this field changed and of transformations we somewhat dimly recall in the absence of more definitive accounts.

Histories of these scholarly and institutional changes will be written, but at the moment we have little more than our own anecdotal accounts. When I recall "what happened," I often forget the intellectual struggles and debates Lenz recounts so well as he interprets Fredric Jameson's efforts to reconcile Marxist theories with poststructuralism and Edward Said's negotiation of the boundaries between poststructuralism and postcolonial studies. Until I began editing Lenz's manuscript, I had forgotten utterly Philip Fisher's special issue of *Representations* on the New American Studies and how the very name itself involved a defense of American exceptionalism. Gerald Graff's academic work and Christopher Lasch's work as a public intellectual did indeed shape the debates about multicultural America that in the 1980s came to be known as the "culture wars" during which the barriers of the ivory tower were pulled down forever.

When I was asked to write a memorial essay in honor of Edward Said for *American Quarterly*, I had barely thought of Said's contributions to American Studies, other than a handful of essays he had written on American authors.[10] Günter Lenz knew long ago that Said was a powerful, transformative figure in the field of American Studies, not just as an influential public intellectual in U.S. culture. Lenz understood well in advance of Jameson's *Postmodernism, Or, the Logic of Late Capitalism* (1991) that Jameson made it impossible to think about the United States apart from its global circulation and international military, political, and economic ventures. Lenz also knew that Jacques Derrida's deconstruction was not just an imported philosophical "fashion," but an approach that had deep appeal and powerful significance for the study of the United States and indeed any postcolonial society defined by its differences rather than homogeneity. Add to this list of impressive contributions to our understanding of how American Studies changed between 1970 and 1990 Lenz's account of the new anthropology. Today we take for granted how the highly self-conscious anthropological work of James Clifford, Paul Rabinow, George Marcus, Marilyn Strathern, Elizabeth Meese, and Michael M. J. Fischer influenced postcolonial theories and American Studies in a period when folklore and ethnography were under increasing attack for their complicity in Western imperial projects.

Günter Lenz did not live to finish the book he wanted to publish on the transformation of the field of American Studies, but what he has written and did plan provides valuable insights into the recent past and the ongoing present of the New American Studies. It is indeed a "critical history," because it recounts so much of what we have forgotten and need today more than ever to manage the vastly expanded responsibilities of our discipline.

A Personal Recollection

I met Günter Lenz thirty years ago, in June 1986, at a conference organized by Winfried Fluck and Heinz Ickstadt at Konstanz University on the topic "Revising American Literary History." I was transforming my own work then from that of a poststructuralist critic to that of a "new materialist," neo-Marxian critic. In my agonistic paper on Melville's *Pierre*, the rack on which so many American literary scholars have been broken, Lenz must have recognized a kindred intellectual, struggling with similar issues. We became friends at that conference and together participated in an extraordinary series of professional and personal events, including the many conferences to which he invited me in Frankfurt and then in Berlin. We met almost every year in the twenty-five years of our friendship, making sure to find time at the annual American Studies Association convention to talk, have dinner, and inevitably attend the incoming president's address. He would not miss the event, no matter how hard I tried to play hooky.

Günter joined the research group I organized on the topic "The Work of Intellectuals" at the University of California's Humanities Research Institute in the fall of 1989, and during his residence in California, my wife, Kristin, and I got to know the entire family: Günter's wife, Ruth, and their two children, Christopher and Katharina. The Lenz family loved Laguna Beach and returned as often as they could, including on several occasions when Günter taught in the University of California, Irvine's Summer Masters in English program. On the occasion of his sixtieth birthday celebration at the Humboldt University, I gave Günter and Ruth a week's vacation at our log cabin in southeastern Idaho, near Yellowstone National Park. Dedicated to his undergraduate, graduate, and former students, Günter rarely took time off from the endless tasks of reading theses, writing recommendations, grading papers and exams. He chose to take this rare vacation at the end of a period of teaching in Irvine's summer program, and I recall his adamant refusal to leave the cabin and visit Yellowstone until he had graded all of his papers. But when he did finish grading the last paper, he turned with youthful joy to witness the herds of American Bison, elk, moose, and trumpeter swans in the Park.

Günter Lenz left Frankfurt University for the Humboldt University only four years after *die Wende*, after the collapse of the old German Democratic Republic and the destruction of the Berlin Wall dividing the city and the nation. He was one of several West German academics who had been chosen to reinvent the old East German universities and coordinate them with West German higher education. Everyone who knows Günter knows how generously and humanely he conducted this crucial work, enabling advanced graduate students and young faculty members in particular to make a difficult transition. Günter put these younger scholars in contact with a network of intellectuals from which they had been barred by the political isolation of the German Democratic Republic. He helped many who had been abandoned by their own mentors. He read, corrected, and supported their work, and he wrote recommendations for them for grants and academic positions. Today, there are numerous scholars at work in German and other universities around the world who were helped and supported by Günter Lenz. When I meet them, we always talk about Günter first and last. They are his great legacy.

His greatest legacy remains his loving family. He was fortunate to attend Christopher and Keiko's marriage in Berlin. His daughter, Katharina, and her husband, Micha, have a beautiful baby girl, Valeska, born three years ago, also in Berlin. And Günter's dear wife, Ruth Weisshaupt Lenz, a talented teacher of music and theater and a fiercely independent Swiss, still lives in Berlin close to their growing family.

A CRITICAL HISTORY OF THE NEW AMERICAN STUDIES, 1970–1990

[1]

AFTER DECONSTRUCTION: RECONSTRUCTING AMERICAN LITERARY AND CULTURAL STUDIES IN THE 1980S

Traveling Theory and the Repoliticization of American Criticism

Late in 1985, the French critic Tzvetan Todorov began his review essay of his American colleague Robert Scholes's new book, *Textual Power: Literary Theory and the Teaching of English* in the London *Times Literary Supplement* with the following statement:

> When a foreigner visiting France asks me, "What's going on in French criticism these days?" I always feel rather stupid; I either remain silent or else change the subject. I am unaware of the trends, being familiar with a certain number of individuals following paths that have no obvious connection with one another. Conversely, in the United States, where I spend only a few weeks a year, I have the impression of observing a coherent picture, and would have no difficulty in responding to the same question.[1]

Todorov realizes that his unified picture of American literary criticism is made possible by the geographic distance—"being no longer a participant but a visitor"—and he knows that this distance also has its drawbacks in any effort to grasp fully what has been going on, but he reads Scholes's book as a corroboration of his own understanding of the critical scene in the United States in the mid-1980s. He considers the new tendencies in American criticism to exhibit a "drastic discontinuity," "post-structuralism," making the traditional question of the New Criticism and of structuralism—"What does this text mean?"—"wholly irrelevant." In Todorov's analysis "post-structuralism" is of two sorts, "deconstruction" and "pragmaticism," each of which answers the traditional question of meaning with a "Nothing" or an "Anything," respectively. Todorov finds both deconstruction and pragmaticism characterized by "dogmatism," "excess," "exaggeration," and "insurmountable aporias"; he accuses them of "lumping everything together" and presenting "empirically false and logically contradictory hypotheses." In spite of their theoretical and rhetorical divergences, he sees them united in their common enemies ("universal values, justice and ethics on the one hand; truth, knowledge and science on the other") and affinities ("praise of force," "subjective idealism"). Even the dissenting forms of criticism that set out to provide a polemical alternative to "this school of criticism," particularly Marxism, are read by Todorov as being part of a unified picture, as establishing no "radical opposition" to "post-structuralism": "Above and beyond their minor disagreements, both are fighting a common enemy, and that enemy's name is humanism." Therefore, it is possible to account for the recent repoliticization in American criticism and see "why there have been so many attempts to hybridize these two apparently hostile schools of thought" ("AAH," 1094).

From Todorov's perspective, then, a totally "coherent picture" of the contemporary critical scene in the United States arises that acknowledges neither any alternative positions in American criticism nor any qualitative changes since French poststructuralism began to dominate leading American critics. He presents French poststructuralism, American deconstruction and pragmaticism, and Marxism as homogenized movements of "schools" that are united in their "anti-humanism": "If we wish to call a spade a spade, we must conclude that the dominant tendency of American criticism is anti-humanism" ("AAH," 1094). Todorov's wholesale indictment of contemporary American criticism does not allow him to reconstruct his own alternative position, "a critical humanism," in any historical manner. Instead, he simply opts for a strategy of forgetting, of repressing a bad dream: "What I would hope, without really believing it possible, is that this whole unfortunate episode of contemporary criticism be rapidly forgotten, in order that we might make a new departure from the former conception of criticism" ("AAH," 1094).

Todorov's sweeping critique raises some general questions of theory and of patterns of influence between cultures. Only if we seriously address the problems of intercultural (mis)understanding, of the appropriation and transformations of theoretical models, concepts, and strategies of one country in the light and context of the indigenous traditions, cultural institutions, and critical demands of the other society can we achieve some kind of working knowledge in the international debate on the objectives and methods of literary theory and cultural criticism. As a society and a culture are never homogeneous, or totally unified, and never "equitemporal" in their constituent parts, we have to allow for tensions, plurality, heterogeneity, discontinuities, displacements, and indeterminacies that continually press for unity, continuity, and totality but question, suspend, redefine, and subvert this drive at the same time. It is with these critical observations in mind that we have to reassess the politics of traveling theory and the repoliticization in American literary criticism.

If the 1970s and early 1980s were characterized by a serious crisis of radical cultural criticism from the Left and by a deconstruction of all the traditional foundations and strategies of critical discourse, by the mid-1980s the time seemed to have come for a critical account of the consequences and the perspectives for the future, for a "provisional reconstruction," as Ihab Hassan put it in an essay.[2] Reconstruction, or redefinition, however, turns out to be a very difficult task. If we want to avoid the trap of a superficial synthesis or a harmonization of oppositions, contradictions, or difference, we must first try to become fully aware of the conflicts that have dominated the crisis and the deconstruction of earlier forms of criticism. This is especially the case in any reassessment of the interaction between Western European philosophical, social, and cultural thought and literary and cultural criticism in the United States. Particularly the recent demands for, and efforts at, a repoliticization of criticism, of a renewed emphasis on the social and political construction or deconstruction of knowledge and discourse, must fail if one form of thought or one national tradition is valorized against another as more "political" or more "radical" and if isolated aspects or concepts of different intellectual and/or national contexts are reassembled in order to overcome the feeling of disorientation and political frustration.

In this chapter I will, therefore, address some of the patterns of influence, of appropriation, of misunderstanding, and of recontextualization that have been at work in the American response to French poststructuralist thought and to West German and English neo-Marxism. I will not offer another European jeremiad on the dismal fate of radical European thought, or theory, in the United States, but will take up some of the assessments, explanations, and critical demands suggested by American philosophers and critics themselves in recent years concerning traveling theory and indicate some problems in the current reconstruction of (radical) cultural and literary criticism in the United States.

Deconstruction and Neo-Marxism in America: Patterns of Misunderstanding and Domestication

Concerning deconstruction, several philosophers and critics, including Rodolphe Gasché, Samuel Weber, and Andreas Huyssen, have shown that

American literary critics have misunderstood Derrida's notion of "deconstruction." By applying a strategy that was "developed in the course of a philosophical discussion bearing upon fundamental tendencies of Western thought in general, and in particular upon the specific form these tendencies took in Husserlian phenomenology and in the thought of Heidegger," to "their regional science of literary criticism," by transferring it into the realm of the discipline of literary criticism, they have falsely turned it into a "method of interpretation."[3] As Rodolphe Gasché argued in his essay "Deconstruction as Criticism" (1979): "The critical malaise of modern critics that makes them long for a 'beyond-deconstruction' and simultaneously allows the attacks of the rear-guard, stems in the first place from a mutual misunderstanding of the notion of deconstruction. It is precisely this misinterpretation that makes its accommodation by American criticism possible, and, by the same token, transforms it into a mechanical exercise similar to academic thematism or formalism."[4]

Though true, this critique clearly can be only a first step in our argument. As this "misunderstanding" has been so pervasive, "too insistent and widespread" (Samuel Weber), the question is, why was deconstruction so quickly and easily assimilated by American literary criticism in spite of its explicit rejection of any traditional disciplinary or methodological claims?

Samuel Weber convincingly argues that the theoretical preoccupations of American literary studies made them particularly receptive to a "theory" that focused on the interpretive power of language:

> By virtue of a practice that consists essentially in reading, informed by the New Criticism and involving the remarking of significant relations within and between texts, North American literary studies were particularly positioned to see in "deconstruction" a confirmation of previous practice and a legitimation of future value. To implement this latter goal, all that was required was to construe the relation of deconstruction to philosophy as one of essential negativity, as the overcoming of philosophy, in order for deconstruction to emerge as a valorization of literature and of literary criticism, as they had been previously understood and practiced here. ["AE," 235]

What had been conceived as a critique of philosophical discourse in general and of disciplinary boundaries could thus be transformed by American literary critics into "a new, global, and undifferentiated Science of Textuality or Method of Deconstruction" that failed to "deconstruct" its own institutional context ("AE," 235).

Therefore, the critique of the misunderstanding, transformation, and appropriation in terms of methodology easily blends into a critique in terms of politics and depoliticization. Maria Ruegg has suggested that Derrida's deconstruction and American deconstructionist literary criticism share common—in her view, false—traditional assumptions about the meaning and function of literature, namely that both "deny history" and are "conservative" in their political implications,[5] a critique even more forcefully argued by orthodox Marxists. But most literary critics on the left *contrast* the "radicalism" of French poststructuralism with its "domestication" in the United States. Frank Lentricchia, for one, insists on the radical potential of French poststructuralism and finds Derrida's deconstruction "profoundly historical in its operations and concerns." If Derrida's historical and political concerns remain general and unspecific, Foucault—in Lentricchia's reading—complements these shortcomings in his work on social institutions and power. In contrast to French poststructuralism, American (or Yale) deconstructionist literary criticism is characterized, as Lentricchia tries to prove in *After the New Criticism*, by an "ahistoricism" that empties its work of radical political implications.[6]

What these political critiques amount to is the thesis that French poststructuralism has been domesticated, incorporated, and depoliticized in American academia. Ironically, as Gerald Graff and Edward W. Said have argued from different political perspectives, forms of radical thought that have questioned both the orthodox Marxist Left and the academic institution and that represented a "bold interventionary movement across lines of specialization" have been "displaced" and appropriated in American consumer capitalist society by the "ethic of professionalism" as elitist critical methods within the traditional boundaries of literary criticism, isolating and canonizing "textuality."[7]

If French poststructuralism has been domesticated and depoliticized in America, the same is said about the use of European neo-Marxism. Edward Said sees American "Left" criticism as part of a profoundly accommodationist academia that robs European Marxist criticism of its political interventionist quality (*WTC*, 158–77). The English Marxist critic Terry Eagleton acknowledges the power of Jameson's or Lentricchia's radical criticism, but accuses these writers of political "unclarity," lingering "pragmatism," and "eclecticism" that transforms Marxism into academic work and interpretive strategies. Cornel West, from an explicitly Marxist point of view, criticizes Jameson's work for being too "theoretical," too "abstract," for "domesticating" Marxism, for having "no political consequences."[8]

Now, what are the reasons for and implications of this process of domestication and depoliticization? Concerning the enormous success of

French poststructuralism during the late 1970s and early 1980s, one reason clearly was that it was critical of Marxism (of the orthodox kind), or "History" as a "grand narrative" of legitimation (Lyotard), of the politics of criticism that had dominated the 1960s and early 1970s (and their use of the Frankfurt school or of the New Left). It seemed to provide a form of criticism that was radical, disruptive, and without politically revolutionary demands and that could radicalize the homegrown tradition of the New Criticism and its interpretative strategies in terms of paradox, irony, tension, ambiguity, and the like, as characteristic qualities of the work of literature and/or literary language. Derrida's celebrated statement, "There is nothing outside of the text (*il n'y a pas de hors-texte*)," and his privileging of "writing" seemed to offer a radical solution to the crisis of literature and literary criticism during the 1960s and valorize the "self-deconstructive" quality of literature and the "answerable style" of literary criticism (Geoffrey Hartman) over traditional philosophical and scientific discourse. Ironically, the "radical appropriation" of deconstruction to literary criticism, sometimes in the philosophical vein of a negative metaphysics, not only was a misreading of Derrida's reasoning, but contained his far more radical questioning of the powers of language, textuality, writing, and history.[9]

The impact of European (neo-)Marxism on the American critical scene has been more contradictory. After the contemptuous rejection of the forms of Marxist or (old) leftist literary criticism of the American 1930s during the postwar decades, the New Left and the student movement of the 1960s seemed to easily absorb neo-Marxist thought in their critique of dominant American society and culture (including the New Criticism). This direct adoption of European Marxist thought in American literary and cultural criticism, however, turned out to be short-lived and often more a matter of moral or political commitment than of critical reflection. Fredric Jameson pointed out, in *Marxism and Form* (1971), that dialectical thinking is "hostile" to the Anglo-American tradition in thought. As the dialectical critic, therefore, can rely neither on a viable native tradition of dialectical thinking nor on a substantial Marxist intelligentsia in the United States, he will not only have to fight against the predominant American tradition, but also have to mediate European Marxist thought with the American context and critical tradition.[10] Clearly, this process of mediation has often led to a loss of the critical, historical, dialectical dimensions or was not pursued in any consistent manner, as Edward W. Said has pointed out in his "Reflections on American 'Left' Literary Criticism" (1979), but even where this very difficult move of revision and reformulation was attempted, it could easily be seen as a "domestication" of the political thrust of Marxism (*WTC*, 166–68).

The Dialectics of Traveling Theory in America

Unless we want to read the transformation of European social and cultural thought by American critics simply in terms of misunderstanding or misinterpretation that could in principle be "corrected," we need, then, a more general framework for analyzing the patterns of influence or interaction between theories of different countries or times. In his essay "Traveling Theory," Edward W. Said talks of a "discernible and recurrent pattern to the movement of the transplantation, transference, circulation, and commerce of theories and ideas," namely "three or four stages common to the way any theory or idea travels" (*WTC*, 226). Said does not talk of theory or ideas in the sense of the combination of concepts and items that can be (re)assembled in different ways and "used" with different political intentions and results. What Said has in mind is the complex constellation and process of critical thought in particular historical and social contexts. The key concepts in his understanding of the pattern of traveling theory are "place" and "time" as specific situations and the "distance" between them. His approach is, therefore, radically historical, particularly as there does not exist any consensus among critics of different times and places on the enclosing limits of literature or literary criticism, and as the critic should not renounce his historical responsibility by "resort[ing] to the theory of limitless intertextuality as an Archimedean point outside the two situations." In studying "the extent to which theory is a response to a specific social and historical situation of which an intellectual occasion is a part," the critic of traveling theory will "judge misreadings (as they occur) as part of a historical transfer of ideas and theories from one setting to another" (*WTC*, 226).

The "historical transfer of ideas and theories," therefore, necessarily entails a *transformation* of their forms and functions, a transformation the critic of traveling theory has to reconstruct and analyze. As significant examples Said discusses the "influence" Lukács's *History and Class Consciousness* had on Lucien Goldmann in France and on Raymond Williams in England, and the response to Foucault's work in the United States. As any theory tends toward "closure, like social conventions or cultural dogma," or "overextension" to a "bad infinity" (in Lukács's case), the critic has to develop the "faculty for locating or situating theory," or, as Said calls it, a "critical consciousness" that is aware of the differences between "situations" and the "resistance to theory" and that opens up theory toward historical reality, society, human needs, and interests. "Theory, in short, can never be complete, just as one's interest in everyday life is never exhausted by simulacra, models, or theoretical abstracts of it." If critical consciousness has to beware of the "closure" of theory, it also has to keep from "overtotalizing" "social reality" and "degrading theory," as Said accuses Foucault of tending to do: "The problem is that Foucault's use of the term *pouvoir* moves around too much, swallowing up every obstacle in its path (resistances to it, the class and economic bases that refresh and fuel it, the reserves it builds up), obliterating change and mystifying its microphysical sovereignty" (*WTC*, 236f., 241f., 245–47).

In his more detailed analyses of traveling theory, Said focuses on examples of an "appropriation" of "revolutionary" theories that have robbed them of their "insurrectionary quality" and have led to "impoverishment" or "rarefaction," but his argument *also* implies the possibility of a "(re)politicization" of a "theory" in another historical, social, or disciplinary situation. One pertinent example would be Leo Marx's wide-ranging and cogent interpretation of the "revolutionary" potential of "pastoralism" in the United States. In his book *The Machine in the Garden* (1964) and particularly in many subsequent essays, he has shown how pastoralism as a "world view," an "ideology," and a "distinctive literary mode" that had taken on a "conservative" meaning in Europe was transformed by Americans in a different ecological, social, and cultural situation into a "progressive" idea and form. The "new," "complex" pastoralism in America, however, seemed to lose its distinctively progressive meaning in the course of American history under an ideology that prevented Americans from facing the urgent problems of social reality. Since the 1960s, however, basic social and cultural changes and the crisis in ecology have revealed the "dialectical mode of perception" that pastoralism implies, the "ineradicable, ultimately irresolvable nature of the conflict at its heart," and have renewed and "reactivated" the revolutionary potential of a pastoralism as a "nascent left-wing ideology" and as a dissident, "counter-cultural" literary mode.[11]

This returns us to the fact that virtually all discussions of the reception of European radical thought in the United States seem to end up in the confession, or accusation, of its depoliticization and incorporation. In a critical discussion of Stanley Fish's *Is There a Text in This Class?* and Fredric Jameson's *The Political Unconscious*, the philosopher and critic Samuel Weber has reflected on this recurring pattern and explained it in a Louis Hartzian vein.[12] With Louis Hartz, he finds the reason for this American domestication of both poststructuralism and (neo-)Marxism in the unique historical experience of the United States. The unchallenged triumph of liberalism in the absence of the feudal tradition and competing models of social organization made it lose the sense of its own historical and social relativity, hypostasize itself as an absolute, and turn the polemical, critical meaning of Locke's universal and naturalist categories and values into an affirmation of the status quo. In Weber's view, this "compulsive liberalism" is characterized by three inclusive strategies: universalization, the delegitimization of social/structural conflict, and individualization (i.e., the reinterpretation of collective, group conflicts as competition among individuals). To Weber the reception of recent French and German social thought is another case in point. What began in France, in a highly centralized culture and society, as an attack on all systems and isms, and as a questioning of the "borders" of disciplines and of the institutionalization of literary studies, was established, in the more decentralized American culture and academia, as a new "paradigm" of literary criticism. Conflict was turned into a "self-standing methodology," into a peacefully coexisting diversity *within* an institution or a discipline that is *not* subject to substantive conflict and controversy.

Nevertheless, Weber acknowledges in his essay that "liberalism" is in crisis today. He also realizes that there are signs of a "relegitimization" of conflict in the United States, at least "within the ethics of intellectual activity." In fact, a closer look shows that even in the appropriation of French poststructuralism in the United States we can discover traces of political "intervention," of an undermining of the liberal delegitimization of conflict, of calling into question prevailing lines of demarcation. There also can be no doubt that poststructuralist theory and criticism have seriously challenged the dominant modes of thought in American philosophy and social thought. More significantly, by the mid-1980s, a new confrontation with (neo-)Marxism seemed inevitable. Whereas orthodox Marxism had been criticized by French poststructuralist thinkers because it claimed to resolve the social, structural conflict of bourgeois society once and for all, in the United States, in the context of absolutist liberalism, Marxism (or socialism) had been excluded as "the other."

In spite of his critical emphasis on the inherent contradictions of "American liberalism," Hartz's argument that eliminates *all* kinds of socialist, Marxist, and alternative radical traditions and movements from the process of American history by principle, and afterward complains about the absence of "conflict" and alternative notions of society and culture, is historically and theoretically very dubious and in a crucial way self-fulfilling. Weber, however, uses Hartz's conceptual framework to argue that Jameson, in *The Political Unconscious*, falls victim to the same three strategies of domestication typical of absolutist American liberalism. Actually, Weber's critique aims less at Jameson's "typically" American appropriation of Marxism or poststructuralism than at his "Capitalizing History," as he calls his essay, at Jameson's refusal to accept the French poststructuralist critique of Marxism. Weber attacks Jameson for his tendency to "contain," to totalize the Marxist notion of history and for arguing within the institution of the university and of literary criticism, instead of allowing a Freudian "hermeneutics of *Entstellung*" and transcending the institutional context, as Weber suggested in his concluding essay to the final and eighth volume of *Glyph* in 1981, "After Eight," in the direction of an inter- or transdisciplinary approach to cultural studies. Weber fails to show, however, how this approach would differ, for example, from the (traditional) project of American Culture Studies and in what sense it would be more "political" than Jameson's radically historicized Marxist hermeneutic ("AE," 327).[13] If Jameson, in some sense, depoliticizes European neo-Marxism in the American context, we may as well ask if he does not also, particularly in his recent work on postmodernism, repoliticize it—or some of its aspects—by confronting the critical strategies of French poststructuralism and the revolutionary historical dialectic of neo-Marxist thought to the most advanced processes and manifestations of American culture and society.[14]

The Repoliticization of American Criticism

If American criticism during the 1970s and early 1980s was characterized by a radical questioning of all traditional approaches and basic terms such as "literature," "social reality," "history," "author," and "subject," it was only in the mid-1980s that a historical and political reconstruction of American "advanced" literary and cultural criticism began to move to the center of critical debates. During these years, these *historical and political reconstructions* of critical theory have been pursued mostly in the form of a revisionary dialogue and confrontation between poststructuralist criticism and a new Marxism, set in the context of the Western postmodern condition. As the organizers and editors of the symposium "Marxism and Deconstruction" at the University of Oklahoma in 1984 asked, "Can Marxism and deconstruction rescue each other from the blindness of each approach? Is there a way of combining Marxism and deconstruction that remains loyal to both? Do Marxism and deconstruction share structural similarities as modes of analysis?"[15]

Let me enumerate some of the results of these revisions in American critical thought:

(1) The powerful, though ambivalent political power of French poststructuralism has been reassessed. The relation of French poststructuralism to the work of several neo-Marxist thinkers (Adorno, Benjamin, Habermas, Althusser) has been scrutinized in a fresh way, beyond the common superficial, reified opposition of poststructuralism and Marxism.

(2) The various, often conflicting strands of contemporary European neo-Marxist thought have been rediscovered, often in the light of a political reading of deconstruction, as in Michael Ryan's *Marxism and Deconstruction* (1982).[16] What makes European neo-Marxist thought attractive is its critique of the self, of history, of enlightenment, not only in terms of an inherent critique of philosophy, but as historical and social process (especially the Frankfurt school).

(3) Even *American* deconstructionist *literary* criticism that had been, and continues to be, attacked by the Left—by, for example, Frank Lentricchia, Terry Eagleton, and Barbara Foley—as accommodationist, elitist, apolitical, or politically bankrupt, has been reinterpreted by a few incisive critics as suggesting, in some of its versions, a new vision of the very meaning of political criticism or politics.[17] The work of Paul de Man in particular, who had been denounced for his nihilistic, neo-Nietzschean, and apolitical stance, has been reclaimed for the project of a new form of radical literary and cultural criticism—for example, his remarks in his essay "The Resistance to Theory" (1982) that "the linguistics of literariness is a powerful and indispensable tool in the unmasking of ideological aberrations, as well as a determining factor in accounting for their occurrence."[18] Such a reassessment is, however, under serious reconsideration after the recent discovery of de Man's World War II essays and reviews in Belgian newspapers.[19]

(4) New forms of critical discourse have been developed in an attempt to move literary criticism toward radical cultural studies and to combine the rhetorical strategies of postmodern critics, such as Ihab Hassan, with the experimental, open forms of the essay as a "radically skeptical form" (Edward W. Said), worked out in reference to Adorno's negative dialectic, Benjamin's redemptive criticism, or Derrida's deconstruction (Said, *WTC*, 16).

(5) The interface between European (French and German) and American contemporary theory and the complex relations between poststructuralism, modernism, avant-garde movements, and versions of postmodernism

on both sides of the Atlantic are perceptively reconstructed in Andreas Huyssen's wide-ranging essay "Mapping the Postmodern" (1985). He shows how different the meaning of seemingly parallel developments such as the end of modernism, the counterculture, the aporias of the avant-garde, and postmodernism has been in Western Europe and the United States.[20]

(6) And most important, the setting, the place, the specific historical social situation, or situations, in which radical literary and cultural criticism has to reconstitute itself and in which the interaction between European and American thought takes place have been analyzed more comprehensively and searchingly. If postmodernism was first understood mainly as an aesthetic movement that was antimodernist and therefore, in some—aesthetic—sense, "subversive," "counterhegemonic" per se,[21] in more recent years versions of an oppositional reading of postmodernism have been worked out. This project joins postmodernism's aesthetic, cultural forms with the social and political issues of a postindustrial society, a multinational capitalist society, a society of the spectacle, and consumerism, and forces us to revise our understanding of the role of culture and of radicalism. Critics such as Hal Foster, Fredric Jameson, and Andreas Huyssen have analyzed various approaches to postmodernism (and their relation to the "project of modernity"—Habermas) and their different political intentions and implications and have delineated the dimensions and problems of an oppositional postmodernism.[22]

Situating Theory: Political Criticism and America

If all these recent developments are major steps in the direction of a more complex and productive interchange between European and American social and cultural thought and of a reconstruction of radical cultural criticism, things are more complicated than this account indicates. Let me point out several problems concerning the current process of a repoliticization of American literary and cultural criticism.

Politics, Dialectics, and Deconstruction

First of all, the repoliticization of criticism cannot be achieved by an unmediated reference to political thinkers or social critics who provide programmatic statements and demands that remain exterior to the interpretative procedures of criticism.[23] Oppositional criticism must work out its own kind of counterdiscourse without simply speaking *for* the excluded, marginalized "others," and it must not impatiently push aside the *difference* between cultural criticism and politics. If the social and cultural changes brought about in an age of postmodernism have profoundly transformed the role of culture, they also force us to reconsider the notion of politics that has been the standard for radical intellectuals for a long time.

Second, even though it is remarkable how similar in many respects Derrida's deconstruction (or some of its applications) is to dialectical thinking in the Marxist tradition, particularly Adorno's negative dialectic, it is mistaken simply to coopt or assimilate deconstruction to Marxism. As Derrida put it several years ago: "Once the amalgam [of Marx and Derrida] is accomplished, the appropriation incorporated, we hear that 'deconstruction' is to be abandoned, since Marx had already said it."[24] It is equally dubious when dialectical thinking, or the dialectic of enlightenment, is reduced to a number of motifs and critical statements, and then integrated as an element, or as a preliminary step, into a version of "political" deconstruction. As Andrew Parker has pointed out, the relationship between Marx and Derrida should not be defined as either "antithetical" or "complementary," as these "solutions" too quickly reduce the heterogeneity of some of their problematics and strategies to a common ground.[25]

There are, however, several studies that attempt a productive confrontation of Marxism and deconstruction. Rainer Nägele carefully compares Derrida's deconstruction and Adorno's negative dialectic. He does not look for an "identity," even though he finds many points of "overlapping," "affinity," and "resemblance," but for a "constellation" that could help him to trace some key notions as "part of an immanent problematic in both discourses, constituted by their specific historical position":

> It might well be possible that there is a mutual interest: an immanent element, inarticulable within each discourse, but articulable through the other. If poststructuralism is able to articulate and reinvestigate the problematic of history, language, and the subject in a way that lays bare some of the unacknowledged, repressed, and therefore very effective bourgeois heritage in Marxist theory, Marxism on the other hand is able to articulate some of the unacknowledged, repressed political and institutional implications in poststructuralist thought.[26]

Nägele does not try to synthesize Derrida and Adorno, but insists on their *differences*, in, for example, their understanding of "history," the "figure of affirmation in the negation," the "utopian dimension of difference," and "language."

In his book *Marxism and Deconstruction* (1982), Michael Ryan also finds that Adorno's negative dialectic bears "strong affinities to deconstruction." His whole project is close to Nägele's objective, but far more ambitious and comprehensive. He "believe[s] Marx and Derrida, critical marxism and deconstruction, are on the same side," and he "articulates deconstructive analyses with marxism" as well as "rereads Marx's text . . . in the light of the deconstructive critique of dialectics." Ryan's close readings of (neo-)Marxist and deconstructionist texts are subtle and mostly pertinent, even though he tries too hard to push Derrida into the position of a declared "communist" or "open marxist" (*MD*, xivf., 1, 82, 102, 117).[27] But his objectives go beyond philosophical analysis: "[This book] consists not only of a comparison of contents, but also of an attempt to develop a new form of analysis which would be both marxist and deconstructionist and would also encompass modes of political and social organization. One of the major arguments of the book is that how we read or analyze and how we organize political and social institutions are related forms of practice" (*MD*, xv, cf. 116). Undoubtedly, in using his theoretical reflections for an elucidation of the "new" political quality of a "critical marxism of the nonleninst left, [of] a postleninist marxism," particularly "British socialist feminism and the Italian Autonomy Movement," Ryan confronts a crucial problem of any contemporary discussion of the political meaning and consequences of a "new" Marxist critique, or of radical criticism on the left. But his drive for synthesis and unity of conflicting or competing theories and of theory and practice seems to me to be too all-encompassing and overly optimistic, perhaps too American in its pragmatic way of complementing everything with everything else, even though he emphatically defines his project as one of "theorizing (and discursively practising) this decentered plurality" and writes in his conclusion: "Unity, rather than authority, is needed, and . . . at this point in history in North America, unity excludes authority. By unity, I mean the articulation of a diverse, differentiated plurality; unity or a whole or identity or a 'totality' is never anything but that anyway" (*MD*, 116, 193, 215).

It is the exploration and articulation of this "diverse, differentiated plurality," I think, that Andrew Parker has in mind when he reformulates the relationship between Marxism and deconstruction as one of "supplementarity" rather than of antithesis and complementation and tries to "open up a space of inter-implication."[28] Similarly, John Brenkman in his concise remarks in "Deconstruction and the Social Text" sketches a program for "reopen[ing] deconstructive reading to the problematic initiated by Freud and Marx" by reinterpreting deconstruction's use of the figurality of language and of intertextuality without positing the unity of the "social text":

> Literature is intertextual in the sense that literary practice actively responds to the entire set of discourses, symbolic formations, and systems of representation that define a particular society's cultural and political life. . . . The general or, if you will, social text comprises all those discourses, each of which has a distinct history, just as the forms of their interaction evolve historically. Moreover, each of these discourses entails its own signifying operations as well as its own libidinal and inter-subjective economy. In other words, these various "textual fields" are not homogeneous nor even necessarily homologous with one another—which is why, it seems to me, that the deconstructive reading of literature, when satisfied with its limited conception of intertextuality, narrows the scope of reading, which it had promised to expand.[29]

Brenkman questions Derrida's generalized deconstruction of history and the subject by emphasizing that history "is the always open interplay between the events that have made the subject's history and the history that the subject makes of those events" and asks for a strategy that would return the "act of radical critique" to "its actual historical, political, and institutional context" ("DST," 188).

Culture and History: Deconstructing America

Another crucial problem of a rehistoricized American criticism "after deconstruction" is the role and the implications of its "location" in the United States. In spite of the strong emphasis on an analysis of the specific sociohistorical and cultural situation of criticism in the critique of traveling theory and contemporary social thought, it is amazing how rarely the *American* context and American traditions have been addressed and studied in a serious theoretical manner. Some beginnings were made by Frank Lentricchia's critical overview *After the New Criticism* (1980) and by the critical essays of Jonathan Arac, Wlad Godzich, Wallace Martin, and others in *The Yale Critics: Deconstruction in America* (1983). These critics touch on the question of "translation" and "cultural transference in general" from the European to the American context and extensively debate the relation of American deconstruction to the New Criticism (which they see as one of continuity), but they mainly attack the Yale critics' "displacement and appropriation" of French theory and their universalizing strategies in defining the power of literature or literary language.[30] We also have Jacques Derrida's reflections on the "adventures of deconstruction" in the United States in his *Memoirs for Paul de Man* (1986):

> Were I not so frequently associated with this adventure of deconstruction, I would risk, with a smile, the following hypothesis: America *is* deconstruction (*l'Amérique, mais c'est la deconstruction*). *In this hypothesis*, American would be the proper name of deconstruction in progress, its family name, its toponymy, its language and its place, its principal residence. . . . But we have learned from "Deconstruction" to suspend these always hasty attributions of proper names. My *hypothesis* must thus be abandoned. No, "deconstruction" is not a proper name, nor is America the proper name of deconstruction. Let us say instead: deconstruction and America are two open sets which intersect partially according to an allegorico-metonymic figure. In this fiction of truth, "America" would be the title of a new novel in the history of deconstruction and the deconstruction of history.[31]

Some aspects of "America" as the history of deconstruction and the deconstruction of history were suggested by Kenneth Dauber in his essays "Criticism of American Literature" (1977) and "American Culture as Genre" (1980), in which he argues that "the distinctiveness of American literature" consists in the fact that its "primary concern has always been its own nature," that it "was unsure of itself from the beginning," that it "*has* no ground," that it is "a literature radically undercut." In this context of deconstructionist criticism, what had seemed a significant liability or problem of American literature turns out to be a "model of models," as it "makes manifest what is implicit in other literatures."[32] This observation, however, needs to be pursued far more rigorously in its social, political, cultural, and literary presuppositions and implications if it is to go beyond a new methodological version of literary American uniqueness, of the post–World War II efforts of defining the essential "Americanness" of American literature.

American deconstructionist or poststructuralist *criticism* of all kinds contends that most American literary criticism is of little value. In a similar vein, neo-Marxist criticism has tended to express only contempt for any *American* tradition of Marxist or radical thought. Not only are the 1930s rejected as a "useless past," but the 1960s are "trashed," too, as the book by the editors of *Social Text*'s special issue, "The 60s Without Apology" (1984), complain.[33] In his critique of Jameson's work, Cornel West finds him "too American" in his conception of utopia—that is, in a Hartzian (or Sam Weberian) vein—but criticizes him, on the other hand, as too much "looking to France" instead of taking up the challenge of important American fellow critics.[34]

In general, radical literary critics of the 1980s tended to emphasize the tremendous power of the "American ideology" or "myth of America" in American cultural and literary history that, in Sacvan Bercovitch's words, has "turned" all forms of dissent "into a force against radical change."[35] They, therefore, usually failed to reconstruct or uncover the radical traditions and the subversive potential within the history or histories of *American* literary critical discourse(s). Only during the past few years have literary critics turned their attention to some figures of a radical or dissenting tradition in American literary criticism. Critics such as R. P. Blackmur, Kenneth Burke, and Charles Feidelson have been rediscovered and reinterpreted, but often under the premise of finding "precursors" of current (deconstructionist, poststructuralist, or neo-Marxist) critical theories, or of reading their works as "prefiguring" contemporary continental advanced thought, or of tracing American criticism's "evolution toward certain Continental positions out of the necessity of its own logic." Fredric Jameson, for example, in his essay on Kenneth Burke, tends to rewrite Burke's critical concepts and the dynamics of his thought in terms of Jameson's own critical system, a form of appropriation that suspends, or destroys, the radical potential of theoretical difference and historical distance.[36]

In the context of the debates on revising the canon and on the rewriting of American literary history that found one of their programmatic manifestations in *Ideology and Classic American Literature*, an outstanding collection of critical essays edited by Sacvan Bercovitch and Myra Jehlen in 1986, the work of F. O. Matthiessen has been rediscovered as representing at the same time a radical vision of American literature and culture and the enabling act of the canonized understanding of the great writers of the American Renaissance. Yet both the "radicalism" of the "classic" American Renaissance writers and the canon of "major" writers established by Matthiessen's *American Renaissance* (1941) have been fundamentally challenged by versions of the "the other American Renaissance" and by a revisionary understanding of the concept of ideology and of ideological criticism in literary studies.[37] But I think the important and necessary process of reconstruction, as well as critical deconstruction of the complex and unresolved and, therefore, potentially very productive tensions that characterized Matthiessen's work, is still at an early stage. Jonathan Arac's and Donald Pease's essays in *The American Renaissance Reconsidered* (1985), for example, are rather reductive readings of Matthiessen's work that argue in terms of a crude distinction between "two

Matthiessens," collapse critical distinctions and the historical dialectic, and provide versions of a "repoliticization" that reify Matthiessen's understanding of "wholeness" and then directly confront it with an ideological construct or "position" such as the Popular Front or the Cold War.[38]

Turning to cultural criticism in a wider sense we find a similar neglect of the dynamics of American history. Until recently cultural critics have ignored the traditions of radical cultural criticism, from Randolph Bourne to early American Studies, for example, and the wealth of oppositional movements, of alternative cultures created in the course of a complex American history that has been characterized as much by diversity and heterogeneity as by consensus, as American working-class history, ethnic histories, and cultural history have convincingly shown. Only if these radical traditions in social and political practice and in thought are reassessed with respect to both their achievements and their failures, as Alan Trachtenberg in *The Incorporation of America* (1982), Giles Gunn in *The Culture of Criticism and the Criticism of Culture* (1987), and Christopher Lasch in some of his recent essays have done, can the "situational" analysis of traveling theory and the potential and the specific critical strategies and perspectives of radical cultural criticism in the United States be more adequately grasped.[39]

Modernism and Postmodernism in the United States

It is mainly in the context of the debate on the politics of *postmodernism*, which began in the *American* 1960s, that American developments, cultural products and processes, and cultural criticism have been given more careful attention. Since the early 1970s, Ihab Hassan has discussed postmodernism as a general question of culture and consciousness, as cultural change that not only affects aesthetic production and perception, but presupposes and demands a change in society and politics as well. As he put it in *The Right Promethean Fire: Imagination, Science, and Cultural Change* (1980), "Innovation in criticism finally aspires not only to epistemological, existential, or aesthetic freedom but also to basic political change."[40] In exploring these multiple and often incommensurable interrelationships, Hassan draws on an immense knowledge of contemporary thought and production in the arts (from the neo-avant-garde to postmodernism), in the humanities, philosophy, the social sciences, and the natural sciences that clearly is on an international scale, but increasingly has been motivated and energized by his critical commitment to an understanding of cultural crisis and change, of desire and dissent in the United States.[41] Early in 1974, in his preface to *Paracriticism*, he answered the question of how criticism could "help to formulate a theory of change, and thus become part of a design of life" by insisting it "go beyond our current shibboleths: disconfirmation, decreation, demystification, deconstruction, decentering, depropriation, difference, etc." In looking for this "beyond," for this "reconstruction" of knowledge and our experience, he drew on new "French theory," but he often found the most controversial or promising "models of change" among recent American thinkers and visionaries increasingly influenced by the pragmatism of William James.[42]

The interface between European (French and German) and American contemporary theory and the complex relations among modernism, (social and economic) modernization, avant-garde movements, neoconservatism, and visions of postmodernism and poststructuralism on both sides of the Atlantic are perceptively reconstructed in Andreas Huyssen's important essay "Mapping the Postmodern" (1984). His essay proves how productive a critical assessment of the political, or, in this context, of the radical, subversive potential of these developments or movements, particularly of a "critical or oppositional" postmodernism, in American culture and society can be when it is based on a careful study of the dynamics and politics of culture, ideology, and social and cultural differences in a specific historical context.

Huyssen points out the nonsynchronism (Ernst Bloch's *Ungleichzeitigkeiten*) in post–World War II Western culture, the development of a "genuine avant-garde movement" in the early phase of postmodernism in the United States during the 1960s, at a time when European critics talked about the exhaustion or the "aporias" (Hans Magnus Enzensberger) of the historical avant-garde of the early twentieth century. Huyssen's argument that the early phase of postmodernism developed as a subversive critique of the canonization of the "high modernism" in 1950s America establishes historically "the specifically American character of postmodernism" ("MTP," 18). It is, however, inadequate to interpret this process basically as a "revitalization" of the "heritage of the European avant-garde" ("MTP," 39). What Huyssen neglects in his subtle dialectical analysis is the complexity of the *American tradition itself*, or the differences and tensions that have characterized the various American traditions in the culture and in criticism—for example, the versions of an American avant-garde in the first decades of the twentieth century or alternative forms of literature, culture, and cultural criticism in the interstices of, or on the margins of, the dominant culture or among minorities and oppressed groups before World War II.

A similar problem arises in his brilliant reassessment of the relations between postmodernism and poststructuralism. He shows that poststructuralism in France must be read as "a theory of modernism at the stage of its exhaustion," and not of postmodernism, as American "deconstructionist" critics have tended to take it. It can, however, be seen, in Lyotard's sense, as a "postmodern" phenomenon, as it replaces the modernism of negativity, alienation, and ambiguity of the "age of anxiety" by a version of modernism that celebrates *jouissance* (Roland Barthes), "playful transgression, an unlimited weaving of textuality, a modernism all confident in its rejection of representation and reality, in its denial of the subject, of history, and of the subject of history." Huyssen's convincing reading of French poststructuralism as a discourse of and about modernism, a discourse that is by no means politically adversarial per se, implies that the common leftist objection to American deconstructionist criticism that it has "domesticated" and "depoliticized" radical French poststructuralism can, at best, be part of the truth. As Huyssen puts it: "The fact is that even in France the political implications of certain forms of poststructuralism are hotly debated and in doubt. It is not just the institutional pressures of American literary criticism which have depoliticized French theory; the aestheticist trend within poststructuralism itself has facilitated the peculiar American reception" ("MTP," 50). It is, however, exactly this "peculiar American reception" that Huyssen seems to take for granted too quickly by simply claiming that "in America, too, poststructuralism offers a theory of modernism, not a theory of the postmodern." There have been very different reactions to the challenge of French theories in the United States and very different and heterogeneous American traditions and contexts at work in recent critical cultural thought. If French poststructuralist thinkers or critics "rarely, if ever, . . . even address postmodernist works," much of recent "advanced" cultural and literary criticism in the United States has been worked out in direct response to the cultural pressures, promises, and productions of the "specifically American character of postmodernism." The fundamental crisis of modernism has opened up many possibilities for creative work, and postmodernism has redrawn the lines between high art, mass culture, and society and redefined the meaning and perspectives of radical cultural criticism. Huyssen points to the "emergence of the problematics of 'otherness,' which has asserted itself in the socio-political sphere as much as in the cultural sphere." The politics of otherness is less evident in a strictly theoretical reading of French poststructuralism than in the "various and multiple forms of otherness as they emerge from differences in subjectivity, gender and sexuality, race and class, temporal *Ungleichzeitigkeite* and spatial geographic locations and dislocations" in which the resources and the directions of a "postmodernism of resistance" lie, as these "forms of otherness" not only characterize the postmodern condition in the United States today, but have permeated the dynamic and the contradictions of modernism and the avant-garde in this country more than anywhere else ("MTP," 50).

Difference, Pluralism, and the Question of Synthesis in American Historical and Cultural Studies

"Difference" and "Otherness": Gender, Race, and Critical Writing

The various efforts since the mid-1980s to advocate for the supplementarity of deconstruction and Marxism, to articulate their constellation as a "decentered" or "diverse, differentiated plurality," to elaborate the intertextuality of the "social text" as a historical interplay of different "textual fields" find a theoretical and political focus in the discussion of the meanings and the implementations of the concepts of "difference" and "otherness" crucial to both deconstruction and Marxism. From the perspective of deconstruction, the problem that has become most urgent is how to recontextualize linguistic difference, how to reinscribe sexual, racial, or social class difference into deconstructive work, and how to adapt its strategies to the voices, critical concepts, and discursive practices created in feminist and black literature and criticism, as well as in those of other marginalized or oppressed groups. For Marxism "after deconstruction," the question presents itself how to deal with social groups, political movements, and cultural projects of difference and otherness that cannot be understood adequately in terms of a logic of contradictions and the traditional concepts of class conflict alone. The strong tendency to confine the analysis of difference and otherness to a general philosophical, rhetorical level (deconstruction) or to reduce them to the negation or reversal of dominant cultural patterns and values (Marxism) not only accommodates the strategies used by the dominant cultural group, but often permeates the theoretical and political strategies of the "other" groups themselves.

In their book, *Kafka: Toward a Minor Literature* (1975), Gilles Deleuze and Félix Guattari have offered a penetrating analysis of the question of "minor literature," a term that comprises the literatures of (marginalized) minorities as well as the forms of literature that are defined and disparaged as "minor," as opposed to "major," "great" literature, within the dominant culture itself, such as "popular," "proletarian," and "regional" literatures. In the chapter "What Is a Minor Literature?" they write, "'[M]inor' no longer characterizes certain literatures, but describes the revolutionary conditions of any literature within what we call the great (or established)." For the radical critic who is critical of the dominant cultural discourse, but at the same time is situated in its institutions and public culture, the problem is "how to become the nomad and the immigrant and the gypsy of our own language." Another way to put this question would be to ask how to achieve (and sustain) "deterritorialization" (of "minor" literatures, of one's own intellectual, interpretive position) without symbolic or cultural "reterritorialization," without a reinvestment in the dominant culture's meaning.[43] For the minority critic, however, the celebration of marginality, difference, and undecidability too easily falls victim to mystifications of "otherness" and overlooks that "plurality" and "marginality" are also produced by the political and economic "center" in order to contain the explosive potential of social and cultural heterogeneity.

It is this set of problems that John Carlos Rowe pursues in his penetrating essay "'To Live Outside the Law, You Must Be Honest': The Authority of the Margin in Contemporary Theory" (1985), a revisionary reading of the "political" deconstructive critics Luce Irigaray, Geoffrey Hartman, and Edward W. Said—that is, at the same time, a self-criticism of his own earlier deconstructive critical work. Rowe writes:

> Each method focuses its intertextual concerns in terms of a very specific discourse that has been considered traditionally marginal to the ruling culture: Irigaray is concerned with the discourse of woman; Hartman with that of literature; Said with that of the "Orient," and more generally with the entire problem of the "Third World." Each method of reading borrows much from the post-structuralist theories of Foucault, Derrida, and Lacan; each method deploys such post-structuralist notions in very particular acts of interpretation designed to "revise" our understanding of western history. In my view, they represent three significant modalities of the appropriation of the post-structuralist notion of "marginality" (defined as it is by linguistic indeterminacy). These modalities do not cover the possibilities of employing marginality and indeterminacy, but they represent some of the inevitable dangers of the approach.[44]

Rowe very much emphasizes that "the culture produces its own margins —margins that only *appear* to be at the boundaries of the picture and on closer examination are determined by yet other framing devices that place such marginal forces in association with the center." Or that the "dominant ideology" produces the illusion of marginality or "cultural subversion" for the purpose of "sustaining its own marginality as a protection for the dominant culture against 'contamination' by what it fears, what it has suppressed." The production of plurality and of marginality is seen as a logical outgrowth, or "surplus," of contemporary Western consumer capitalism, even though Rowe does not specify his argument in any detail. If the dominant culture powerfully "appropriate[s] differences and construct[s] an other" in order to strengthen its "internal regularities," the critics of marginality in contemporary theory—Irigaray, Hartman, and Said—"cannot escape their own sets of mystifications" and "hypostasizations" by their "fetishizing of multiplicity, difference, aporia, undecidability" ("TLOL," 39, 42, 25 ff., 49, 58 ff.).

Rowe traces this process of "mystification" of the "other" in feminist discourse (Irigaray) as well as in the discourse of the "Third World" or of the "other culture," of non-Western cultures. In his critique of Said's *Orientalism* (1978), he confronts the problem of "self-marginalization" when he writes that Said "must conceive of this tradition [from romantic idealism through Nietzsche to the contemporary strategies of Foucault, Derrida, and Lacan] to be a sort of 'anti-tradition,' or 'counter-culture,' which marginalizes itself with respect to the dominant culture" and argues that Said "mythologizes" this process of marginalization "until it clusters into a single, albeit complex, image of a margin inhabited by: the avant-garde artist, the Orient, Woman, the 'third-world,' and the genealogical critic himself" ("TLOL," 62). Rowe's strong sense of the ideological "production" and "appropriation" as well as the "mystification" and "mythologizing" of the "Other," of "indeterminacy," "hetero-geneity," and "marginalization" in "contemporary theory" makes him, however, overestimate the omnipresence and total power of the social and ideological system of consumer capitalism and neglect the presence and the power of alternative radical traditions. It also prevents him, in this essay, from questioning and transcending his own radical reading of deconstruction, his own (self-critical) process of "self-marginalization," by confronting the critical voices of the "other" groups themselves that are not part of "contemporary theory" *qua* deconstruction. His final remarks may point in this direction, but they remain highly programmatic and hypothetical, couched in a rhetoric of radical morality.

American deconstructionist criticism, particularly Yale deconstructionism, not only rarely touched on American literature or American literary criticism, but virtually ignored feminist and black literary and theoretical perspectives. Barbara Johnson, a leading deconstructionist at Yale at the time, attacked her colleagues' "manifesto" *Deconstruction and Criticism* (1979) for its exclusive male list of contributors, and she planned, with Shoshana Felman, to publish a complementary volume, *The Bride of Deconstruction.* Yet in the mid-1980s, she self-critically remarked that "no book produced by the Yale School seems to have excluded women as effectively as [her own] *The Critical Difference.*" In her later work, collected under the title *A World of Difference* (1987), she set out to "re-referentialize the notion of difference," to "transfer the analysis of difference . . . out of the realm of linguistic universality or deconstructive allegory and into the context in which difference is very much at issue in the 'real world.'"[45] She set herself the task of "actually translat[ing] what deconstruction has done into the realm of historical and political action."[46]

For feminist critics and black critics it was not necessary to "position" their work in American society and culture and to *re*inscribe sexual, racial, or class difference into their "deconstructive" and historically "reconstructive" work. In feminist criticism and in black criticism, these differences have, in different ways, always been inscribed from the very beginning. Their critical utterances have always been seen as historically positioned utterances, which does not mean, of course, that their critical strategies are per se fully conscious theoretical expressions of their complex social and cultural situation of difference and otherness. Only during the 1980s have feminist critics and black critics forcefully redefined and transcended the earlier commitment to rediscovering and reclaiming literary traditions of their own or a potentially "essentialist" understanding of "women's writing" or of the "blackness" of Afro-American cultural expressions, both notions that very strongly demanded a separatist space for Women's Studies or Black Studies. In recent years they have worked out powerful forms of a criticism of "difference" that situate theory and critical practice as minority discourses in the complex and conflictual intellectual, social, and political dynamic of American culture and turn its intra- and intercultural tensions into visions of American identities characterized by "self-difference" and "double- (or multi)voicedness."

This actually also means that the whole project of "re"-referentializing or "re"-contextualizing critical discourse has to be seen in a new perspective. Rereferentializing and recontextualizing deconstruction cannot mean to confront its interpretive strategies as a "different world" of minority discourse or to achieve a "separate" identity of difference. What it comes to is the experience and insight, as Barbara Johnson realized in her work on the black writer Zora Neale Hurston, that writings by "minority" or "ethnic" "noncanonical" writers constantly undercut and set in motion common oppositions as well as critical key concepts of "minority discourses." These writings dramatize and reveal in the inner dynamics of their forms that the emphasis on "double-voicedness" in black American discourse, for example, has regularly "assumed without question that the black subject is male" and that black politics is "racial politics," and thus made the black woman and her "sexual politics" invisible (Johnson, *WOD*, 166). And they enact in their discursive strategies the project of identity not as the growth toward an "authentic voice" *qua* "self-identity," but as a process of *self-difference* or "*self-differentiation*" of the "double-voiced" utterances of a developing, discontinuous self that again and again returns the self to the world: "If I initially approached Hurston out of a desire to re-referentialize difference, what Hurston gives me back seems to be difference as a suspension of reference. Yet the terms 'black' and 'white,' 'inside' and 'outside,' continue to matter. Hurston suspends the certainty of reference not by erasing these differences but by foregrounding the complex dynamism of their interaction" (*WOD*, 183).

Pluralism and Synthesis

In recent years the critical debate on the politics of interpretation has found one focus in the question of the meaning and implications of *pluralism* in American criticism, culture, and society. The question of pluralism does not only refer to the general problem of the interactions among the dominant culture and various kinds of group cultures, subcultures, and alternative cultures, but is particularly pertinent to the *American* situation, as it directly addresses the conceptual and political model of understanding American society and culture as a multiculture, a society and culture of immigrants, as an ensemble and force field of ethnic and minority cultures and literatures. The "crisis" of American society and culture during the late 1960s and the 1970s undermined a false, ideological unity and hegemony and led to a strong emphasis on (and institutionalization of) difference, separateness, and multiplicity. While pluralism and ethnicity were rediscovered during the time as concepts and perspectives of a complex, heterogeneous America "beyond the melting pot" (N. Glazer; D. P. Moynihan), as liberating forces in a dangerously homogenizing consumer society and dominant white middle-class culture, they have been attacked in recent years as producing, for example, "sectarian and fragmented histories of American literatures (in the plural) instead of American literary history" that prevent us from seeing the interactions and contours of the whole picture.[47] Pluralism, it has been argued, far from being free of ideology or politically progressive or radical, must be seen as deeply imbued with dogmatism and ideology (W. T. J. Mitchell), as originating in its American versions as "cultural pluralism" (Horace Kallen) and in "ambiguous racialist assumptions" (Philip Gleason), and as having played a dubious role in the post–World War II ideological fight against totalitarianism (Werner Sollors). As Sacvan Bercovitch has suggested, even the "new pluralism" signals an "ideological trap" of its own by "avoiding the issue of dominance," by turning "what might have been a confrontation into an alternation of opposites": "Ideological analysis . . . reminds us that multiplicity is not necessarily opposite to hegemony: the two may simply be different sides of the same coin."[48]

In many respects, this critique of the consequences of pluralism or ethnicity—if qualified as "pure pluralism" or "the ethnic perspective taken exclusively" (Sollors)—is well taken, as sheer multiplicity and lines of separation can easily obscure or distort the many crosscurrents and "the cultural interplays and contacts among writers of different backgrounds, the cultural mergers and secessions that took place in America".[49] And the demands for a new synthesis are by no means per se a counterattack by neoconservative ideologues against the "liberations" of the radical 1960s—as the essays by Herbert G. Gutman and Thomas Bender on the need for a "new synthesis" in American history show—though they often *are* signs of a "political call to reconciliation and consolidation" (Annette Kolodny).[50]

As early as 1981, Gutman published a short piece in the *Nation* in which he praised the remarkable achievements of the new social history of the 1970s, but pointed out that the focus on "segments (such as blacks, workers, or women)" had also "reinforced the disintegration of a coherent synthesis in the writing of American history." And he concluded, "A new synthesis is needed, one that incorporates and then transcends the new history," a new synthesis that could succeed in creating a different, critical understanding of American history in the public at large ("TMS," 554). Four years later, Thomas Bender took up Gutman's remarks, placed them in a wider context, and indicated ways of realizing the "new synthesis" without "sacrificing the rich harvest—as well as the cultural and political point—of recent studies of particular groups." Bender is certainly right when he states that the "*interrelations* of races, classes and sexes in the formation of American society and culture—or in the making of individual lives" have not been studied by the new history in sufficient detail. But he tends to oppose the histories of segments, of minorities, of ethnic groups to "American" history as something synthetic or whole, as if the histories of groups and segments (and their interrelationships) are not American history or do not constitute manifestations of the American historical experience(s). Therefore, his demand in this essay to "restore the center" seems to me an ambiguous undertaking, as the many meanings of its title reveal: "Making History Whole Again" ("MHWA," 42–43).

However, Sollors and Bender have worked out critical perspectives of American cultural and social history "beyond pluralism" and "beyond ethnicity." In *Beyond Ethnicity: Consent and Descent in American Culture* (1986), Sollors revises the common understanding of "ethnicity," drawing on Fredrik Barth's notion of "boundary-construction processes" and Andrew Greeley's use of "ethnogenesis." In his analysis, the "persistent conflict between consent and descent in America" is the new key to understanding the "creation of an American culture out of diverse pre-American pasts" and the "socialization into the codes of Americanness." Sollors briefly discusses the role of class and race in his model, but then neglects them in favor of the "conflict between contractual and hereditary, self-made and ancestral, definitions of American identity—between consent and descent." He regards this conflict as "the central drama in American culture" and concentrates on the "construction of new forms of symbolic kinship among people who are not blood relatives." In its emphasis on the achievement of consent and consensus "in a country whose citizens are of such heterogeneous descent," the book mainly pursues the fascinating cultural processes by which a common "identity," central rhetorical codes of Americanness, and a "common typological language" have been worked out that provide the consensual terms for discussing "consensus" as well as "conflict" in American culture. "My interest is not in the raw data of the so-called ethnic experience, but in the mental formations and cultural constructions (the codes, beliefs, rites, and rituals) which were developed in America in order to make sense of ethnicity and immigration in a melting-pot culture."[51] But I think it is doubtful if the conflict between consent and descent as the central drama in American culture can really provide a principle of critical synthesis for the various conflicting literatures and cultures in the United States that has a critical and differentiating potential similar to Thomas Bender's notion of the "public culture(s)" or the "public realm(s)."

In some ways, Bender's comprehensive and sophisticated essay "Wholes and Parts: The Need for Synthesis in American History" (1986) can be read as establishing the wider contexts for Sollors's reading of the conflict between consent and descent as the central drama in American culture. He elaborates his earlier suggestion that the "new synthesis" can be achieved by studying the "public realm," by "reconceptualiz[ing] public culture," that "essentially civic arena where groups interact, even compete, to establish the configuration of political power in a society and its cultural forms and their meanings" ("WAP," 131). He also hopes that by exploring the "public realm" in the making and remaking, as a contested and constantly changing "civic arena," historians can regain their general audience and contribute to a "revitalization of public life." Bender brilliantly discusses his notion of "public culture" as a "principle of synthesis" that "crystallizes in narrative form" an "image of society" and brings together politics, power, and their forms of "symbolic meaning." "At the center of such a synthetic narrative, as a focus and as an analytical device, we must develop a historical notion of public culture, at once an arena for the play of cultures and interests in society and the product of that play—the constituted definition of power and meaning" ("WAP," 132). Some questions remain. Does Bender's claim of the central role of public culture and the public realm—apparently influenced by Jürgen Habermas's work on the public sphere in bourgeois society—adequately take into account the functional changes they have undergone in this century, particularly in the United States, the distortions and limitations of the power of public culture and the public realm and their dispersal as an ensemble or constellation of different public culture*s* and potentially oppositional public realm*s*? Does his aim to write history as "a synthetic narrative," "a *single*, complex narrative that stresses the interplay of various groups, usually characterized as *homogeneous*, whether defined socially (for example, ethnic groups) or as private worlds (for example, the family), and the larger, heterogeneous, and contested political and cultural realm of the nation" (my emphases), do justice to the experience of "difference in America" if this difference supposedly "does *not* assume a discontinuity in social and individual experience" (my emphasis, "WAP," 132).

In general, the models of new "synthetic" and "postpluralist, postethnic approaches" to the study of American society, culture, and literature show quite clearly that the call for "a synthesis" beyond pluralism and ethnicity faces many problems that should not be prematurely and impatiently put aside. On the contrary, before the "new pluralism" is dismissed as conceptually vague and politically evasive and "ideological," the theoretical and political implications of the recent emphasis on multiplicity, difference, otherness, discontinuity, and competing interests and critical strategies have to be studied even more rigorously (which, of course, includes their interrelationship to hegemony, power, tradition, and the claims of "the whole"). The notion of a new pluralism still produces far-reaching consequences and insights into the dynamics of postmodern American culture and society and the forms, interfaces, and objectives of American cultural criticism. I think of W. J. T. Mitchell's program of a "dialectical pluralism" that "insists on pushing divergent theories and practices toward confrontation and dialogue"[52] or of Hayden White's "historical pluralism" that makes us aware of a multiplicity of "senses of history" as "modes of emplotment," as "mutually exclusive narrative interpretations of the same historical phenomenon." It emphasizes a multiplicity of "narrative accounts of real historical events" that "admit of as many equally plausible versions of this representation as there are plot structures available in a given culture for endowing stories, whether fictional or real, with meanings." For White, "the whole question of pluralism, in both criticism and historiography, is linked in some crucial way to a narrativistic notion of historical representation." It is equally possible and legitimate to envisage an "anti-narrativistic account of historical phenomena" that is written on deconstructionist principles, as "there is nothing in historical events themselves to require that accounts of them be cast in a narrative mode." If this anti-narrativistic approach is taken, very different standards and strategies apply that cannot be judged in terms of the limits of pluralism.[53]

In contradistinction to White's "radical relativism in matters having to do with *historical knowledge*," Ihab Hassan takes up pluralism as a positive challenge to a critical understanding of postmodernism: "Pluralism in our time finds (if not founds) itself in the social, aesthetic, and intellectual assumptions of postmodernism—finds its ordeal, its rightness, there." A "limited critical pluralism" is "deeply implicated in the cultural field of postmodernism" and "is in some measure a reaction against the radical relativism, the ironic indeterminancies, of the postmodern condition; it is an attempt to contain them." The "containment," the "reconstructive" turn, is not arbitrary, or ideologically imposed on the "ironic indeterminancies" of postmodernism, but a tendency inherent in its very work of deconstruction of traditional unities, consensus, and dichotomies, as Hassan's short "definitions" of postmodernism indicate. The potential anarchy of critical pluralism finds its limits in "cognitive, political, or affective constraints," but the constraints of "power," "politics," and "desire" remain only "partial," as they fail to "create consensual theory or practice." To Hassan, William James's "will to believe" suggests a *tentative*, "pragmatic," and "local" foundation of "a wide consensus on discourse" in our postmodern epoch.[54]

Writing New Histories of American Literature

All these programmatic essays show how much the relationship of a dialectical, historical, or critical pluralism to the problems of synthesis beyond multiplicity, pure pluralism, or ethnicity in American culture and cultural criticism is implicated in the contemporary theoretical debate on the meanings of history and the *writing* of history. The controversy over history as *a form of discourse*, over narrativity, testifies to the influential role recent developments in *literary theory* (writing, textuality, and discursive practices) have played and can play in defining the functions of cultural and historical criticism at the present time.

The current projects of *writing new histories of American literature* have to face directly the "fundamental tension" between "the attempt to unify, to provide coherence, organization, and continuity" (the "centripetal impulse") and the "divergent or centrifugal impulses pulling away from the center toward plurality of method and diversity of authors and texts," as Emory Elliott, editor of the *Columbia Literary History of the United States*, has put it.[55] Their challenge is to work out this literary history "in the dialogic mode," this "diverse and multi-layered approach" (Elliott), this "re-historicizing of American literature" (Sacvan Bercovitch), *without* "containing" and "abbreviating the mapping of alternative landscapes" of recent American literary scholarship, *without* reducing, to quote Annette Kolodny, the "complicating intersections of race, class, and gender" to the common model of incorporating the "contributions of women and minority group writers within these [traditional] categories and periods."[56] *Revising the canon* is not simply a matter of including new writers and renegotiating the ranking of writers, but of questioning the presuppositions and the very notion of a canon itself. The debates about the canon force the literary critic and historian to draw critically on the various approaches to pluralism and relate them to their institutional contexts in universities.

The new American literary historians must respond to the "respect for diversity, plurality, and heterogeneity that marked the outburst of innovative criticism and scholarship in the 1960s and 1970s" (Kolodny), to a "distinctive generational experience (of discontinuity, disruption, dissensus)" (Bercovitch). This experience taught young American literary scholars that "if there was something uniquely 'American' about our nation and our literary inheritances, it was not a harmonious commonality or shared traditions but diversity, division, and discord" (Kolodny).[57] At the same time, their work must show the awareness that the critique of myth, ideology, and utopia in history and of consensus, continuity, and unity does not exhaust itself in debunking, unmasking, and demystifying the lies and repressions of the dominant culture, but also has to uncover, as Bercovitch writes, "the positive and enabling aspect of ideology," the "empowering force" of myth, ideology, and utopia in the culture (subcultures, countercultures, radical traditions).[58] Myra Jehlen has traced in detail the emergence of a new understanding of "ideology" congenial to literary analysis in American criticism and reconstructed its theoretical sources, or resources, in the two forms of ideological critique in Europe, put succinctly, the Marxist and the Weberian traditions.

The *Columbia Literary History of the United States*, edited by Emory Elliott and published in 1988, shows how difficult it is to realize these programmatic statements. The book fulfills its aim "to make pluralism of method and diversity of materials the primary goal of a contemporary literary history" by including a wide variety of approaches and giving considerable space to "the conditions of women writers and of writers of racial and ethnic minority groups." It also acknowledges the multiple "beginnings" of "American" literature. Yet it often fails to elaborate how the "dialogic oppositions" of literary history have worked, leaving it to the reader to trace some of these developments by "cross-indexing." It also tends to overemphasize matters of cultural life and literary politics, particularly with "minority literatures," which sometimes leads to the strange result—as with Afro-American literature—that the literary works themselves are not interpreted at all.[59]

Sacvan Bercovitch has tried far more rigorously than Elliott to determine the specific cultural potential of language, of the literary dynamic of American literary history. In a number of penetrating essays he has traced and analyzed the complex historical "cultural dialectic" and the "distinctive form of expression" it demands. To him, the crucial importance of history and the problem of ideology asks for a "flexible, open-ended and self-reflexive approach," an "open-ended dialectic between literary and historical analysis," an "open-ended engagement between history, the reader, and the text." Most important of all, Bercovitch tries to define the "contribution of literary theory to the study of ideology": "I have in mind a cultural dialectic, attuned to the power of language no less than to the language of power, sensitive to the emotional and imaginative appeal of myth while insisting on the cognitive dimensions of art." The new emphasis on language as "an intrinsic part of the material of history, and hence a central category of historical analysis," has opened up an understanding of the "text" as "invested with all the subtleties of historical process so that history may be understood through the subtleties of literary criticism."[60] This project of reconstructing American literary history has found one focus in the revaluation of the American Renaissance, in the paradoxical expression of American literary radicalism, or of a radical tradition in American literature, namely of an "antagonistic literature that is somehow also culturally representative."[61] There are very divergent and contending answers to the question of the "radicalism" of "classic" American literature, as the essays in *Ideology and Classic American Literature* (1986), edited by Sacvan Bercovitch and Myra Jehlen, demonstrate. But the contributors to Bercovitch's literary history projects share the conviction, as he has put it in his preface to *Reconstructing American Literary History*,

> that race, class, and gender are formal principles of art and therefore integral to textual analysis; that language has the capacity to break free of social restrictions and through its own dynamics to undermine the power structures it seems to reflect; that political norms are inscribed in aesthetic judgement and therefore inherent in the process of interpretation; that aesthetic structures shape the way we understand history, so that tropes and narrative devices may be said to use historians to enforce certain views of the past; that the task of literary historians is not just to show how art transcends culture, but also to identify and explore the ideological limits of their time, and then to bring these to bear upon literary analysis in such a way as to make use of the categories of culture, rather than being used by them.[62]

Many questions remain, and we look forward to the realization of Bercovitch's program in the multivolume *Cambridge History of American Literature*, but the two collections of essays by its contributors show that the project of a critical de- and reconstruction of the historical "dynamics of dissensus inherent in the very notion of an American literature" is well under way, "beyond transcendence."[63]

[2]

NEW HISTORICISM, NEW AMERICAN EXCEPTIONALISM, AND NEW AMERICAN STUDIES: VERSIONS OF A NEW SYNTHESIS

AFTER A PERIOD OF DIVERSIFICATION, the fragmentation of the field into new interdisciplinary studies programs, an emphasis on difference and pluralism, and new experimental and often conflicting approaches and concepts appropriated from various disciplines, we are seeking a "new synthesis" or "New American Studies." As Elizabeth Fox-Genovese puts it in an essay in *American Quarterly*, "Between Individualism and Fragmentation: American Culture and the New Literary Studies of Race and Gender" (1990): "Today the most pressing question appears to be whether any new synthesis is possible or even desirable. How, in other words, are we to weave the various cultures that we are learning to recognize and appreciate into a general view of American culture?"[1] What are these New American Studies all about? In what sense do they represent a new synthesis of the scholarship of the 1970s and 1980s? What is new about their conception of America and of cultural studies?

In her critical review of the "new scholarship of race and gender," Elizabeth Fox-Genovese finds that the new studies have embraced fragmentation, diversity, and pluralism rather than "engag[ed] the battle for American culture as a whole" ("BIF," 10) or worked toward a "systematic view of the central dynamics of American society and culture" ("BIF," 23). If, as she argues, the most compelling results of the new scholarship are, on the one hand, its analysis of cultural processes and social and political relations in terms of strategies of textualization and, on the other hand, the exploration of the "inescapable relations between culture and power" and the "privileged positions" ("BIF," 28) race and gender must enjoy in our understanding of American culture, the search for the New American Studies must define and elaborate the old question of text and context in interdisciplinary American Culture Studies in a new way. This problem is discussed by Robert F. Berkhofer, Jr., in his penetrating and wide-ranging essay "A New Context for a New American Studies?," also published in *American Quarterly* (1989), in which he systematically analyzes the potential and the limitations of the current "cultural or textual construction of social reality." He distinguishes three conflicting meanings of "context" in use today that make any "attempt to find a single methodology for the new cultural studies" a futile adventure.[2] As a "textualist poetics" and a "contextualist politics" basically "oppose, even deconstruct, each other," a "new synthesis" in American Studies could be achieved only at the high price of discounting and repressing much of the recent work in cultural studies. Berkhofer concludes: "So methodological stands upon the use of poetics or politics in explicating texts and contexts in the human sciences lead inevitably to a reflexive poetics and politics of the human sciences themselves as texts and contexts" ("NC," 599). In practical terms, however, the New American Studies should look for "a new historicism or historicization to mediate the differing approaches to context and thereby steer a middle course among the pitfalls opened by modern theory," a way out Berkhofer seems to endorse tentatively: "The new trend to historicization in American Studies seeks a construction of the United States past that would provide a firm foundation to constrain the free play of interpretations [of poststructuralist textualist criticism] while at the same time being sensitive to the problems of representation and textualization that form so important a part of the new trends" ("NC," 602).

This search in American Studies for what Berkhofer terms a "new realism based upon cultural pluralism without lapsing into any extreme conceptual relativisms" ("NC," 603) has been pursued, if we follow Fox-Genovese's and Berkhofer's many examples, less in a critical revisionary debate on the concept of culture and its newly (re)discovered dimensions of historical difference than in American literary historical studies. After more than a decade of a strong impact of European philosophy or "theory" and a neglect of critical American traditions and approaches, the debate has finally been taken up on native grounds, and literary and cultural studies in the United States have explicitly and self-consciously become *American* literary and cultural studies.

This *rehistoricization* of critical discourse and *recontextualization* of the analysis of literature and culture in terms of "America" as some kind of synthesizing principle, at a closer, particularly a European perspective, turns out, however, to be a very ambiguous adventure. I will critically discuss three different responses to the challenge of history and context, of rearticulating textualist readings and the fragmentation of literatures und cultures in terms of cultural studies and America that seem to me of crucial importance for the current efforts of reconceiving American Cultural Studies.

(Dis)entangling History: The New Historicism

The internationalization of the debate on the "postmodern condition" in recent years has also brought about American efforts to resolve or undercut the controversies that have dominated the philosophical interpretation of modernity and postmodernity in Europe. I think it is an important step in American thought when Richard Rorty in his essay "Habermas and Lyotard on Postmodernism" (1984) interprets the debate between Jean-François Lyotard and Jürgen Habermas in the light of the *American* tradition of pragmatism.[3] Rorty writes in the introduction to *Consequences of Pragmatism*, "James and Dewey were not only waiting at the end of the dialectical road which analytic philosophy travelled, but are waiting at the end of the road, which, for example, Foucault and Deleuze are currently travelling."[4] The consequences Rorty draws from this teleological narrative are, however, to give up the search for a general philosophical legitimation of cultural norms and values as equally mistaken, futile, and superfluous. Rorty's solutions to the debate seem to me to minimize crucial problems Lyotard and Habermas have argued about and to foreclose the exploration of fundamental differences and discontinuities that we should *not* try to reinterpret as only apparently antagonistic, incommensurable, or irrelevant. Rorty's "postmodern bourgeois liberalism" is "unashamedly" "ethnocentric," as Cornel West writes in the afterword to *Post-Analytic Philosophy* (1985).[5] He celebrates American political culture and American society without seriously questioning key terms such as "our society," "our political traditions," or "our intellectual heritage." Christopher Norris points to the similarity of this strategy to the "end of ideology" debate of the 1950s:

> Like the "end of ideology" argument propounded in the 1950s, it holds out the prospect of a new social order based on widespread consensus and no longer needing to criticize its own ideological assumptions. Basic to that earlier movement was the premise that real social conflict had to come to an end, so that now there was simply no reason for mounting any kind of radical critique. . . . It ignored, for one thing, the differences of interest between those within and those outside the established dominant consensuses.[6]

In arguing in his essay "Pragmatism without Method" that "anti-ideological liberalism is the most valuable tradition in American literature," Rorty seems to reaffirm Louis Hartz's thesis in *The Liberal Tradition in America* (1955), but without Hartz's critical, sharply polemical thrust.[7]

The problems of a neopragmatism that is supposed to transcend or to undercut the questions and validity claims of philosophy and "theory," that denies to theoretical questions any consequences for practice, and that still sets out to work out an explicitly "historical" mode of critical practice characterize also the work of the New Historicism of Walter Benn Michaels, Stephen Greenblatt, and the other founders of the journal *Representations*.[8] Greenblatt has defined his scholarly work in English Renaissance studies as "trying to situate myself in relation to Marxism on the one hand, and poststructuralism on the other."[9] His wide-ranging studies and a few of his more general and theoretical short essays or introductions to his books, especially to *Renaissance Self-Fashioning* (1980), *Shakespearean Negotiations* (1988), and *Learning to Curse* (1990), have set the agenda for the New Historicism's analysis of literary and nonliterary discourses in terms of power. As the Elizabethan period was also the "Age of Discovery," of the colonialist adventure, Greenblatt's changing conceptions of colonialist discourse and of the response or the articulation of the colonized peoples themselves have become in our time of the critique of neocolonialism and colonialist discourse the most controversial part of his scholarly work, the crucial issue for judging the meaning and the political implications of "history" and "historical criticism" in the New Historicism.

The Totalizing Power of the Culture of Capitalism: Walter Benn Michaels

In *American* literary studies, Walter Benn Michaels's book *The Gold Standard and the Logic of Naturalism* (1987) and his later essays have been the most provocative and influential efforts of the New Historicism. He originally worked out his own New Historicist approach in a direct response to the New Pragmatism of Richard Rorty and Stanley Fish. Rejecting his own earlier deconstructionist work, he argued in the manifesto "Against Theory," jointly written with Stephen Knapp in 1982, that theory per se, be it deconstruction, poststructuralism, hermeneutics, Marxism, or the quest for objective meaning, is misguided and should be given up, as long as it attempts to "govern interpretation of particular texts by appealing to an account of interpretation in general." As "the meaning of a text is simply identical to the author's intended meaning" and "knowledge and true belief are the same," there just cannot be any need or possibility of "grounding" meaning in something "outside" itself or of uncovering hidden meanings or different meanings in a text changing over time.[10] If this argument wipes out the philosophical objectives of Marxism as well as of deconstruction, Michaels and Knapp's own account of interpretation in terms of "intention" is said to have *no* consequences for practice, to be "useless as a guide to practice"—that is, methodologically useless. They argue that it is "compatible with (or indifferent to) all modes of critical practice" as well as "all ways of organizing that practice."[11]

How, then, can the project of a New Historicism be conceived? Michaels and Knapp write, "To insist, as we do, that the object of interpretation is always a historical intention is, once again, not to justify or even to recommend, the pursuit of historical scholarship." Yet this "historical intention" that was said to be identical to the "author's intentional meaning" as the "object of interpretation" turns out to be a free-floating construct, as it is anchored neither in a notion of the historical author of the text nor in any conception of historical process: "In our view, the object of all reading is always the historical author's intention, *even if the historical author is the universal muse*" (my emphasis). As Michaels and Knapp claim that their account of interpretation "describes the way interpretation *always* works" in practice, all the talk about "historical intention" or the "historical author's intention" as well as their account of critical practice turns out to be tautological and empty ("RC," 103–105). If these reflections may be taken as another example of the futility of "grounding" a New Historicism "theoretically," they also seem to me to make this whole project a contradiction in terms.

Yet Michaels and Knapp's "radical" version of pragmatism and their closing remark in their final contribution to the "Against Theory" debate, that "in practice [the critics] are all pragmatists," indicate the direction Michaels's New Historicism was to take "in practice."[12] In his book *The Gold Standard and the Logic of Naturalism*, his New Historicism works through constellations and confrontations of various, often seemingly very different contemporaneous discourses from literature, economics, sociology, or law, which he deconstructs in critical readings that reveal their inherent dialectics, their highly complex, often self-contradictory or multiple rhetorical strategies, and their often stunning and spectacular interrelationships.

Brilliant and illuminating as these "practical" readings are, they raise several questions that refer us back to Michaels's controversial version of a New Pragmatism. If the meaning of a text is its historical author's intention, but not necessarily the intentions of the historical author or cultural or social conditions and processes as historical scholarship can (try to) reconstruct them, in what sense, then, can there be any historical interpretation of texts at all? Michaels's answer is a version of "intertextuality" that places texts in something like a Foucauldian *épistème* that is dominated by the omnipresence of power and complicity with power.[13] Michaels elaborates this in his readings of literature and other discourses in the era of naturalism in an understanding of the "logic of capitalism" around the turn of the twentieth century, which sees it as a total structure of consumerism and circulation in a market economy that finally makes any individual dissent or critical distance impossible as well as irrelevant. As he writes in the introduction to his book, he "needed to transform an argument about the affective relation of certain literary texts to American capitalism into an investigation of the position of those texts within a system of representation that, producing objects of approval and disapproval both, is more important than any attitude one might imagine oneself to have toward it" (*GS*, 19).

Capitalism is read in terms of a logic that turns it into a total "system of representation," into an omnipresent, basically homogeneous system of "consumption," "circulation," and "exchange." The capitalist market economy is transformed into a system or force field of tropes that obscures by "textualizing" them economic, social, and cultural differences and their material production and change in a society that is as heterogeneous as it is permeated by the drive toward unity and consensus.

Michaels briefly refers to the historical account of the genesis of consumer society by Alan Trachtenberg, Richard Wightman Fox, T. Jackson Lears, and Ann Douglas, but rejects their efforts to trace and reconstruct "alternative views of American culture" and some "subversive" potential in the "radical" literature and cultural criticism of the time as "moral handwringing" and "nostalgia" that overlook the "radical acceptance of the logic of consumption" by their heroes, as he puts it ironically (*GS*, 14–17). For Michaels's new literary history, this means that the focus is shifted "from the individual text or author to structures whose coherence, interest, and effect may be greater than that of either author or text" (*GS*, 174–75). Unquestionably, the claims for a radical tradition in American letters have often been made too carelessly by critics who have seen the "great works" of American literature as per se oppositional, but certainly this applies only to a part of earlier American radical literary and cultural criticism. Moreover, as many recent "radical" critics have shown, the questioning of the notion of a radical tradition in American literary and cultural history does not demand its wholesale rejection, but its reformulation in terms of discontinuity, differences, and counter-discourses, in the plural.[14]

In his emphasis on "structures," Michaels attempts to go beyond Foucault's critique of the "constituent subject," but by eliminating the last traces of the constituent subject he also eliminates the dimension of a "critique of ideology" altogether: "But can economies be subjects? Can they have intentions, desires, beliefs? Can they have interests? Individuals obviously can, classes can, but insofar as an economy is neither an individual nor a class, it is hard to see how it can be said to have interests. Indeed, from a certain standpoint, the whole point of the analysis I have attempted here has been, by subverting the primacy of the subjects in literary history, to subvert also the primacy of interest" (*GS*, 178). Everything, *every* text, in this reading, is a "corporate fiction" (*GS*, 213). Not only is *every* text implicated and immersed in the total system of representation or circulation of capitalism, but according to Michaels—in a Foucauldian move of the omnipresence of power that produces its own "subversion" in order to contain it—*every* mode of discourse can be shown to be "equivalent" *and* "complicitous" with it, whatever the author may have "intended" to express and communicate (certainly an ironic turn after his earlier emphasis on authorial intentions in "Against Theory").

Instead of making use of the recent work in revisionary Marxist literary and cultural critique from Fredric Jameson to Edward W. Said and of the alternative historical critical practices developed during the past decades in feminist or African American criticism, Michaels so rigorously restricts the discursive space in his readings of American literary history and abstracts it from social, political, economic, and cultural processes that his argument concerning the "complicity" of any "oppositional" criticism can only tautologically reconfirm itself.

Michaels's New Historicist interpretation of naturalism, literature, or literary "representation" does not offer anything in particular that makes it different from other discourses. Whereas other critics such as Amy Kaplan, Philip Fisher, and Lee Clark Mitchell have read novels of American realism and naturalism as working out new fictional modes or models of understanding a rapidly changing culture and society and of re-encoding and transfiguring traditional literary strategies and genres as competing contemporary forms of representation of a new urban public culture, Michaels uses the multiple meanings of "fiction" (or "fictionality"), especially in the fields of literature and of law, to dismiss the question of the specific potentiality of literature altogether (*GS*, 56, 58,

212–13). In his reading, Dreiser's novels are not in any meaningful sense "oppositional" to capitalism, but wholly complicitous with it.

Concerning the concept of culture and cultural studies, Michaels argues in a daring move that there can be no "space outside culture"; therefore, the project of "interrogating the relation between that space (here defined as literature) and the culture makes no sense" (*GS*, 27). On the one hand, in his ambiguous, or "slippery," use of the term "culture" Michaels takes up the tradition of cultural anthropology by defining culture as an all-encompassing concept that challenges and transcends the divisions of realms (social, cultural, political, economic) and of the various specialized discourses in modern industrialized societies. This concept has often led to diffuse generalizations, but it was intended, especially in early American Studies, to implicate scholarly work in a critical engagement with the force field of differences and was implicitly comparative, intercultural in its method.

On the other hand, Michaels focuses his analysis on modes of representation in the realm of culture, on the construction of different discourses by the social forces or groups in power, and then takes the patterns of homology and containment he discovers among the contemporaneous *discourses* as identical with the *social, material processes* of American society at large. In his notion of the "logic of capitalism" around the turn of the century, which posits a more or less holistic view of culture as circulation of social energy, the heterogeneity of American society, the coexistence of different stages in the development of American "consumer capitalism," and the inevitable tensions, material struggles, and alternative modes in and of American culture(s) and literature(s) become invisible. As the question of opposition or subversion is seen exclusively from the perspective of the totalizing system of the dominant discourse, never in terms of the agency of the oppositional groups themselves, their alternative experiences and countercultural representations must necessarily appear as deluded acts of opposition that turn out to be nothing but complicitous parts of the system. Put another way, the totalizing understanding of the public discourse of American consumer capitalist society in the late nineteenth and early twentieth centuries entails a notion of opposition and "subversion" that is equally totalizing; that is, it is considered subversive only when it is free from any involvement with dominant discourse. As this obviously is impossible, Michaels denies the possibility of any oppositional practices of minorities and other dissenting groups instead of exploring the complex double- (or multi)voicedness of alternative discourses in terms of class, race, ethnicity, and gender in specific historical contexts. Also, Michaels's version of the New Historicism has no place for any notion of *inter*cultural relations and differences.

Thus, in spite of his penetrating deconstructions of various discourses of capitalism, Walter Benn Michaels's critique becomes curiously disembodied and ahistorical, and his strong commitment to intertextuality and interdisciplinarity tends to result in a repetitive discovery of sameness. His approach does not allow us to distinguish in a historically productive manner between our own reading of a historical (literary) text and the (reconstruction of the) reception during the time of its production. Consensus and a homogenizing synthesis, again, replace the exploration of difference, heterogeneity, dissent, and multicultural perspectives as the agenda for literary and cultural studies.

"America"—A New American Exceptionalism?

The renewed interest in American literary, critical, and philosophical traditions finally brought about by the rehistoricization of criticism since the mid-1980s has turned out to be highly ambivalent. Concerning the New Historicism, however, what had seemed to be a commitment to a critical confrontation of deconstruction with the different historical discourses of social and cultural power in the United States has ironically tended to become a reconfirmation of the American ideology and the traditional literary canon.

Another increasingly influential assertion of an American historical critique after deconstruction tends to reverse the former orientation toward European intellectual developments by claiming American priority and primacy in the philosophical critique of the Western tradition. In this vein, the renewed awareness of important historical differences between the United States and Europe is turned into a strong emphasis on unique American social and cultural conditions and a unique democratic system that are said to make the problematics and ordeals of European philosophical thought and its notions of cultural and social critique inapplicable and irrelevant to the United States.

Clearly, this *New American Exceptionalism*, as I would call it, has taken different forms in the various disciplines. It can have widely divergent political aims or implications, just as the earlier version of the 1950s led to a glorification of American uniqueness as well as to a critique of the "irrationalism" of the American consensus (Hartz). Whereas the old exceptionalism was closely—and consciously—tied to the political and sociological question as to why there had been no socialism in the United

States, the New American Exceptionalism challenges the whole notion of the political in traditional political science and philosophy and/or tends to slight or redefine issues of political power and of the social struggle in terms of *readings of American culture.* I think it important, particularly in a time of talk about the "end of history" and the loss of any utopian perspectives, to analyze more carefully some of these tendencies in American political theory, philosophy, and literary and cultural studies.

Emerson, Whitman, and the Culture of American Democracy: George Kateb

The specific dynamics and the range of problems involved in reassessing the meaning of "politics" and "culture" and their interrelations in the United States, as they characterize the project of a New American Exceptionalism, can perhaps be paradigmatically identified in the work of the political theorist George Kateb. In several remarkable essays, Kateb has argued that in a time of nuclear threat of human extinction it is not "statism" or "state activism" but the "theory of democratic individuality" of a rights-based constitutional democracy that is indispensable and thus the best resource for the survival of mankind. Nancy L. Rosenblum explains that Kateb uses the terms "statism" and "state activism" to refer to political movements and concepts such as nationalism, civic republicanism, and communitarianism.[15] Kateb finds the theory of democratic individuality most perfectly expressed and alive in the United States, as he writes in his essay "Thinking about Human Extinction (II): Emerson and Whitman" (1976), "though the United States has only an imperfectly democratic system of political power" ("EW," 7). That is, Kateb clearly distinguishes democracy as the political system and as "the culture of democracy." Yet this culture of democracy in its espousal of moral identity and democratic individuality is "unthinkable without the functioning of the system of power—without the functioning of constitutional democracy"—and is sustained by it ("EW," 7). If democracy is a "distinctive culture, made and kept so to a significant degree by its political system," and if this system is "full of faults" in reality, the culture of democracy can find the realization of its idealism "more perfectly outside [the political system], in nonpolitical life," in "all the nonpolitical sectors of life" ("EW," 3, 7). Thus democratic individuality is basically conceived as "an existential condition" that *transcends* the sphere of the political power struggle and an active daily involvement in political life. What it refers to is "the way an individual in certain moments or in certain respects withdraws from her or his immediate world in order to enter into a relation to all that lies beyond it," to what Kateb calls an "attachment to existence as such" ("EW," 7).

Kateb's strong emphasis on the "culture of democracy" and the political effects he finds inherent in it leads him to the discovery of Emerson, Thoreau, and Whitman as political philosophers who have given us the "greatest formulations concerning democratic individuality" ("EW," 1). He finds in their work the most powerful representation of "constitutional democracy as a morally expressive system" ("EW," 11). He reads their work less as a critique of the pitfalls and social dangers of the doctrine and practice of individualism and of the shortcomings of American society or as the projection of alternative social visions than as a "transcendence" of "the social" as well as of the "self": "[All] three are transcendental: what they ask us to transcend is the social altogether, even if only in moments, so that one may enter into what Emerson calls 'an original relation' to reality" ("EW," 15). What at first had been addressed as "democratic individuality" is replaced by "moral identity" or "a radical spiritual equality that in certain respects is shared with all natural existence" ("EW," 15–16). As Kateb puts it succinctly, "The telos of the encouragement of democratic individuality is to transcend not only the social but even the individualistic, and to attain impersonality" ("EW," 16).

Kateb's emphatic rejection of "rootedness in social life," in "what is superstitiously called reality," in the "merely social," is based on a reductive understanding of the meaning of social and political relations that he opposes to the truly "human" ("EW," 17–18). He accepts conventions and laws as necessary even in a democracy, but dismisses their constitutive role insofar as being changeable cannot provide the "locus of ultimacy." Instead, he turns democracy as culture into a celebration of a "democratic estheticism" he characterizes in Kantian terms as a "detached attachment to one's immediate world, a disinterested interest in it," but also as the "attachment of love" ("EW," 16–17). "Supreme individuals" learn to think that one is "only playing, no matter what one does." This move implies, however, that the locus of ultimacy Kateb looks for is a purely formal one, a move "beyond good and evil" open to every person, an "individuality that goes beyond itself," a detached attachment to existence as such ("EW," 18).

Now, if the "American Romantic democrats" most powerfully help us to see "that democracy, truly understood, is a change of heart," Kateb qualifies his invocation of these democratic individualists by pointing out a fundamental weakness in their thought, especially in its Emersonian version, that Americans in the nuclear age have to revise in order to repossess their great tradition. Not only does he accept the common charge against Emerson, Thoreau, and Whitman that their formulations of democratic individuality in mid-nineteenth-century America are "too exuberant, too prone to suggest that everything can be accepted, too eager for reconciliation," a faith we can no longer share, but he also discovers a more serious flaw related to their notion of the "locus of ultimacy": "When we try to determine what upholds Emerson, Thoreau, and Whitman in their radical democracy, in their insistence that democracy can and should realize itself in impersonal individuality, we come across a religious spirit. This is their greatest weakness" ("EW," 21). It is not in later American philosophy or cultural and social critique, but in the radical antireligious, antimetaphysical thought of two *European* philosophers, in Nietzsche's and Heidegger's sense of the "inessentiality of all things and the wonder at the uncomposed indefiniteness that contrasts with nothingness" that Kateb finds the "right and true replacement for an untenable religiousness" in Emerson and his followers ("EW," 22). Paradoxically, the explicitly "antidemocratic individualism" of the two German philosophers is chosen to revise and reinvigorate the "idealism of democratic individuality" in the United States.[16]

However, in a later essay, "Walt Whitman and the Culture of Democracy" (1990), Kateb seems to have turned his call for an intercultural dialogue, for a correction of the "Emersonian tradition" by the radically demystifying work of Nietzsche and Heidegger into a compelling reassessment of the critical deconstructive potential of mid-nineteenth-century American writings. A rereading of Walt Whitman's poetry, especially of his "Song of Myself" leads one to rediscover among the American romantic democrats themselves America's own "indigenous resources" for countering the "exuberance," "innocence," and "inexpungeable religiousness" of their theory and practice of democratic individuality. Kateb readily admits that there are contradictory forces at work in Whitman's poetry, but he strongly argues for the decidedly secular and antiessentialist strain, particularly in "Song of Myself," that is free of Emerson's "metaphysics," his "moralizing," his "analogical" or "symbolical" thinking, his quest for reconciliation, and any "reference to a Creator or to any assimilation to a Creator" ("WCD," 560). Instead, Whitman's best, radical work constructs and deconstructs the self, the "great composite democratic individual" as "unexpressed individuality," as "permanent difference," as "ambiguous and ambivalent," and does *not* conceive it as an "indivisible," "fixed identity" or an "indestructible core" ("WCD," 554, 561–62). If Whitman emphasizes, as does Emerson, receptivity and responsiveness, it should not be understood, Kateb argues, as what he sometimes takes "adhesive love, or love of comrades" to be, but as an acceptance of "otherness" and the "mutuality of strangers," as an openness to the potentiality in other human beings, as the potential for a more experimental life and for seeking "heterogeneous accumulated experiences" ("WCD," 556, 563–64, 569).

Again, Kateb acknowledges some problems with Whitman's notion of the culture of democracy, particularly concerning the "moral and mental limits to sympathy or empathy" ("WCD," 568). What is much more important to him, however, is that Whitman's perspectivism, which corresponds to a person's "inner multiplicity," finds a powerful and self-reflective expression in the specific "formal qualities" of a poetic discourse that can be read as "a work in political theory," as the "new forms . . . of the artistic beauty appropriate for a new world, for a democracy," for "America" ("WCD," 548, 555). Kateb points out and strongly valorizes the poem's "discontinuities, abrupt transitions, and sudden eruptions into different tones," reading "Song of Myself" in the manner of poststructuralist theory as a self-deconstructive text as well as a text deconstructing the unitary self into an "indefinite multiplicity" ("WCD," 551, 555).

This interpretive move that could have returned Kateb's reflections to a reengagement with the political contradictions of democratic culture and the political system of American democracy, however, results in a disengagement of Whitman's "teaching" from the "aims of political action," a pedagogy that can at best influence political action indirectly ("WCD," 563). Indeed, the final lesson Kateb sees in Whitman is a "democratic transcendence of democratic culture" open to everyone, a "solitary relation with something unconceptualizable—perhaps the sheer fact of existence, of one's own being and the being of anything else," a message of "solitude, not the adventures of human connectedness" ("WCD," 570).

It is at the end of "Walt Whitman and the Culture of Democracy" that Kateb seems to endorse again the American tradition of anti-institutional, antisocial thought that removes his stimulating interpretation of the American "culture of democracy" too radically from the sphere of political action and the reality of the democratic political system. He must again face the charge of political irrelevance or inconsequence raised against the Emersonian tradition by its critics. As Nancy L. Rosenblum argues in her critique of Kateb's essay, in his "poetic vision of democracy as a spectacle of diversity . . . democratic *politics* recedes into the background."[17] Unfortunately, Kateb has not confronted as yet more directly the inevitable tensions between the theory of rights-based democracy and the political, social, and economic inequality and difference in the multicultural United States. These tensions and contradictions are not so much suspended or transcended by the culture of democracy as inscribed and dramatized in its very forms of representation and its institutions. His reaffirmation and revision of the Emersonian tradition by confronting it with the antihistorical thought of Nietzsche and Heidegger and, more recently, by displacing this philosophical critique in a radically deconstructive (and reconstructive) reading of Whitman's poetry seem to leave him with what Leo Marx has called his "unabashed affirmation of American exceptionalism."[18] Obviously, it is a very rich and self-reflective version of American exceptionalism, but in its wholesale rejection of "statism" and "state activism" it fails to engage democratic theory in a critical analysis of the crucial transformations in American capitalist society, in public culture(s), and in the representations of democracy in recent decades.

The Literary Redemption of Philosophy and Emersonian Perfectionism: Stanley Cavell

In many ways, George Kateb's powerful reflections on the American democratic political system and the culture of democracy can be read as defining and redefining or, potentially, also questioning the boundaries and contours of the various versions of a new, self-consciously revisionary American philosophy of culture and politics in the United States.

In literary and cultural studies, the two most complex and challenging versions of this New American Exceptionalism can be found in the works of the philosopher Stanley Cavell and of the literary critic Richard Poirier. Both are aware of the strong impact of European philosophy and respond to the fundamental critique of the Western philosophical tradition, but their work is focused on an authoritative revisionary reading of American literary and philosophical thought. The Emersonian tradition they rediscover and reappropriate in American philosophy, literary criticism, and literature is offered as the fulfillment and transcendence of European antisystematic (and poststructuralist) thought as well as a unique way of philosophical, or poetic-philosophical, practice that finds its manifestation in a new, enabling mode of American cultural and literary critique. It is exactly their specific reconstruction of an Emersonian tradition and the far-reaching philosophical and political claims associated with it that raise serious "historical" questions about the New American Exceptionalism.

In *The Senses of Walden* (1972), Cavell raised the question "Why has America never expressed itself philosophically? Or has it—in the metaphysical riot of its greatest literature?"[19] His long quest for the philosophical meaning and power of "America" has from its beginning been motivated by the ambitious endeavor to engage the two competing (European) philosophical traditions of Germany and the Anglo-Saxon world in a dialogue (and transcend them), as both have faced in the twentieth century, though in different ways, the radical challenge of the end of systematic philosophy and turned it into reflections on the *modes of philosophical discourse itself.* In his critique of metaphysics, epistemology, and the truth claims of representations in language, Cavell does not draw on Derrida's philosophical deconstruction of the logocentric discourse of the Western tradition (and he occasionally explicitly distinguishes his own critical work from deconstruction in the Derridean vein). Instead, he relies on J. L. Austin's ordinary language philosophy, Wittgenstein's *Philosophical Investigations*, and, finally, the essays on the experience of thinking of the later Heidegger.

Cavell reads Wittgenstein's remark in *Philosophical Investigations* about philosophy and the use of language, "philosophy leaves everything as it is" (*SW*, 124), as a radical critique of culture, as a rejection of any kind of false transcendence. Positively, he takes it as asking us to relinquish our desire to impose our own (philosophical) will on language, "so that language itself, as if beyond me, exclusively takes over the responsibility for meaning," as he puts it in his book *This New Yet Unapproachable America: Lectures after Emerson after Wittgenstein* (1989) (*TN*, 57). This emphasis on the "emptying out" of language, on "look and see," on "listen and [hear] the word" helps Cavell to propose a connection between Wittgenstein's philosophy and Heidegger's notion of letting truth happen, of "thinking" as responsiveness, as "letting-lie-before-us," as "being on the way towards language" (*TN*, 13, 46). By blending or merging Wittgenstein's philosophy and Heidegger's poetical thinking, Cavell can define philosophical thinking as "responsiveness" and "reading" that "position" the philosopher as a "prophet" (*TN*, 75).

If Cavell's thoughts on the "end" of philosophy and on philosophical thinking as reading, however, find their legitimation in Wittgenstein and Heidegger, he draws on philosophers who in different ways set out to liberate philosophy from the spell of intellectual history and its "classic" texts. What, then, can "philosophy as reading" mean? Which texts can we read or interpret without getting entangled again in the snares of traditional (systematic) philosophy?

For Cavell, Heidegger's mythologizing interpretation of Hölderlin's poetry testifies to the power of a philosophical reading of *literature*. Whereas the deconstructionist literary criticism of Paul de Man or J. Hillis Miller exposes the self-deconstruction of literary language in a never-ending process characterized by negativity and a dismantling of the claims to "presence," Cavell's philosophical reflections are directed at a "presentness (which is about me and my world)," as he writes in his book *In Quest of the Ordinary: Lines of Skepticism and Romanticism* (1988), which we can experience or read in certain literary texts he valorizes as "sacred scriptures" (*IQO*, 174).

It is here that Cavell's quest for the specific form and achievement of *philosophical thinking in America* becomes crucial. The common notion of the "poverty" of American philosophy, of the "American belatedness" (*TN*, 6–7, 28) compared with European philosophy takes on a completely different meaning for Cavell. In the perspective of his readings of Wittgenstein's and Heidegger's work, the poverty of American philosophy reveals itself as its richness, the belatedness as the priority *and* primacy of American philosophical thinking. To Cavell, Emerson and Thoreau *anticipated* the critique of systematic philosophy later found in Nietzsche, Wittgenstein, and Heidegger. More than that, they had already *put into practice* the utopian hopes for a new constitution of meaning projected in the crisis of metaphysical thinking. This "anticipation," this "underwriting as grounding" (*TN*, 77, 79), as Cavell defines the relation of Emerson and Thoreau to Austin, Wittgenstein, and Heidegger from the perspective of twentieth-century philosophical thought, finds its complement in the fact that Cavell recognized the crucial role of the ordinary, of the common, the near, the low (*TN*, 34), of everyday language as a form of life in the works of these philosophers only after having carefully reread Thoreau's *Walden* and Emerson's essays. Emerson and Thoreau are to Cavell the "founders of American thinking" as well as of American literature, the "origin" and the "inventors" of a hitherto neglected or repressed tradition of thinking that acquires its *philosophical* significance in the distinctive quality of its *literary* discourse.

This close connection between literary and philosophical writing and thinking relates Emerson's and Thoreau's work to European romanticism, and Cavell has increasingly devoted some critical attention to Wordsworth and Coleridge. In Cavell's reading, however, Emerson's essays are the practical solution to the program of romanticism, the realization of the poetic philosophizing or philosophical poetry/poetics (especially of Friedrich Schlegel, whom Cavell with some hesitation mentions in *This New Yet Unapproachable America*) as well as romanticism's own theory, "announc[ing] and provid[ing] the conditions under which an Emersonian essay can be experienced" (*TN*, 103; *IQO*, xii). If professional philosophers have complained about the fuzziness, the inconsistencies, and the discursive impurity of Emerson's essays, Cavell discovers in these texts "a mode of thinking, a mode of conceptual accuracy, as thorough as anything imagined within established philosophy," a "foreign rigor" (*IQO*, 14), a "terrible exactness" (*SW*, 152). To him, Emerson's essays and Thoreau's *Walden* are "prophetic texts" that recover the lost "sense of intimacy with existence" (*SW*, 152) and answer to the "romantic demand for, or promise of, redemption" (*IQO*, 26). This quest for a "philosophical redemption" (cf. *IQO*, 32) by means of a specific kind of literary-philosophical discourse finds its fulfilment in the claim that "they are their own Hölderlins" (*SW*, 134).

In *The Senses of Walden*, Cavell declares, "The literary redemption of language is at the same time a philosophical redemption; the establishment of American literature undertaken in *Walden* requires not only the writing of a scripture and an epic, but a work of philosophy" (*SW*, 93). His powerful reading of *Walden* tries to prove that this work is America's first "epic" and "sacred text" and offers in its specific verbal gestalt at once "literary and philosophical redemption." Not just a book about Thoreau's experience at Walden Pond in the years 1845–47, it is to Cavell also a book about the writing of the book *Walden*, about writing and reading as such, the "original, or initiating [philosophical] text," written at a "pre-philosophical moment of its culture" (*SW*, xiii, 3–5).

Cavell notes the "impurity" and complexity of *Walden*'s literary discourse, its "puns and paradoxes, its fracturing of idiom and twisting of quotation, its drones of fact and flights of impersonation" (*SW*, 16). Yet he interprets all these puns and paradoxes in a manner reminiscent of the later Heidegger's often pseudo-etymological ruminations as revelations in and of language itself, as "scriptural procedures or . . . revisions of mythology" (*SW*, 20). This reading uncovers in the ordinary, in the common a "deeper" meaning, while bracketing its literal, sociohistorical meaning.

Through these moves Cavell establishes the primacy of American philosophy as it found expression in Emerson's and Thoreau's works. The "finding" of this "origin," of the "founding" of philosophical thinking means, at the same time, a discovery, a finding and founding of a new "America." It is a rejection of the as yet "uncultivated," "forbidding" America of the time, but also a "rebirth" of the idea of America in the "prophetic," "sacred texts" of Emerson and Thoreau (*TN*, 92; *IQO*, 185). When Cavell argues that it is the task of American literature in the tradition of Emerson and Thoreau "to rescue the word from both politics and religion" (*SW*, 31), he himself claims to save it from being mixed up with religious dogma, ideology, or therapeutics. Yet at the same time Cavell lifts philosophical thinking about "America" out of its real, historical context in the United States, its "American location" (*SW*, 37; *TN*, 92–93).

In his essay "The Politics of Interpretation (Politics as Opposed to What?)" (1982), reprinted in his book *Themes Out of School: Effects and Causes* (1984), Cavell addresses directly his "political liability" in his acceptance of Emerson and Thoreau, "namely, their interpretation of what you might call the politics of philosophical interpretation as a withdrawal or rejection of politics, even of society, as such" (*TOS*, 49–50). Earlier, in *The Senses of Walden*, he mentioned a few passages in *Walden* where Thoreau refers to the political problems of his time, particularly the question of slavery. To Cavell, *Walden* is also "a tract of political education for membership in the polis" (*SW*, 85), but in his reading this "political education" has to be an act of *withdrawal from society*, an "education for isolation." Thoreau's withdrawal, the writing of *Walden*, is taken as an "act of civil disobedience" that does not, however, return the writer to society, but replaces it. In "The Politics of Interpretation," Cavell concludes, "So the writer's silence (that is, this writer's writing) declares itself redemptive religiously, aesthetically, and politically" (*TOS*, 51). Cavell understands Emerson's and Thoreau's ambiguous, or unelaborated, uses of "society" as a necessary abstraction, because a citizen cannot "reject" politics or society "as such," only particular "representations" of politics or social movements or processes. In effect, Cavell substitutes his own abstractions of such terms as "society" and "politics" rather than interpreting carefully their different connotations in the writings of the Transcendentalists. Thoreau's efforts to redefine the terms "politics" and "economy of living" in the long first chapter of his book and his later political reflections in *Walden*—not to mention his "reform lectures"—are contracted, in *The Senses of Walden*, into an "epistemology of conscience" (*SW*, 88), which transcends the "false consciousness" (*SW*, 93) of history that has kept all of us prisoner: "Who knows what our lives will be when we have shaken off the stupor of history, slipped the drag of time?" (*SW*, 93).

Similarly, Cavell again and again returns to what he calls in *Conditions Handsome and Unhandsome: The Constitution of Emerson's Perfectionism* (1990) Emerson's "famously outrageous passage" from "Self-Reliance": "I shun father and mother and wife and brother when my genius calls me. I would write on the lintels of the door-post, *Whim*. I hope it is somewhat better than whim at last, but we cannot spend the day in explanation. . . . Do not tell me, as a good man did to-day, of my obligation to put all poor men in good situations. Are they *my* poor?" (*TOS*, 50; *CHU*, 79, 97, 134–35). What others have criticized as Emerson's slip into a "religion of selfishness" (Harold Bloom) Cavell reads as Emerson's "gesture to claim that his [philosophical] genius is redemptive beyond himself" (*TOS*, 50), as a message of "withdrawal," the "announcement of nothing to assert" (*CHU*, 79), or if to "assert" something, "that what he is withdrawing in order to do is done for the poor," namely "writing": "This announces his act as moral, as announcing moral principles whose application will rebuke those who rebuke him for failing his moral obligations" (*CHU*, 136–37). Cavell's sometimes rather involved interpretations and arguments raise the question, why does he feel obliged to defend Emerson at any price? Does not his obsession with the quasi-infallibility and consequentiality of Emerson's thinking, with the "sacred texts" of his essays and the "genuine Scripture," "our Scripture" of Thoreau's *Walden* (*SW*, xv, 19), contradict his own philosophical engagement with skepticism and compromise his commitment to the supreme values of American democracy?

If Cavell's philosophical work can be understood as a critical engagement with skepticism, he has set out neither to subscribe to skepticism nor to refute it, but to "reconceive" its basic premises, as he put it in "Thinking of Emerson" (*SW*, 122), and to turn its negative thrust, its demystifying spirit into a positive dynamic, an enabling aesthetic, moral, and political way of thinking and acting. His central term "acknowledging existence" refers not only to the epistemological problems of knowledge and the alternative vision of "thinking as receptive" (*SW*, 133), but also to our relation to other human beings, to getting involved in dialogue, in a reciprocal acknowledgment, accepting the "responsibility" of working out our relationship with others in the world.[20]

In *Conditions Handsome and Unhandsome*, Cavell calls this position "Emersonian Perfectionism," a "(secular) perfectionist outlook" (xix) that is characterized epistemologically by a "withholding of assertion" (*CHU*, 79; *TOS*, 51), by a notion of the self as "always attained and always unattained" (*CHU*, xxxi, cf. 12), and by a concept of society and politics not of a privileged and principled elitism, but of "social conditions that escape the extremes of chaos or of tyranny," of the "compromise" and the negotiations of conditions of "good enough justice" (*CHU*, xxii). In social and political terms Cavell's Emersonian Perfectionism is not offered as a new and ultimate "competing moral theory," but as "a dimension of any moral thinking" (*CHU*, 62) that "places tremendous burdens on personal relationships and on the possibility or necessity of the transforming of oneself and of one's society" (*CHU*, 2).

Conditions Handsome and Unhandsome addresses the "doubleness" of the self and of society (*CHU*, xxi, xxxi, xxxv), the "open-ended thematics" of democracy, and powerfully argues that Emersonian Perfectionism is not "inherently undemocratic, or elitist," but "essential to the criticism of democracy from within" (*CHU*, 3, cf. 18, 28). In his reading, Emerson's sense of "thinking" is of "a double process, or a single process with two names: transfiguration and conversion," or, when thinking is "oppositional, or critical," "aversion" (*CHU*, 36, referring to Emerson's "The American Scholar") as a "*continual turning away* from society . . . [and] thereby a continual turning *toward* it. Toward and away; it is a motion of seduction—such as philosophy will contain" (*CHU*, 59). Cavell finds this continual (and therefore discontinuous) process of "responsiveness to society" (*CHU*, 28), of "conversion" and "aversion" in democracy most perfectly articulated in Emerson's writings, in their "incessant conversion or refiguration of society's incessant demands for his consent—his conforming himself—to its doings," as well as in their equally incessant movement of his "aversion to society's demands for conformity" and of being "the object of aversion to society's consciousness, to what it might read in him" (*CHU*, 37).

Cavell's understanding of thinking as "reception" or "reading" rearticulates the relationship between philosophy and literature and assigns literary texts a crucial role in our "reading" of American democracy. Yet the tension in the incessant refiguration of conversion and aversion at the heart of his philosophical response to skepticism and his philosophical understanding of democracy all but vanishes in Cavell's commitment to "saving" and reappropriating Emerson's essays and Thoreau's *Walden* as American Scripture or sacred texts. In trying to "listen" to Emerson's and Thoreau's words, in suspending his own historical subjectivity and philosophical will in favor of an open response to the revelatory power of language, his readings risk paradoxically leading to arbitrary, sometimes pseudo-etymological evocations and rather subjective associations. Obviously, this danger is inherent in the active response to literary texts and an experimental, exploratory perfectionist thinking, and misreadings can be corrected by rereadings and the interpretive community. However, by conceiving of some literary texts as sacred texts, Cavell eliminates their historical differences and homogenizes them in the pursuit of an omnipresent, coherent meaning, a process that—in spite of, as well as because of, its fundamental challenge and opposition to the "fallen" world of society—suspends the dimension of secular criticism and cultural revision. If a philosophical "(secular) perfectionism" and American democracy are to be permeated by dialogue and by reciprocal acknowledgment, we must respond to Emerson's and Thoreau's texts as voices of a historically different time with different philosophical and literary problems and options, as secular, sometimes mistaken voices that are important challenges for us, because they also speak to us in terms of otherness and difference. Instead of claiming again and again Emerson's "direct anticipation of Heidegger's [thought]" (*CHU*, 38), it could be more productive for a critical understanding of the achievement of American literature and philosophy to reconstruct and expound the specific problematic of "sacred" thought and its secular critique in the formative period of the American Renaissance and *contrast* it to the "(secular) perfectionist" perspectives of American democratic culture and society today.

In some of his more recent works Cavell clearly indicates that he is more and more willing to confront these questions. In *Conditions Handsome and Unhandsome*, a long meditation on the fate of democracy in America, he confesses that he finds it more and more urgent to think about the "political implications" not only of Heidegger's work but also of "his connection, through Nietzsche, with Emerson" (*CHU*, xvi). At the end of "The Politics of Interpretation," he talks about the "cultural difference between American and European intellectual life," deploring the "absence" of "sacred intellectual texts" in America "whose authority the intellectual community at large is anxious to preserve at all costs" (*TOS*, 59). Even though this final statement does not apply to contemporary Europe and certainly cannot explain the "absence" of "the concept of ideology" in American intellectual life, Cavell's observation leads him to qualify his lament over the lack of a "common cultural inheritance" in the United States (*TOS*, 8): "Since my paper rather deplores the absence of Emersonian and Thoreauvian texts as something like sacred common possessions, I should add here that this absence is not wholly, or just, deplorable" (*CHU*, 59). He has, however, not elaborated the cultural implications of this insight. Instead of proposing a "theology of reading" (*TOS*, 53) of a number of sacred texts by white male authors (see also his long list of names of the tradition of "perfectionist texts," *CHU*, 5), Cavell could follow more closely his own discovery of "difference" in his engagement with Emerson's writing (which "works out the conditions for my recognizing my difference from others as a function of my recognizing my difference from myself," *CHU*, 53) and with contemporary political and scholarly debates. He could turn the "instability" he finds "constituting Emerson's capture of philosophy for America" and the possibility he suggests that Emerson may have wished "to write in order to deprive us of a philosophical founder, of all foundation of a certain sort" (*CHU*, 133–34) into a version of "secular perfectionism" that resituates Emersonian thought in history and opens up his American philosophy to a full acknowledgment of *other* voices and *different* traditions and forms of thought.

Cavell writes at the end of "Hope Against Hope" (1986) that for him "Emerson's prose enacts in this way the state of democracy—not because it praises the democratic condition we have so far achieved but because its aversive stance toward our condition only makes sense on the assumption of democracy as our life and our aspiration" (*CHU*, 138). He has made a beginning by responding in his unique style of philosophical writing to Emerson's and Thoreau's "founding texts," to the challenge of the most influential philosophers beyond philosophy of our time, and also to an important area of American cultural representations in what is called popular culture, but his work has been highly selective in its representation of the complexity of American culture. His preoccupation with, and powerful reconstruction of, "specifically American thought" that suspends and transcends the separation of philosophy and literature and is said to renew the promise "yet to discover America" (*IQO*, 181–82, 185) has led him to an invocation and construction of an Emersonian tradition that has transformed the *historical* inscriptions in these texts of the ruptures and discontinuities of American culture and society "in this restless, nervous, bustling, trivial Nineteenth Century," as Thoreau put it in his conclusion to *Walden*, into tropes of a "visionary union" (*SW*, 111). In Cavell's version of American exceptionalism, the United States is turned into a transhistorical myth of America that in its practical political implications could easily be used as an ideological instrument to claim a unique political supremacy for the United States.

The literary and cultural critic Richard Poirier, in his important book *The Renewal of Literature: Emersonian Reflections* (1987), has pursued similar questions in his reflections on Emerson's legacy and on literary modernism and more pertinently compared Emerson with the work of American pragmatist philosophers than has Cavell, who confesses to his awkward relationship to pragmatism.[21] If the "Emersonian tradition" as well as its continuation and revision in the American pragmatist philosophy of William James is to become a *critical* and *enabling* force in American literary, cultural, and political thought in a secular, multicultural society, it has also to be deconstructed, I think, in its political limitations and in its complex cultural and political dialectic. Cornel West's book *The American Evasion of Philosophy: A Genealogy of Pragmatism* (1989) and Sacvan Bercovitch's work on the "paradoxes of dissent" in *The Office of "The Scarlet Letter"* (1991) and his recent essays are important steps in this direction.[22]

The New American Studies

Civil War over Representation in an American Society without Ideology: Philip Fisher

Philip Fisher's introduction to the collection of essays from the journal *Representations* published in 1991 as *The New American Studies* joins the objectives and strategies of the New Historicism and the New American Exceptionalism.[23] The collection represents "a new generation within American Studies," "a new idea of what it might mean to do American Studies and how one would go about doing it," and the "rich diversity of explanations and materials in the study of American culture" ("Intro.," vii). What is *new* about the New American Studies is, Fisher contends, the emphasis on *rhetorics*, the "open" and "plural" work within culture, as against *myth* and *ideology*, which are said to claim a "monopoly on representation," a "fixed, satisfying, and stable story that is used again and again to normalize our account of social life" ("Intro.," vii).

In a sweeping critique of the post–World War II American Studies movement and its institutionalization in the universities, Fisher repeats the common indictment of the so-called myth-and-symbol school as having focused its work on the search for unifying myths in American culture or a "central myth of America" that was to capture "American uniqueness and national identity" in the politically charged Cold War atmosphere ("Intro.," viii). Fisher clearly is aware of the critical dimension of the early American Studies movement, from F. O. Matthiessen's *American Renaissance* to Henry Nash Smith's *Virgin Land*, Leo Marx's *The Machine in the Garden*, and Richard Slotkin's *Regeneration through Violence*, but he reads this critical emphasis in terms of an opposition between the "purity" of the "promise" and the "disappointment" over the "betrayal" of the myth in social and political reality over time ("Intro.," x). Because he fails to see that it was exactly the attack on the very notion of a central myth of America and its antihistorical and antisocial implications and repercussions that was the major objective in the best work of the period and not the opposition of a monolithic ideal and the failure in reality, he is bound to reduce the manifestations of adversarial cultures in American history and of radical cultural critique to what he labels rather disparagingly "a utopian or even moral radicalism combined with or concealing the resentment of artists and intellectuals at their rather small voice in a national life dominated by business and politics" ("Intro.," xi). If in Fisher's sense "within American studies the study of America had become the study of dissent" and if the key figures of the American literary tradition such as Emerson and Whitman had been claimed as great "defiant, adversarial figures," Fisher, in a typical revisionary New Historicist reading, *reverses* this critical assessment and announces that "the very greatest figures of our literature were not oppositional," "having imagined themselves to have seen into the philosophic and temperamental depths of those two systems [of democracy and capitalism] and to have found them both profound and humane, exhilarating and enduring" ("Intro.," xii.).

Fisher's foreshortened and undialectical view of post–World War II American Studies and its forms of a radical critique of American culture also affects his discussion of what he calls the "counter element to unitary myths within American Studies" ("Intro.," viii), a "second element [that] shared the stage," the "claim of pluralism within American culture" ("Intro.," xii). This "claim" of pluralism within American culture is seen as a "diversity, which resists the single shelter of myth and ideology, [and] has again and again risen to dominance in what we might call the episodes of regionalism in American cultural history" ("Intro.," xii). He continues: "Cultural life in America swings like a pendulum between a diversity of sectional voices and an ever-new project of unity, between the representation of the nation as made up of weakly joined districts and the representation of a central national order." Fisher argues that these "episodes of regionalism," such as sectionalism in nineteenth-century America and "ethnic regionalism" early in the twentieth century, always have led to a "new identity" and "unity" on a "new plane of association" ("Intro.," xiii). Yet Fisher's model of the pendulum swing between diversity and unity reduces the manifestations of pluralism and difference to "episodes" produced *only* in times of "a highly politicized atmosphere" ("Intro.," xiv), to merely "regional" (in his idiosyncratic use of the term) interests that challenge the existing notions of cultural unity, but are absorbed by it in a redefinition of the "representation of a central national order." Thus the historical dialectic of American culture(s) is not explored in its theoretical implications for understanding "American culture" *as* a "multiculture" in its various and conflicting "representational" dimensions and social and political processes of identity and difference. Fisher conceptualizes it, instead, in the geographical tropes of a swing between "regions" or "districts" and a "center" that does not allow him, finally, to understand the powerful manifestations and critical discourses of the groups that "represent" themselves in these "regionalisms" as *inherent* in the dynamics of American culture and American cultural critique. Therefore, he reduces the forces of "pluralism" of our own time, what he calls the "regionalism of gender and race" ("Intro.," xiii), to political "identity movements"—"Native American, Chicano, gay, black, lesbian, female"—which he attacks for their intolerance, for their "unnegotiable identities," that is, for challenging Fisher's notion of the "open unity" of American culture and for defining their objectives in terms of clear-cut *oppositions* and demands for *institutionalized territory.*

Fisher defines the New American Studies as an "alternative or aftermath" to the forms of a regionalism of gender and race. He identifies the regionalism of gender and race as *part* of a broader "civil war:" "Regionalism is always, in America, part of a civil war within representation" ("Intro.," xiv). But in the following sentences, Fisher *excludes* gender and race as illegitimate, politically motivated oppositional movements from his notion of the New American Studies:

> The new American Studies has stood outside this regionalism by locating a set of underlying but permanently open national facts around which all identities are shaped and with which the many rhetorics of our culture are engaged. Among these permanently open, that is, never won or lost, national facts are democratic culture and its demands; the culture of freedom that permits conditions of dominance, whether economic, sexual, or cultural, and has permitted even permutations of slavery as one aspect of the nature of freedom itself; the creation of a national life that is economic rather than religious, or in the anthropological sense, cultural. This troubled utopian core of enterprise, freedom, and democratic culture baffled by the preexisting social facts while never surrendering to them is part of the essence of the cultural analyses present in the essays of this book. ["Intro.," xiv]

By situating the New American Studies "outside" the regionalism of gender and race, Fisher not only puts aside their cultural politics and critique of American public culture, but redefines their theoretical and practical work that has articulated *alternative* positions and discursive strategies of cultural critique from his own terms of a homogenized American culture characterized by some "permanently open . . . national facts." He ignores that feminist or minority discourses in the United States have continuously addressed exactly these supposedly "permanently open" questions and their status in terms of power in the culture at large and asked *who* defines and answers these questions.

The rest of Fisher's introduction elaborates the cultural and political implications of the uniqueness of "this troubled utopian core of enterprise, freedom, and democratic culture" in the United States.[24] Fisher takes up his concept of the plurality and openness of rhetorics and introduces the notion of the "civil war within representation" as the central, "normative" experience of American culture that is said to dispose of concepts like the American Renaissance and its "unified set of ideas and aesthetic practices" and concomitant notions of ideology, dissent, and period identity. "The conditions of civil war can be taken as the fundamental alternative to the condition of monarchical power, self-display, uniform discourse, ideology, and controlled representation" ("Intro.," xv). As Fisher identifies ideology with a total unifying control of a society, the representational situation in the United States transcends ideology and dissent.

If the recent New Historicism has drawn on Foucault's work on the omnipresence of power and on the analyses of the fate of representation in "absolutist states or societies," Fisher claims that the New Historicism *as applied to the United States* finds "its basis in the representational situation not of monarchy but of civil war" ("Intro.," xv). The United States is defined, in a strange use of the terms, as "an economy rather than a culture," an "economy" in which competing versions of rhetoric achieve local and temporary, fundamentally "unstable" and "incomplete" dominance over representations. As in Walter Benn Michaels's version of the New Historicism, these "rhetorics" succeed one other and compete with one other as representations of disembodied forces, such as "railroads," the "passenger automobile," and the "new telephone industry," in a system of capitalism that is understood as omnipresent ("Intro.," xii–xiv). But Fisher goes beyond Michaels to claim explicitly that the very concept of power is dissolved, in some sense "circulated" out of existence in the United States, as it lacks a substantive basis in reality, which according to Fisher depends on the inheritance of land and a landed gentry. "Power," Fisher contends, is *not* the "topic" of this American New Historicism, but "its weak long-term expectation within a culture where economic power is not located in land, that one genuinely scarce, readily transferable, and not easily variable basis of power" ("Intro.," xvi).

Therefore, according to Fisher, the essays in the volume focus not on the relations of "power" and the manifestations of "dissent," but the "contest" or "discord" of "rhetorics" *within* the frame of the "public sphere" or "democratic culture" in the United States. That is, Fisher does not so much celebrate an American "consensus" or paint an idyllic picture of American society as argue for "alternative rhetorics" and the "rhetorical struggles of the culture." Yet he situates this struggle *within the confines* of a democratic public culture that is no longer questioned and sets the terms for the legitimacy of any voice in the cultural "conversation." In the realm of public culture, the "civil war over representation" produces a "surplus of energy" (cultural capital) and reformulates conflicts over power, social class, and ideology as questions of rhetoric. In some kind of essentializing move, Fisher argues that "each culture has its central problem within representation." For the United States this "fated . . . problem of representation" is the problem of race, of the "mutual projection of white and black identity as an ongoing, ever-reconstructed cultural matter" ("Intro.," xvii). This move entails, however, that *other* key social and cultural issues are suspended (such as class, which he assigns as the central problem in English culture) or subordinated as secondary effects (such as feminism). "Causation" and (social) "energy" can flow between the individual or the wider culture in both directions, historically defined or constrained by "the limits of the specific resources of that culture" ("Intro.," xix).

Fisher finds in the New Historicism two basic models in its analysis of the Civil War over or within representation and its transfer of energy in the United States. It traces the replacement of one rhetoric by another, and it shows the "paradoxical" evasion of choice, coexistence, or systemic blending of two alternative rhetorics and strategies "we would only expect to see in conflict and opposition" ("Intro.," xix). The historical existence, experience, and conscious awareness of clear contradictions, of "subversion and collusion," of "opposition or participation," of resistance are, however, said to be "less significant goals within representation than we usually imagine" ("Intro.," xix). The "fusion," "compounding," or "blending" of rhetorics—of "opposite vocabularies"—which one can too easily claim by pointing out homologies or the occurrence of similar or equal terms in different discourses without reconstructing differences in use and cultural (or countercultural) functions, rhetoricizes cultural, social, and political conflicts in the historical process. Fisher quite rightly emphasizes the remarkable capacities of American society to accommodate and neutralize contradictions and dissent, but endorses this evasion of conflict as the achievement of the unending "flow" of "energy" in a culture without ideology. Thus he reaches the conclusion: "We find ourselves with a picture of a culture living on in spite of the requirements of facing up to its contradictions and improvisations, a culture making successful, short-term use of opposites precisely because it has no interest in finding its way to any long-term stable, integrated identity or ideology" ("Intro.," xx).

Fisher grounds this conceptually homogenizing and generalizing picture of "a culture," of American culture as rhetorical, in a particular phase of American history, in the nineteenth century, that is the focus of the essays collected in the volume. If most of the essays examine "alternative rhetorics within the public sphere of the mid-nineteenth-century experience of the war over slavery, its abolitionist foreground, and its reconstructionist and New South aftermath" ("Intro.," xvi), Fisher rarefies this experience of slavery, racial oppression, segregation, and struggle for freedom and literacy of black Americans to the contest of rhetorics in a public sphere from which they were excluded. The great nineteenth-century American texts of Emerson, Hawthorne, Melville, and Whitman are seen as representing the crucial "shifts in national self-conceptions," the replacement of the rhetoric of the "Puritan Mission" by the rhetoric of a "secular and liberal politics" ("Intro.," xvii). Yet as works of "high culture" have always been exposed to the "constraints on representation by ordinary culture" ("Intro.," xviii), the works of the "classic American writers" are reinterpreted as containing—now in a double sense—the contradictions and the "adversarial rhetoric" (Sacvan Bercovitch) of American culture. These New Historicist "deconstructive readings" of the "tropes and layers within representation" ("Intro.," xx) lead to forms of rhetorical analysis that in spite of declarations to the contrary do *not* "historicize this rhetoric," but either *universalize* specific individual experiences, such as Emerson's in his essay "Experience," into a "triumphant affirmation" of a notion of "experience itself" *or* "localize" cultural analyses in a *totalizing* view of "American experience."

Philip Fisher's tentative and exploratory use of critical terms attempts to suspend their traditional determinate meanings and ideological implications (which he relates to European historical conditions and intellectual fashion) and to (re)appropriate them to an American society and culture he considers characterized by a unique flexibility and mobility. Yet, at strategic points in his argument, he collapses this process of experimental and probing analysis of culture and society in American history by reducing their heterogeneity and complexity to blunt evaluative statements that reaffirm their ideological thrust, as the concluding paragraphs of his introduction show again. American uniqueness as distinct from European tradition—the rest of the world does not figure at all—finds its legitimation in a repetition of the argument of the "absence" of the "state" and of the "centralization of the power of representation and self-conception" ("Intro.," xxi) in the United States. The observation of differences in the organization of power and the state in the United States—drawn mainly from studies of nineteenth-century American society—is transformed into a celebration of a culture without ideology, a so-called Emersonian or speculative society oriented toward the future that finds its real democratic foundation in the economy: "In my reading those resources [of American culture] were always richest and most democratic on the economic plane" ("Intro.," xix). When Fisher argues that for this speculative society a "commitment to self-destruction in the name of its own next possibility is far more important than its interest in the transfer of the forms of the past to a future generation," it comes as a surprise when he claims that analysis in American Studies will "always be historical not anthropological" ("Intro.," xxii). It is unclear in what sense he uses the term "historical," and we do not learn what school of anthropology today permits him to *oppose* historical to anthropological studies. If we look at work in symbolic anthropology, the anthropology of experience, the anthropology of praxis, feminist anthropology, or postmodern anthropology, Fisher's opposition clearly is meaningless. Fisher concludes his introduction with an affirmation of the openness and mobility of democratic American society which is permeated by the reification and totalization of key concepts and clear-cut oppositions that seem to be far from the complex and contradictory reality in the United States as well as in Europe: "In the absence of a state we find ourselves freed of the intellectual component of the systematic state: ideology. We have rhetorics because we have no ideology, and we have no ideology because we lack the apparatus of ideology: a national religion, a unitary system of education under the control of the state, a cultural life and media monopolized by the state either by means of ownership or subsidy. Ideology is a cultural mechanism of stabilization and transmission, neither of which are a primary topic of a culture of speculation" ("Intro.," xxii).

[3]

AMERICAN STUDIES AND LITERARY AND CULTURAL CRITIQUE: THE QUESTION OF RADICAL TRADITIONS [IN THE 1980S]

Reconstructing American Studies from the 1930s to the 1960s

In the 1980s, scholars in American Studies became more conscious of the methodological problems of their work and made wide-ranging use of the developments in various disciplines in the humanities and social sciences.[1] They also discovered the importance of a critical perspective on the history of their discipline.[2] But there clearly was a feeling of a loss of direction, an uneasiness about the purposes and objectives of American Studies. Often the appropriation of new methods and approaches was pursued under the old premises, and awareness of the history of the field reduced to a stereotypical periodization of phases characterized by key concepts or dominant methods. Whereas during the late 1960s and early 1970s the work of the myth-and-symbol school (from Henry Nash Smith to Leo Marx) was criticized as methodologically unsound by Bruce Kuklick and politically conservative or even reactionary by Christopher Lasch and others, some of its work, particularly by Leo Marx and Richard Slotkin, was condemned by Kenneth Lynn as "regressive," "reductionist," or simply "anti-American Studies."[3] This confusion about the origin, objectives, political implications, and "legacy" of the early period of American Studies, from the 1930s to the 1960s, and the development and changes in literary and cultural criticism and in historiography during these decades is one reason for the precarious relationship between history and theory in American Studies in the 1980s.[4]

In order to understand what might be termed the disciplinary crisis of American Studies in the 1980s, we need to reconsider the historical development of the field between the 1930s and the 1960s. This reconstruction must be written with an awareness of contemporary developments that I can indicate only very briefly, which make it more difficult and more urgent at the same time. One is the recent polemical critique of American "cultural radicalism" of the 1960s and 1970s as theoretically mistaken and pseudo-revolutionary, and as reinforcing only those aspects and developments of the capitalist society and dominant culture it claims to criticize and reject, as Daniel Bell, Gerald Graff, Eugene Goodheart, and Christopher Lasch have argued variously. This reassessment of the politics of culture during the 1960s and 1970s, however, usually fails to develop the historical dialectic of leftist criticism it discovers, as it approaches its material from a general and often ahistorical perspective and with a contemptuous dismissal of the 1930s as a useless past. The concomitant revision of the "Red Decade" as "not so turbulent years" (Melvyn Dubofsky) has eroded further consciousness of the existence of alternative programs and perspectives in American cultural history and of a "radical" past in American Studies.[5]

The current debates on pluralism and synthesis in American historiography initiated by Thomas Bender and Herbert G. Gutman and on the scope, principles, and writing strategies of a revisionary American literary history provide a stimulating context for reconstructing the contours and conflictual dynamics of history and histories in the United States and of American culture as a multiculture.[6] They also enable us to clarify the specific historical forms of American radical cultural and literary criticism. It is due to the central role of textuality and intertextuality, of self-consciously historical and self-reflexive modes in the criticism of literary as well as nonliterary texts in some versions of deconstruction and poststructuralism, and in the neo-Marxist critique of the ideology of forms and the use of tropes, that radical cultural and literary criticism can contribute in a crucial manner to a new understanding of radical traditions and alternative forms of discourse in American culture and society. Such radical literary and historical criticism has produced important new insights into the rhetorical quality of myth, history, and ideology and the role of narrativity and fiction in literary and historical discourse. The rehistoricization in critical theory is directed at the historical and social context as it is inscribed and dramatized within the formal properties and codes of the text itself (Hayden White). It explores the dimensions and limits of the complex and open-ended cultural dialectic in forms of ideological analysis that critically mediate between literature and history, between aesthetic judgments and political norms, between expressive form and social structure, and the power of language as well as the language of power (Sacvan Bercovitch).[7]

I want to address, then, the question of what "radicalism" meant, and how it changed, in cultural criticism, historiography, and American Studies from the 1930s to the 1960s. It was during this period of fundamental political, social, and cultural change and the institutionalization of American Studies in universities that redefinitions and transformations in American cultural criticism occurred that are crucial to our understanding of the direction of cultural and political radicalism in the United States and the meaning of a radical tradition.[8] If the theoretical debates of the past two decades have cogently questioned and deconstructed the very foundations of traditional cultural criticism and history and the meaning of terms such as "radical" and "Left," they have also led to a renewed interest in the social, political, and institutional presuppositions and repercussions of theoretical discourse and to a "reconstruction" of knowledge.

The close analysis of modes of radical cultural criticism in 1930s America provides a particular challenge to both the historical and New Historicist reorientation in American cultural and literary theory in the 1980s. It was during the 1930s that for the first time in American history the forms, roles, and functions of literature, of American culture, of documentary realism, of modernism, of the institutions of art were fundamentally questioned, contested, and redefined in public culture at large as well as in critical thought. During the decade the most radical and wide-ranging works of (white) American modernism in literature appeared, which, at the same time, laid bare its aesthetic and ideological presuppositions and inherent dialectic. The boundaries and approaches of the traditional disciplines in the humanities and the social sciences and their relationship to public discourse were challenged and revised. The crisis was answered by new experimental, often "interdisciplinary" or strikingly "impure" modes of writing and criticism and a new openness to alternative expressive forms of ethnic, regional groups, and minorities. From our perspective, we can see that during the years of the Depression and World War II, deconstructive and reconstructive strategies and forms of critical cultural discourse were explored in the undeniably heterogeneous United States that were virtually ignored or repressed during the consensus-defined postwar decades. These radical cultural practices in the 1930s offer American alternatives or complements to more recent theories appropriated from European sources. They certainly do not provide ready-made solutions to our problems after deconstruction and after the powerful critique of history in French poststructuralist philosophy, but they enable us to articulate more clearly what can be meant by new contemporary forms of historical cultural criticism, as long as we remain attentive to their historical differences.

Therefore, I do not want to offer a new general overview of the developments in literature, culture, society, politics, and criticism during the 1930s and 1940s that had some bearing on cultural radicalism in America. Whereas Richard H. Pells's wide-ranging synthesis, *Radical Visions and American Dreams* (1973), had reinterpreted the culture and social thought of the 1930s as basically conservative, during the 1980s a new interest in the so-called Red Decade developed that reopened the question of its radical or leftist impulse.[9] In addition to critical and biographical studies of individual writers and critics, we have a large number of autobiographies and memoirs of many of the participants in the critical controversies of the time, which add many details to the picture but more often than not were written under the premises of a politics of memory that tries to reestablish a revisionary account of the author's place in history. We also have a number of scholarly studies of the New York Intellectuals, particularly the *Partisan Review* group, that set out to give a more complete portrait of radicalism in American culture and society during the Depression and World War II. Studies by Terry A. Cooney, Alexander Bloom, and Alan Wald enrich our understanding of the literary, cultural, and social politics of the New York Intellectuals, but they more or less cover the same, well-known ground and set of characters (Wald's study is an exception) and hardly offer a new reading of American cultural radicalism during the 1930s and 1940s that is informed by modes of the recent "rehistoricization" in cultural criticism.[10]

In his magisterial overview of the problems and works of liberal and leftist intellectuals in the 1940s and 1950s, *The Liberal Mind in a Conservative Age*, Richard Pells convincingly traces the revisions and redirections in radical political, social, and cultural thought during these decades of consensus, but he does not devote more than two paragraphs to the major books in American Studies.[11] I think that some of the most consequential redefinitions of the American radical tradition in history and cultural criticism and its interpretive methods were worked out in the wider context of the early American Studies movement.

I want to concentrate on the problematic that was the rationale in various forms of radical cultural criticism of the late 1930s and early 1940s and that also gave the critical edge to American Studies and some of the cultural and historical "revisionary" criticism of the 1950s and 1960s. The discovery of an American culture and of the culture concept during the 1930s (Warren Susman) often led to cultural nationalism or chauvinism, a shallow popular front "Americanism," or emphasis on an ahistorical unity and integration in what the anthropologist Ruth Benedict termed "patterns of culture" in the United States. But it also opened up radical cultural criticism to an understanding of "American culture" as a *multiculture* of regional, class, and gender differences, of ethnic and marginalized groups, of spectacular contrasts and conflicts between high, folk, and mass culture, of subcultures and radical traditions in a society characterized by a strong consensus as well as by unequaled heterogeneity. The critical, self-reflexive use of the culture concept helped to transcend the dominant patterns of Marxist criticism of the time, to reassess the discourse of modernism, to radicalize the work of American cultural and social anthropology in their intra- and intercultural dimensions, and to produce a radically new understanding of the relationships of language, culture, and society.

My critical approach focuses less on the changing ideological positions and the programmatic statements of writers, critics, and scholars, as these have been documented and evaluated often enough, than on the historical dynamic in their practical work and on the formal properties of their critical discourse. What I find most pertinent to the new American Studies is the search for and the revision and transformation of different forms of radical cultural criticism—that is, the specific strategies, modes, and tropes of cultural criticism as critical discourse and counterdiscourse. Radical cultural critique from this perspective will always be a "double-voiced discourse," as it reads culture as a social text or drama in the sense that it enacts a dialogue (or polylogue) and struggle over the realization of power and desire, of remembering and anticipation, over the construction and revision of identities and communities, and acknowledges the irremediable moment of otherness and difference in the very act of understanding itself. Radical criticism will see American culture(s) both in its (their) inner dynamic and from the margins and will set out to explore critically the potential of America's original meanings and the utopian visions of a new social order.

This kind of radical cultural criticism will particularly be found in the work of critics and writers, male as well as female, who wrote on the boundaries of scholarly disciplines and on the margins of discourse in criticism and art. A closer look at the works of F. O. Matthiessen, Caroline Ware, Henry Nash Smith, and Leo Marx (among others) can show us both the historical discontinuities and the continuities of the problems cultural critics faced and the strategies they tried to develop in their radical cultural criticism during the Depression, World War II, and a period of postwar "affluence"—continuities *and* discontinuities that in many ways remain vital to our own thoughts on cultural criticism and social change today.

[In what follows, Lenz considers how these legacies of Left criticism from the 1930s and 1940s, as well as post–World War II liberalism, structure the efforts of four influential American Studies scholars of the 1980s: Gerald Graff, Christopher Lasch, Sacvan Bercovitch, and Alan Trachtenberg.]

The Crisis of Cultural Radicalism and the Politics of Interpretation: Gerald Graff

If the New Historicism of Walter Benn Michaels contemptuously dismisses a radical tradition in American literary and cultural thought and makes the whole question meaningless, the "New American Exceptionalism" of George Kateb, Stanley Cavell, and Richard Poirier has rediscovered and reappropriated a specifically American critical tradition as a viable and promising alternative to European neo-Marxism and poststructuralism, but has tended in different ways to lift it out of its historical context in the United States and turn it into some kind of transcendent truth. Philip Fisher's program for a New American Studies equally rejects the claims of a radical tradition in American literature and in the American Studies of the post–World War II decades. It registers the "exhaustion" of "oppositional criticism" and reinterprets and reevaluates F. O. Matthiessen's "Emersonian tradition" of a critical commitment to the realization of democracy and turns it into a celebration of the unique success story of American society as a "culture of speculation" energized *and* contained by a "civil war over representation." Obviously, political developments at home and abroad, and particularly the demise of socialism in the Soviet Union and Eastern Europe, have led to a serious crisis of oppositional criticism from the Left, but it is amazing how easily and ritualistically what had been a complex, multivoiced, and continually changing critical movement of radical literary and cultural critique is rejected without second thoughts as a useless past at the same moment criticism is claimed to be in the process of "repoliticization" and "rehistoricization."

Undoubtedly, as the critical discussion in the preceding chapter showed, it is much more difficult to redefine politics and history as well as culture and literature after their cogent deconstruction in poststructuralist thought than critics of the late 1980s and the early 1990s have supposed. But the wholesale dismissal of the radical traditions in American literature, culture, and critical thought is also a result, I think, of the polemical rejection of what was termed "cultural radicalism" of the 1960s (and of earlier decades) by influential cultural and literary critics during the late 1970s and early 1980s who denounced it as politically dangerous, self-deceptive, and theoretically spurious. Critics such as Gerald Graff and Christopher Lasch castigated a pseudo-radical counterculture or "culture of narcissism" as symptomatic of the bankruptcy of serious radical criticism that they saw reinforced to various degrees by the more recent fashions and movements of deconstruction, feminism, and minority discourse. Graff's *Literature against Itself* (1979) and Lasch's *The Culture of Narcissism* (1978) were highly polemical, often reductionist and self-contradictory books, but it would be a mistake to discuss them as mainly sensationalist tracts of the time. Both Graff and Lasch have taken pains to argue that their books were written as self-critical works from a basically leftist position. They set out to expose what they consider the self-deceiving naïveté of the cultural radicalism of the 1960s and 1970s that failed to realize its own precarious historical and political position in a fundamentally changing world and the ways its radical ideas had been co-opted by the dominant culture.

In *Literature against Itself*, Gerald Graff points out the historical dialectic that had worked in the development of American radical cultural criticism since the 1960s and, in later essays, the tenuous and changing relationship between culture and politics in the history of American literary criticism. In "The Politics of Anti-Realism," he indicates the implications of a cultural radicalism that turns its force against itself. "In exposing objective reason as an ideology, radicalism leaves itself no means of legitimizing its own critique of injustice and exploitation." Or, most succinctly, "in the name of radical egalitarianism, criticism has to be liquidated."[12]

Graff does not understand this process in the radical cultural criticism he discusses either to liquidate itself or to affirm the dominant capitalist society and culture, but simply to exhibit a failure of critical nerve symptomatic of "social changes" in the United States:

> Cultural radicalism ignores the disappearance of the paternalistic repressions it seeks to dissolve. . . . Whereas power once required the appearance of sanction by the spiritual ideas of high culture, [corporate] power today finds it possible to do without such sanctions, to exploit a culture of radical pluralism and ideological dissonance. . . . Insofar as radicalism makes the extirpation of high cultural snobbery the central objective, it encourages the illusion that mass culture is the democratic expression of the people, as if mass culture were not owned and operated by private interests. [*LAI*, 95]

As the traditional basis of capitalist society and the use of bourgeois culture for legitimizing corporate power have dissolved in contemporary "consumer society," the leftist critique of ideology seems to have lost its basis and has "diverted [radical thought] from legitimate targets—injustice, poverty, triviality, vulgarity, loneliness—to a spurious quest after psychic liberation and expanded sensibility." In the introduction to *Literature against Itself*, Graff sums up his thesis about the "belatedness" of cultural radicalism: "One of my central arguments is that the real 'avant-garde' is advanced capitalism, with its built-in need to destroy all vestiges of tradition, all orthodox ideologies, all continuous and stable forms of reality in order to stimulate higher levels of consumption" (*LAI*, 8). By vastly overrating the homogeneity of contemporary "consumer society" as a totally closed system and the effectiveness of the manipulative and seductive power of "mass culture" (and the political impact of "cultural radicalism"), Graff maneuvers himself into a situation in which the only way out seems to be a total rejection of contemporary culture and society in the name of a transhistorical ideal of "reality," "objective truth," and "coherence" that he had to find, or invent, somewhere in the past. Graff's effort to keep alive for the future the critical tradition of bourgeois culture, with its consciousness of opposition and alternative perspectives, may have been a laudable undertaking, but how could it work if we take his own remarks about fundamental social and cultural changes in the United States since World War II seriously? How can his notion of the adversary core of "realism" in criticism and the culture be exempt from the historical dialectic that, according to his own argument, has subverted the oppositional potential of all versions of "radicalism"? How can he escape the crisis or dilemma of criticism in a postmodern era he finds dominant everywhere in society and culture? It certainly is not sufficient to claim, as he does in *Literature against Itself*, that "the notion, then, that there exists an objective reality 'out there,' independent of our perceptions of it, far from being an ideological rationalization for the existing order, is a prerequisite for changing the existing order, which has to be understood as it is before it can be altered" (*LAI*, 27).

In subsequent work, Graff tries to work out a more complex historical view of American radical cultural criticism. In "Textual Leftism" (1982), he goes beyond polemics by focusing his attention on the "politics of language," the "literary politics of the textual left," the "hermeneutics of power," as they have developed in the United States (and France) since World War II, a historical reconstruction that allows for a more subtle judgment of the various critical approaches and their political implications from the 1940s to the 1970s. Instead of "denounc[ing] the sins of structuralism, deconstruction, and other exotic, critical methodologies," he now tries to "look into the reasons why these methodologies have arisen and why they have been embraced by so many." Graff understands the new theories as genuine attempts at continuing the "political promise" of the 1960s and reemphasizing the "cultural and social context" of literary studies. In an unusually careful assessment of what he calls "textual leftism" in the work of Derrida, Foucault, and Barthes, he explains the "current conflation of language and politics," the role of "master-codes of interpretation," of "institutional conventions," and of "alternate codes," and the "clash of interpretive systems" as a mark of the "global conflict of ideologies." Yet he finds this "hermeneutics of power" lacking in analytical rigor. Graff judges the basic reason for the political contradictions in poststructuralism to be its simplistic "parallels between linguistic and social constraints" and its "leap to conclusions about what epistemologies are subversive or reactionary." He has clearly failed to apply this critical insight to his own political use of a "realist," "objectivist" epistemology.[13]

Graff has elaborated his understanding of the problematic relationship between interpretive systems and political meaning in general in his article "The Pseudo-Politics of Interpretation" (1983), in which he argues that "the politics of any theory is as much a matter of empirical investigation as of logical analysis." This clearly is true, but Graff too neatly distinguishes between ideas or concepts and their political consequences, between theories or systems and their uses or political alignments: "the political motivations and effects of a theory are irrelevant to its truth" and "theories . . . are politically *ambidextrous*; they can be appropriated by the Right, Left, or Center." If it certainly is important to criticize the often careless identification of critical theories with political positions and their continuous transvaluations, especially the totalization of politics and power in some theories, Graff's notion of what constitutes critical theory is clearly reductive. His reading of French poststructuralism and of the tradition of dialectical criticism should have taught him that a critical theory cannot be reduced to the combination of fixed ideas, concepts, and a vocabulary that then can be used or appropriated in a more or less arbitrary manner.[14]

In another essay of 1983, "An Ideological Map of American Literary Criticism," Graff holds onto his notion that "history presents many instances in which the same idea (or intellectual system) has produced different or opposed social effects in different circumstances." But the essay shows a clearer awareness of American literary criticism as an institution and offers a more detailed account of the complexity of the history of "American Criticism Left and Right" (as he called another version of this essay, published in 1986). He traces the "elusiveness of the connections between ideas and their social uses" in American literary criticism and acknowledges that the "logical dilemmas posed by inquiries into ideology may themselves alter in character with changing historical circumstances." Yet Graff's approach still seems to be marred by reified notions of ideas, systems, and doctrines and by a historically abstract understanding of their uses and appropriations. Once again, what he objects to in his critique of leftist criticism in an age of "co-optation" and of "consumerist pluralism" is mirrored in his own use of ideas as commodities in critical discourse.[15]

Clearly, in these essays of the early 1980s Graff has gone a long way from his polemical critique of the politics of antirealism in *Literature against Itself*, but in his historical and political "reconstruction" fails to meet the challenge Jane P. Tompkins poses in her essay, "Graff against Himself": "The textuality of history makes literature and history responsible not simply to but for each other. By removing the ontological distinction that separates literary from historical texts, deconstruction forces literary studies to re-define its territory. . . . It invites us to examine, in detail, the network of custom, beliefs, institutional structures, and practices of which the literary text is an extension and which it, in turn, helps to construct."[16] How this historical political analysis should actually proceed, how radical criticism could be redefined were open questions in the 1980s. Graff himself leaves us with a full awareness of the cultural critic's dilemma in that changing decade: "Although it has become a commonplace that literary criticism itself is a political act and is inseparable from power, this view has arisen at a moment, when criticism has become peculiarly closed off within the university, a fact that complicates further the problem of how the political effects of criticism should be measured."[17]

The Dialectics of Modernity and the Radical Potential of Residual Cultures: Christopher Lasch

In his commentary on Graff's essay "The Politics of Anti-Realism," Christopher Lasch heartily agreed with most of what Graff had said about the decline of American cultural radicalism and the historical dialectic characterizing its more recent phase:

> Those positions that seem most radical—most uncompromising in their opposition to bourgeois cultural hegemony—often turn out today to render the

> most effective reinforcement of the status quo. As Gerald Graff shows so clearly, the problem goes deeper than our society's well-known capacity to absorb dangerous ideas. The ideas associated with the politics of "cultural revolution" have in fact ceased to be dangerous. The cultural vanguard has become a rear guard. It attacks bastions long since surrendered: the patriarchal family, repressive sexual morality, the conventions of literary realism. Proponents of "cultural revolution" merely give the sanction of enlightened opinion to changes already brought about by the corporation, the advertising industry, the mass culture industry, and the propaganda of commodities.[18]

What Graff developed in the field of literary and cultural criticism, Lasch claimed to ground in a more comprehensive and a consciously historical analysis of contemporary American society and culture, written from the perspective of an American leftist. Countering the "waning of the sense of historical time" he observed everywhere in American society, he writes *The Culture of Narcissism* to keep alive the historical consciousness at the heart of American cultural radicalism and thus to renew the basis of the "very concept of criticism," of social and cultural radicalism.

Unfortunately, however, his own book, by offering only a very foreshortened analysis of the historical dialectic of culture and society and by often substituting polemics for historical interpretation, reinforces the "devaluation of the past" about which he complains (*CN*, 9). If pseudoreligious and neoconservative trendsetters of the 1970s repudiated and denounced the political movements, programs of social reform, and projects of an alternative culture of the 1960s as un-American, dangerous, or irrelevant, Lasch does not see anything viable and usable in these efforts either. At one point he distinguishes between the "corruption of radical politics in the late 1960s by the irrational elements in American culture" and "the validity of many radical goals," but he does not take this up in the rest of his book (*CN*, 29). If the "historical sense" is vital for survival and for envisioning a "better society," it must be more than a feeling of all-pervasive decline and loss.

Where do we, then, find a positive tradition of radicalism in the United States? In *The Culture of Narcissism*, Lasch mentions "a well-established American tradition of social thought," a "critical tradition" that "still has much to tell us about the evils of untrammeled individualism," but adds that "it needs to be restated" (*CN*, 9). Lasch claims that his analysis has heavily relied on "a well-established theoretical tradition" of "culture-and-personality studies" and "social criticism," on the work of his "predecessors in the sociology of culture," and that he tried to "revise the work of Riesman, Fromm, and the Frankfurt School" and used "psychoanalytical ideas" to "uncover patterns, both cultural and psychological, that remain far from obvious and largely inaccessible to common sense."[19] Yet if we see his strong emphasis on social psychology as a key to understanding American society and culture of the 1970s in the historical perspective he himself provides in his critique of American cultural radicalism, we might ask if his emphasis is not itself part of a historical phase of Marxist and radical social and cultural criticism that has been superseded or undercut by more recent developments.

Lasch's neglect of a precise historical analysis becomes obvious again in his own conclusions when he suggests that the "new movement for radical reform" will have to build on "traditions of localism, self-help, and community action"—ideas that clearly were a vital part of the counterculture of the 1960s and 1970s he condemns. He argues, in a rather dubious turn, that "any radical movement that seeks to transcend the progressive and socialist pieties of an earlier time" must show "a 'conservative' respect for order and authority" and that it should look for its constituency in "middle America," in "the people who cling to family life, religion, the work ethic, and other ostensibly outmoded values and institutions" ("PST," 199). He does not, however, elaborate these "conservative" roots or dimensions of American radicalism.

In the early 1980s, Lasch clarified his intentions in his critique of cultural radicalism and revised some of his most controversial positions. The most important and far-reaching publication is his essay "Mass Culture Reconsidered" (1981), which appeared in his short-lived journal *Democracy*.[20] Lasch reconfirms the historic "vision" of the Left, "which embraces not only political democracy but economic democracy and the democratization of culture," a "democracy in the fullest sense" that does not yet exist. At the same time, he repeats his attack on the Left's belief in a conception of "enlightenment," of the "modernization process," and of "modernity" that equates growth and the democratization of culture with the dissolution of "traditional" modes of thought and the cutting of roots.

It is this "myth of progress," this "model of enlightenment," the "prevailing understanding of the 'modernization' process," that Lasch wants to reconsider. He suggests two lines of critique:

> The first uncovers the persistence of allegedly outmoded forms of particularism—family ties, religion, ethnicity, black nationalism—that have not

> only proved resistant to the melting pot but continue to provide people with the psychological and spiritual resources essential for democratic citizenship and for a truly cosmopolitan outlook, as opposed to the deracinated, disoriented outlook that is so often confused, nowadays, with intellectual liberation. The second line of inquiry tries to explain why the homogenized mass culture of modern societies gives rise not to enlightenment and independent thinking but to intellectual passivity, confusion, and collective amnesia. ["MCR," 9]

In his essay, Lasch follows the second path of what can be called an immanent critique of the dialectics of modern culture. He relies on the critique of mass culture by Dwight Macdonald, Irving Howe, Theodor W. Adorno, Max Horkheimer, and Leo Lowenthal and tries to "refine and restate it" by separating their dismissal of "mass culture" from their commitment to (high) "cultural modernism" as the only realm of opposition to mass culture and by distinguishing between "mass culture" (of the "mass media") and "real popular culture" that, contrary to the belief in the total manipulation of the masses, has *not* been completely destroyed ("MCR," 10).

Yet Lasch's pursuit of the second line of inquiry then leaves him at an impasse. If the dialectic of enlightenment, of the "modernization process" has produced only negative results, if the adversarial role of (high) modern culture has been domesticated, if mass culture is to be seen in a totally negative light, and if the mass media "by their very nature" are only "effective instruments of social control," Lasch's critical venture of "revision" and "restatement" does not affect the historical development of the "project of modernity" as such. In Lasch's essay, there are a few indications of a new reading of modernism, particularly in the arts, that could be used as a starting point for a revised understanding of "modern culture as a whole" as the product of interactions between traditions and innovation or change ("MCR," 21).

Unfortunately, Lasch too quickly elaborates these new approaches to modernism in terms of *residual* forces, as areas that have withstood or not been affected by the destructive impact of the modernization process of consumer capitalism. That is, Lasch returns to the "first line of inquiry" and asks the Left "to ally itself . . . with the forces in modern life that resist assimilation, uprooting, and forcible modernization." At the beginning of the essay, he had mentioned "family ties, religion, ethnicity" and, surprisingly after its condemnation in Lasch's earlier books, "black nationalism" and finally the oppositional quality and sustaining power of "real popular culture." Now he is content with a vague general assertion that modernism, modern culture "never represented a simple repudiation of 'traditional' patterns," after all ("MCR," 9).

Lasch's next book, *The Minimal Self* (1984), does not answer these questions either.[21] It takes up, instead, his reassessment of the process of modernization (the "second line of inquiry" in "Mass Culture Reconsidered") and tries to reestablish the *residual* quality, the *persistence* of "outmoded forms of particularism" against the destructive impact of the dialectic of enlightenment and of instrumental reason at the center of the history of modern subjectivity ("MCR," 9). In his efforts to define a viable concept of "selfhood" in a postindustrial society, Lasch strongly embraces dialectical thinking and the dialectical interpretation of history in order to discover a perspective for overcoming the purely negative assessment of recent cultural and social history in the United States. But he still fails to indicate the social and cultural developments, ethnic and class differences, and oppositional or alternative groups and "forces" that could represent sources of "democratic renewal" to manifest and communicate this vision and experience. Instead, he undialectically separates the good from the bad side of the Western tradition of individualism and refers to "what remains valuable in the Western, Judaeo-Christian tradition of individualism (as opposed to the tradition of acquisitive individualism, which parodies and subverts it)," confining his perspective to a basically *individualist* concept of "conscience," to a "selfhood" that expresses itself in the "painful awareness of the gulf between human aspirations and human limitations" (*MS*, 20). In *The Minimal Self*, Lasch does not follow up his own suggestions in "Mass Culture Reconsidered" of a line of inquiry that uncovers the oppositional (or alternative) experience and practice of "traditional forces" or oppressed groups. Although he approaches feminism in a more sympathetic manner than in his previous works, he does not concretize his vision of renewal in a comprehensive critical theory of contemporary American society.

In his work since *The Minimal Self*, however, particularly in some essays on American critics of culture, he has rediscovered an important dimension of radical cultural criticism in the United States, a rediscovery and revision that returns him to his two early books on the history of American radicalism. His new defense of the New Left (and the counterculture) of the 1960s against critics who claim it was ahistorical, his qualified approval of Philip Rahv's reconciliation of high modernism and political radicalism and of Lewis Mumford's critique of the myth of the machine, as well as his awareness of the *positive* potential of the critical traditions of modernity are complemented by his strong support of Randolph Bourne's work on the culture of modernism and his conception of cultural pluralism. Lasch praises Bourne's cosmopolitanism as a defense of diversity and particularism, his awareness of the connections between cultural renewal and social or political change, and his undogmatic, "eclectic" cast of mind, searching for new forms of thought. Bourne's work "remains a standard" for Lasch, which means above all that it renews the question of an "understanding of American radicalism and its history" that does not "force it into European categories" and/or make "its very resistance to this procedure the basis of a general condemnation of the American Left."[22] Lasch's own early books, *The New Radicalism in America, 1889–1963* (1965) and *The Agony of the American Left* (1969), contained important contributions to a history of American radicalism, both in terms of the emergence and the later development of the radical intellectual as a social type and in terms of the specific origin and constitution of radical political movements in American history since the populist revolt.[23] But in the final analysis, his history of American radicalism turns out to be one of "confusion," "decline," "degeneration," "defection," "defeat," "agony"—in one word, "failure."

Myth, History, Ideology, and Rhetoric in American Studies: Sacvan Bercovitch

The problems of the strategies and functions of a radical tradition, or of radical traditions in the plural, in American social, cultural, and literary history, as well as of the theoretical implications and the interpretive power of radical historical cultural critique, have been the driving forces behind the most challenging work in American Studies since the 1930s. It was during the Depression of the 1930s that the view of the "great" American literature as a fundamentally critical tradition was established by such scholars as Granville Hicks, Bernard Smith, and F. O. Matthiessen. In addition, the work of the earlier generation of American "critics of culture," such as Randolph Bourne, Van Wyck Brooks, and Waldo Frank, and V. L. Parrington's critical historical synthesis of the 1920s were taken up and adapted to the demands of a deep social, economic, and cultural crisis. The meaning, the forms, and the roles of literature, American culture, documentary realism, modernism, and the institutions of art were fundamentally questioned, contested, and redefined in public culture and in critical thought. During the decade the most demanding and complex works of American literary modernism, or modernisms in the plural, appeared and laid bare their aesthetic and ideological presuppositions and inherent social dialectic. The boundaries and approaches of the traditional disciplines in the humanities and social sciences and their relationship to public discourse were challenged and revised.

For American cultural critique, a crucial change that occurred after World War II was its wide-ranging institutionalization in the universities, particularly in academic programs of interdisciplinary American Studies. The institutionalization of the "radical" versions of cultural critique in American Studies programs during the 1950s and 1960s had very ambivalent effects. It sometimes contained and appropriated the critical impulse, the questioning of the boundaries of traditional disciplines, or the commitment to the heterogeneity of an American multiculture and turned them into projects of interdisciplinary research and teaching that once more translated and rarefied the tensions and contradictions in the society and culture at large and the division of labor among the disciplines into rhetorical tensions and paradoxes within the limits of an ideological consensus in the Cold War. The relentless search in American Studies for unity as a field with a method of its own often absorbed the self-critical objectives of earlier American cultural critics and neglected any comparative perspective. The obvious failure of its quest for unity, however, made American Studies aware of the tremendous political impact of symbols, myths, and ideologies and of the self-reflective quality of American Studies in the United States. The common identification of American Studies with a conservative "consensus history" or a "counter-Progressive explanation-form" (Gene Wise) has prevented us from realizing that in the process of institutionalization the discourses of radical cultural critique of the 1930s and early 1940s were also redefined and transformed into new dissenting modes of cultural criticism and public culture inside and outside academia.[24] Contrary to the usual denunciation of the myth-and-symbol school that dominated American Studies from the late 1930s to the 1960s, the work of scholars such as Henry Nash Smith and Leo Marx by no means exemplifies the political conservatism and its ideology of consensus or even the "defection of intellectuals from their true calling—critical thought" (Christopher Lasch), but actually constitutes an important expression of the strengths and the difficulties of American radical cultural criticism in a period of cultural conservatism and social change (Lasch, "CCW," 323). In spite of its obvious shortcomings, its failure to engage fully in a critical assessment of the role of class, gender, race, and ethnicity in American culture, American Studies provided a public forum for dialogues for many of these different critical voices.

If we try, then, to reconstruct and reclaim the radical tradition in American cultural and literary history, we have to acknowledge after our critical analyses of Graff's and Lasch's works that this project is not simply one of rediscovering a usable past and its revision. In a formidable manner it forces us to confront the question of *how* we can write a critical history of radical cultural critique in the specific *American* context and what we mean by favorite *critical terms* such as "myth," "history," "ideology," "criticism," "radicalism," and "America." In his work of the late 1970s and early 1980s, Sacvan Bercovitch made important contributions in his efforts to answer these questions.

In a brilliant review essay, "American Studies: A Life and Times" (1980), Burton J. Bledstein reinterprets the work in the dominant tradition of American Studies as critical of American culture and society from the beginning and discovers an increasing radicalization of this critique, which he takes Sacvan Bercovitch's work to represent.[25] Bercovitch's radical critique of America has become so total and comprehensive that it indicates to Bledstein virtually the end of American Studies: "After Bercovitch's radical rejection of the American historical experience, continued pursuit of American Studies would seem to be barren" ("AS," 419). I do not think that Bercovitch's work is characterized by "cynicism" and a total denial of the "capacity for constructive imagination," as Bledstein claims ("AS," 418, 419). Yet it has clearly radicalized the *critique* of the American consensus that Louis Hartz developed in *The Liberal Tradition in America* (1955), in which he argues that American society has uniquely been permeated and dominated by a liberal consensus of the middle class since the American Revolution. Bercovitch goes even further back in American history and writes: "The New England Puritans . . . obviated . . . the distinction between secular and sacred revolution. They bequeathed their peculiar figural mode to Enlightenment America, and ultimately the patriot Whigs, who mystified secular change as divine progress, and redefined the errand as a rite of passage into the sacred meaning of the American Revolution."[26]

Bercovitch has made important contributions to the specific methods of a rhetorical, literary, and ideological interpretation of American cultural history, drawing on the work of Antonio Gramsci, Clifford Geertz, Victor Turner, Roland Barthes, Raymond Williams, and others. American cultural history is understood in his work as a unique venture in the exegesis of the meaning of America, and literary criticism as cultural critique moves to the center of American Studies. In his books *The Puritan Origins of the American Self* (1975) and *The American Jeremiad* (1978) and in numerous essays written during the following years that continue the story told in *The American Jeremiad* beyond the mid-nineteenth century to the present, he has offered a radical deconstruction of the myth of America, the quest for and the critique of an American identity, the continuity and change of a transhistorical hermeneutic of "America," and the movement from sacred errand to manifest destiny.[27] The myth-and-symbol school in the American Studies tradition was centrally attentive to the powerful historical "reality" of symbols and myths in the popular imagination and in mass culture and had tentatively interpreted the relation of these "myths" to political ideologies. Bercovitch revises and radicalizes that critique by understanding myth in Roland Barthes's sense as "depoliticized speech," by interpreting religion and myth as "cultural systems" (Clifford Geertz), and by defining American "dominant culture" (Raymond Williams) as "hegemony" and as "a historically organic ideology" (Antonio Gramsci). He has raised the old debate of conflict versus consensus to a new level and has worked out in a powerful way the tensions of rhetoric and history, problems of the interaction of language, communal myth (Victor Turner), and the social order, or the relationship among rhetoric, myth, ideology, ritual, and their political functions in a culture dominated by the "middle class." He points out that the "ideological consensus" is a "series of . . . rituals of socialization," and the "comprehensive, officially endorsed cultural myths" are "equally 'real'" as a "quantitatively measured 'social reality'" (Bercovitch, *AJ*, xii). Bercovitch convincingly questions the effectiveness and adequacy of a form of radical cultural critique that sets out to uncover the contradictions between myth and reality in American society and its inherent tensions or polarities and of the identification of radicalism with a particular set of dogmas, intentions, or organized movements. Instead, he emphasizes the all-pervasive influence of the "rhetoric of consensus" and of the "ritual impact of the jeremiad" that have established an "increasingly pervasive middle-class hegemony" and succeeded in absorbing all forms of dissent and opposition by turning them into forms of ritual *within* the myth of America.

All this reveals more clearly than ever before the tremendous difficulties radical movements have had to face in American history. Bercovitch's interpretation leads him, however, into denying the existence of any viable American radical tradition whatsoever, as "radicalism itself was socialized into an affirmation of order" and social control. "[The myth] was a web spun out of sacred history and middle-class ideology which allowed virtually no avenue of escape" (*AJ*, 168). Or, put differently, "The revelation of America serves to blight, and ultimately to preclude, the possibility of fundamental social change" (*AJ*, 179). Historians and cultural critics have again and again tried to find—or invent—in American history one period, one great intellectual and/or social movement, or one strain of political ideas and goals that they could use as a standard of a substantive "radical" democratic culture and society. Bercovitch, however, offers the disillusioned view that the United States, or "America," has been destined—or designed—since the establishment of the Puritan Covenant in New England after the Great Migration to become a capitalist society and culture, committed to a "fusion of secular and sacred history" and to the process of modernization. Whereas the critical work of early American Studies had set out to reclaim the radicalism of the "great tradition" (Hicks and Parrington), of the American Renaissance, particularly of Walt Whitman (Matthiessen), and to revise and redirect it, Bercovitch discovers only failure and defeat. In *The American Jeremiad* he writes: "All our classic writers (to varying degrees) labored against the myth as well as within it. All of them felt, privately at least, as oppressed by Americanism as liberated by it. And all of them, however, captivated by the national dream, also *used* the dream to reach beyond the categories of their culture" (*AJ*, 179, 180). Thus he appears to support emphatically the radical impulse in American literature: "To be American for our classic writers was by definition to be radical—to turn against the past, to defy the status quo and become an agent of change" (*AJ*, 203). But he continues:

> And at the same time to be radical as an American was to transmute the revolutionary impulse in some basic sense: by spiritualizing it (as in *Walden*), by diffusing or deflecting it (as in *Leaves of Grass*), by translating it into a choice between blasphemy and regeneration (as in *Moby-Dick*), or most generally by accommodating it to society (as in [Emerson's] "The Fortune of the Republic"). In every case, "America" resolved a conflict of values by reconciling personal, national, and cultural ideals, and by transform[ing] radicalism itself into a mode of cultural cohesion and continuity. [*AJ*, 205]

As he sums it up in his essay "The Rites of Assent: Rhetoric, Ritual, and the Ideology of American Consensus" (1981): "The autonomous act that might have posed fundamental alternatives, imaginative or actual, became instead a mimesis of cultural norms. The works of our classic writers show more clearly than any others I know how American radicalism could be turned into a force against radical change."[28] For American radical critics, there is no "great tradition" to build on: "Insofar as we render *The American Scholar* or *Democratic Vistas* the basis of native radical dissent, we make literary criticism a version of the American jeremiad—which is to say, part of a continuing ritual of socialization."[29]

But Bercovitch's approach to American history in general and radicalism in particular in terms of an interpretation of the meaning of "America" raises some questions. Does not his own hermeneutic of the total "myth of America" rely so much on its inherent claim of a unique all-encompassing and incomparable social and cultural truth, of an "ideological consensus—in moral, religious, economic, social, and intellectual matters," that it by definition must perceive everything in the frame of the rhetoric and the cultural rituals of American society he criticizes ("RA," 5)? Clearly, a historical dialectic of consensus and dissent *has* been at work, but it must *not* be dissolved more or less completely in the direction of the ideology of consensus. Does the totalizing claim of the "ideology of consensus" not necessarily imply that any form of radical dissent or alternative vision can finally be seen merely as affirming "by negative" the myth of American exceptionalism? Predictably, in Bercovitch's readings this also applies to the great "anti-jeremiads" of twentieth-century American literature, from Fitzgerald's *The Great Gatsby* and Dos Passos's *U.S.A.* to the Beat writers and Pynchon's *Gravity's Rainbow.* This perception—or hermeneutic circle—tends to overlook that the presence of aspects and rhetorical motifs of the myth of America in the manifestations of radical criticism, literature, or social and political movements does not mean per se that they affirm the myth of America. It can also have an "alternative" meaning and function within the context of the public culture of the dissenting group or sub- and counterculture, as in the more recent discussions on the meaning of working-class culture or feminist readings of sentimental fiction.

Bercovitch does not, of course, contest that from its beginning, but particularly since the nineteenth century, American society has been characterized by serious conflicts and ethnic and class divisions, but primarily as America is "seen from outside the [ideological] consensus." For Bercovitch, labor leaders, feminists, abolitionists, as well as socialists, blacks, and Indians, whatever their critical intentions and their manifestations of social criticism, still confirm the norms of the culture. Yet how could his own hermeneutical approach to the texts of the myth of America ever notice and reconstruct those forces and movements in history that did *not* affirm or were *not* part of the total "ritual of assent" and the "redundant intra-cultural dialogue"? Does not his general interpretation of the course of American history as the unfolding and realization of a "wholly middle-class culture" necessarily see all dissenting minorities, different ethnic groups, and subcultures only *within* the horizon of the myth of America that originated with New England Puritans, leaving *himself* no way to approach them from their own points of view, experience, and history and leaving *them* no alternative to incorporation into the "middle-class American Way"?

The "question of Southern ideology," not mentioned in *The American Jeremiad*, is dismissed in "The Rites of Assent" in a footnote that acknowledges that "the 'peculiar institution' gave the South a strong *regional* identity," but, he continues, "as a mode of cultural cohesion that identity was undermined by a basic commitment from the start to the tenets of free enterprise" ("RA," 12). Bercovitch again and again points out the precarious relationship between myth, history, and ideology in American history, and he criticizes the myth of America for "plainly substituting symbolic for social analysis," for "explaining history away." But in his own book he himself transforms history into hermeneutics, both in the sense of his understanding of the process of American history itself and in his own notions of how historical cultural criticism is to be realized. We should not be tempted by the totalizing power of the myth of America into separating myth and history as completely as he does, even though he does this to unmask the historical power of the myth and the ideological uses of the myth and to deconstruct this confusion of "myth and history." As a sign of hope, Bercovitch mentions "the recent incursions of history upon the myth of America" that might open up a perspective for a different view, the "discovery of America as a cultural artifact" ("RA," 13), and for an intercultural and comparative analysis of American culture and society that could, finally, destroy the fixation on American exceptionalism. But I think this notion, which you can find at the end of most of the well-known books in American Studies (and also at the end of Hartz's *The Liberal Tradition in America*), ignores the fact that history is not something that "encroaches" upon the ideas and the myths and rituals of a culture from the outside, but has always worked within them, and that their negation and potential sublation have always been part of their very power, questioning their claims to total domination. They could have and have been turned against themselves, used with different meanings and functions by various groups and in various situations in the course of American history, all of which gets lost in the exclusive emphasis on the integrating power of the American myth.

We can fully understand the myths and rituals of the dominant culture only by reconstructing their relationship to other alternative forms, manifestations, and contexts in the culture and society at large. Bercovitch radicalizes Hartz's sweeping critique and emphasizes the persistence of the Puritan Jeremiad, based on a revisionary reading of Perry Miller's work, and substitutes Puritanism for the Lockean Enlightenment as the origin, the source of the American consensus. He virtually eliminates the radical, egalitarian strain in politics and society and political and social thought since the American Revolution by turning it into one aspect or part of the rhetoric and the ritual of a secularized millennial faith and consensus permeated by a sense of continuity. All this prevents him from exploring in earnest the often conflicting and contradictory cultural consequences of the fundamental changes—their *dis*continuity—in American society since the mid-nineteenth century brought about by industrialization, urbanization, and large-scale immigration that have greatly increased the heterogeneity of cultural and social life in the United States. It also keeps him from studying the complex relationship between social and intellectual change and from seeing the dialectic working within history that in the latter part of the nineteenth century produced in the United States a secular, historical consciousness. If Bercovitch charges that the rhetoric of the myth of America "plainly substitutes symbolic for social analysis," his own book does not wholly escape the same objection, as he tends to equate the repercussions of the myth of America with the process of American history and the dominant culture with the persistence of New England Puritanism in the United States in general.

Radical Traditions in American History: Alan Trachtenberg

If Sacvan Bercovitch's work in the 1970s and early 1980s renewed American Studies as radical cultural critique, it ironically *rejected* any viable radical traditions in American history that were not domesticated by the omnipotent myth of America or the American ideology. Yet his radical approach poses some problems that ask us to relate his "totalizing" view of American culture and society to the strategies and insights of the new cultural, social, and intellectual history of the time. I think that Alan Trachtenberg's book *The Incorporation of America: Culture and Society in the Gilded Age* (1982), another study written in the critical tradition of American Studies, suggests some alternative views of the dynamics of American history. Trachtenberg shows in what ways the debate about the symbolic meaning of America in the Gilded Age was a ritual of consensus and socialization not only within a wholly middle-class culture (or ideology), but also among other groups, about survival, working conditions, social and political organization, cultural identities, and the quality of future life in the United States.

The process of the "incorporation" of America is analyzed as a fundamental restructuring of the American economy and society, its institutions, and its systems of transportation and communication across the continent, but at the same time as a "remaking of cultural perceptions" and "values," of the sphere and function of "culture." "By 'incorporation of America' I mean, then, the emergence of a changed, more tightly structured society with new hierarchies of control, and also changed conceptions of that society, of America itself."[30] Trachtenberg's main aim in his book, therefore, is to trace the "relations . . . between the literal and figurative meanings of incorporation," but as a process of social change that "proceeded by contradiction and conflict":

> The corporate system in business, politics, and cultural institutions engendered opposing views, however inchoate and incomplete that opposition remained. The deepest changes in these decades of swift and thorough industrialization and urbanization lay at the level of culture, difficult for contemporaries to recognize, and baffling for historians. The deepest resistances and oppositions also lay there, in the quality as well as the substance of perceptions, in the styles as well as context of responses. [*IA*, 37]

In drawing on the work of the new social and labor history of Herbert Gutman, David Montgomery, Eugene Genovese, and others, Trachtenberg traces among the working-class and dissenting groups the forms of political resistance and radical alternatives to the tightening hegemony of the corporate system of business. In contradistinction to Bercovitch, he discovers a great variety of forms of native radicalism, of radical social and economic thought, of "residual" as well as "emergent" forms of culture (in Raymond Williams's sense) that are oppositional or alternative to the dominant culture.

In studying "the realms of culture," in exploring and clarifying "the dialectic between mind and world, culture and society," Trachtenberg is especially drawn to the power of myth as ideology, to "figurative language," "figures of speech, types, images, metaphors" as "vehicles of self-knowledge," as active forms of control of social reality. He is careful to point out the contradictory meaning of cultural symbols such as "the West" in chapter 1 and "the Machine" in chapter 2. Instead, he emphasizes the dialectic working in their manifestations in social and cultural reality, a dialectic that reveals how Americans tried to grasp and control the "radical discontinuity with the past," the radical changes characteristic of their time.

Trachtenberg also emphasizes the struggle over the meaning of "the word America," but he is careful, at least in most cases, to make clear that "America" was both a myth and a geopolitical reality. He emphasizes the agonistic and antagonistic implications and repercussions of the term, the "unresolved ambiguities within the word 'America' itself," the fact that "the consensus, unstable even at the height of the campaign against slavery and the execution of the war, split asunder in the crisis of the 1870's": "From Appomattox to White City—the temporal range of this study—controversies over the meaning of America symbolized struggles over reality, over the power to define as well as control it" (*IA*, 38).

Radicalism at the time was understood as "restoring America to original meanings," as going back to the substantive democratic roots, and discovering the "utopia" of a "new social order," embodied in experimental utopian communities or represented by third-party movements advocating radical change. Trachtenberg argues that Walt Whitman's attack on capitalist "anti-democratic disease and monstrosity" in *Democratic Vistas* (1871) insisted on an "antebellum egalitarian dogma, that America and democracy are convertible terms," and called for a "radical change of category, in the distribution of precedence," on a "programme for culture" based on equality (*IA*, 39). He demanded a revolution in culture that overcomes, in Trachtenberg's words, the "identification of America itself with a privileged culture distributed and administered with condescension from above" and realizes the promise of more democracy. Workers tended to view wage labor as another form of slavery and the moneyed classes as usurpers, but they saw themselves "as the true inheritors of the republican tradition, the genuine upholders of free labor" (*IA*, 39). At first, they refused to accept the wage system as a permanent fixture of American life: "Dominated by craftsmen and seasoned industrial workers, labor organizations early in the period refused to accept this change and still drew on a free-labor rhetoric while proposing cooperatives and collective ownership of factories and businesses" (*IA*, 39). Contrary to what Bercovitch's brief reference to labor spokesmen implied, the fact that they used the "language of republicanism and fervent Americanism" does *not* mean that "labor remained in these years within the middle-class consensus" (*IA*, 39). Instead, labor thought of itself as "upholding nothing so much as the fundamental American traditions of republicanism and equality—indeed, as the most vigorous defenders of that tradition: so far from 'foreign' as to be the most authentic voice of America itself" (*IA*, 39). In these years of "the fact and perception of a widening class rift" and of the development of a new, multiethnic

American working class that introduced "cultural difference into American life on an unprecedented scale," "a distinct labor culture" developed, a "commonality of the work experience" (including strikes), an "ethic of cooperation, of mutuality," a "movement toward producer cooperatives," "a collectivist counterculture in the midst of the growing factory system" (*IA*, 39). This distinct labor culture was characterized by a "radically different outlook" that sharply diverged from the individualist values of business and middle-class aspirations and found its expression in labor unions and "alternative institutions of everyday life": "We know little of this evolving labor culture which developed as a conscious alternative to the culture of competitive industrialism, of acquisitiveness and segregation. It was short-lived, although its legacy reappears throughout the later history of labor. A residual culture of ethnic identity, religious and republican communitarianism, it was also in some instances fostered by class-conscious radicals" (*IA*, 39).

Populism also set out to restore America to its original meaning, to "restore," as the resolution of the convention of the People's Party in Omaha on July 4, 1892, put it, "'the Government of the Republic to the basis of the "plain people" with whose class it originated. We assert our purposes to be identical with the purposes of the National Constitution, to form a more perfect Union and establish justice'" (as quoted in *IA*, 173). Based on an authentic mass movement of farmers and incorporating the radical objections by workers to industrial capitalism, the Populists were an expression of native radicalism that "aimed at no less than a total revision of the conventional picture of American life" and established an "opposing culture, an alternative view not only of 'politics' and 'economics' but of the world as such" (*IA*, 177). The Omaha platform proposed a coherent program of economic change by means of government action, not by revolution. Its program may have been permeated too much by an idea of a "producer's commonwealth" that had become impossible in the reality of the new urban, corporate society they worked to change. But the Populists went beyond looking back to the past, beyond nostalgia for the original forms of realizing the promise of a fully democratic America. They struggled to explore what the meaning of utopia in America could really mean—that is, if it meant "restoring" the "original America" or if it demanded the realization of a "new social order," a "utopian revolution" (*IA*, 40)

Trachtenberg is, of course, keenly aware that many of these efforts to develop a radical critique of capitalist America were "incorporated" by the dominant culture, that the process of "incorporation" by business helped to "cloud" the public perception of the conflicting interests of capitalist employers and workers. He also points out that the "spirit of mutuality" did not lead to an effectively unified working class, that the unions failed to overcome the "divisions among workers such as ethnic antagonism, language and religious differences between skilled and unskilled workers." And he describes how and why Populism failed as a third-party movement. If it foundered, as Trachtenberg puts it, "in the ill-assorted mixture of culture and politics at the core of its vision," one should add not only that it left a legacy of an indigenous American radicalism that later radical movements could, or should, be aware of and respond to, but that its "ill-assorted mixture of culture and politics at the core of its vision" revealed a fundamental conflict, or contradiction, between culture and politics as well as within the realm of culture that itself has, in different ways, dominated American society since the Gilded Age (*IA*, 41).

Trachtenberg shows how politics was converted into "mass spectacle, into cultural event," how it "displac[ed] economic and social issues by appealing to cultural issues," and how culture was turned into an institution that was to provide "a middle ground," a "vision of a harmonious body politic," "social control," "pacification," "a domestic island of virtue and stability," and "stimulate even greater production of consumer goods" (*AI*, 42). The chapters "Mysteries of the Great City," especially in its treatment of the social spaces of public parks, the department stores as city spectacle, "The Politics of Culture," "Fictions of the Real," with its focus on literary realism, and "White City" offer a wealth of details and brilliant insights into the institutionalization and affirmative social role of culture in the Gilded Age. But Trachtenberg makes clear that the very same process of the "politicization" of culture also produced its very opposition or negation. If the official representatives of "high" culture hardly voiced substantial resistance to the incorporation of American culture, many other groups and individuals used the realm of culture to dramatize and communicate opposing and alternative visions of a democratic America, to create countercultures in America. For the first time, a group of alienated writers and political thinkers developed that produced a form of cultural critique they used to "describe and judge their times against the measure of their own alienation" (*AI*, 42). Trachtenberg takes the White City of the World's Columbian Exposition of 1893 in Chicago as an "ironic" "conclusion" of his narrative, because it exemplified "contradictions held in momentary balance—not a confusion of values—, but an effort to incorporate contrary and diverse values under the unity of a system of culture in support of a system of society" (*AI*, 42). Both in the fight over its architecture between Burnham and Sullivan and its strategies of inclusion and exclusion of cultural and social groups, it seemed to dramatize the triumph of a view of America as "a whole society," as the "alliance and incorporation of business, politics, industry, and culture" (*AI*, 42). Yet it was unmasked in its shallowness when in May 1893, at the time of its opening, banks and factories closed in the worst financial panic of American history and a year later the great railway strike spread over the nation. Therefore, the tension, the unresolved conflict about the meaning and control of "America" has persisted and renewed itself from the margins, as have radical traditions, both continuous and discontinuous, as a project of radical cultural critique and counterdiscourse and a nonteleological form of American history writing.

[4]

AMERICAN CULTURAL CRITIQUE: TOWARD A POLITICS OF POSTMODERNISM AND POSTCOLONIAL DISCOURSE [1970–1990]

The Dialectics of History in Postmodernity: Fredric Jameson

The different reactions to the crisis of the Left or of radical literary and cultural criticism and the controversies about the existence and uses of a radical tradition in American literary, cultural, and social history that were characteristic of the late 1970s and the 1980s helped to bring the theoretical debate in literary and cultural studies back home to the United States. The critical works discussed in the preceding chapter focused on the question of the specific forms and traditions of American literary and cultural radicalism, on the achievements and failures of writers and critics to discover, explore, and elaborate analytical strategies and affiliations of a radical cultural critique that could complement or provide American alternatives to the European challenges of fundamental deconstructions of traditional notions of knowledge in the humanities and social sciences. They also raised the question, in different ways and mostly rather tentatively, as to how the recent far-reaching changes in Western and, particularly, American society and culture force us to reconceptualize our notions of radicalism and cultural critique. This also means opening up the debate to a more international perspective on revisions of radical thought in literary and cultural studies and on a more explicit engagement with the critical implications of postmodernism as a theory of contemporary culture and society in the United States.

It is in this context that the extraordinarily complex, wide-ranging, and self-reflective work of Fredric Jameson can be used to bring together many of the crucial insights of the critics of American cultural radicalism and to provide a focus for some of the most urgent controversial issues. Jameson's vast historical dialectical synthesis has taken up the contending perspectives and demands of many other critical positions and has increasingly tried to situate the theoretical demands, the status, and the prospects of radical cultural criticism in a penetrating analysis of contemporary American and Western societies and cultures that reassesses the role and status of the cultural sphere itself.

Fredric Jameson opens his book *Marxism and Form* (1971) with the following sentences: "When the American reader thinks of Marxist literary criticism, I imagine that it is still the atmosphere of the 1930s which comes to mind. The burning issues of those days . . . generated polemics which we may think back on with nostalgia but which no longer correspond to the conditions of the world today."[1] Against this useless past Jameson offers an extensive and careful analysis of German and French Marxist criticism in order to expound and communicate "dialectical thinking at work" (*MF*, xi). For Jameson, twentieth-century European dialectical theories of literature are exceedingly difficult for Americans to understand, because their national tradition has been characterized by "the absence of any genuine Marxist culture in academic circles" and by "that mixture of political liberalism, empiricism, and logical positivism which we know as Anglo-American philosophy and which is hostile at all points to the type of thinking outlined here" (*MF*, x). Jameson, therefore, sees the political and philosophical contribution of his book in its demolition of the "anti-speculative bias" of the American "liberal tradition" that has not lost its prestige and ideological potency in spite of its obvious political and philosophical "bankruptcy." At the same time, Jameson revises the common understanding of Marxist literary criticism prevalent in the United States, as the title of the book, *Marxism and Form*, provocatively indicates by emphasizing the relevance of Marxism to the interpretation of aesthetic and social forms. The task Jameson sets himself in this study, namely to work out "a genuine Marxist hermeneutic," the "hermeneutic dimension of dialectical thinking," through a critical dialectical reading and rewriting of the works of Adorno, Benjamin, Marcuse, Bloch, Lukács, and Sartre, defines the first stage of a critical project that has been at the heart of his critical writings ever since (*MF*, 61).

In *Marxism and Form*, he emphasizes the "central role" literature plays "in the dialectical process," as he understands the operation of dialectical thought itself as "the elaboration of dialectical sentences," as "discourse" ("tropes and rhetoric"), as "process or figure" that "hermeneutical exegesis of a text" must decipher. Jameson's Marxist political hermeneutic has two coordinates, two "irreconcilable characteristics," a *negative hermeneutics* as "demystification," as the "destruction of illusions," as the critique of ideology, and a *positive hermeneutics* of "restoration of some original, forgotten meaning," of "renewed access to some essential source of life," indicating a future utopia. It comprises the Hegelian and the Marxist mode of dialectics: they "in no way contradict each other, even though their precise relationship remains to be worked out." Most of Jameson's work pursues the Hegelian form of dialectical criticism and concentrates on the "ideology of *form*": "The sociology of culture is therefore first and foremost . . . a *form*: no matter what the philosophical postulates called upon to justify it, as practice and as a conceptual operation it always involves the jumping of a spark between two people, the coming into contact of two unequal terms, of two apparently unrelated modes of being" (*MF*, 62).

The unbridgeable tension between "incommensurable" or "discontinuous realities" and the notion of a "unified world," of the "unity of the cultural field," can be overcome, as Jameson points out in his reading of Adorno's *Philosophy of the New Music*, *Negative Dialectics*, and *Aesthetic Theory*, only in "a glimpse," a reconciliation that in our world can never be claimed as "real," but without its "form" "the new historical and dialectical consciousness" cannot work, cannot "come to its truth in the language of events." In his dialectical vision of historical change, Adorno's *Versöhnung* (reconciliation) is "nothing but a logical possibility" that cannot be projected into the realm of "historical chronology," either as "metaphysical nostalgia" or as "Utopianism." But in the cultural realm, in the world of art, that "unique reconciliation" can find expression at a particular moment in the history of the art form, due to the inner logic of historical development itself. For the dialectical critic in a "fragmented universe" this means that he can "keep faith with the Hegelian spirit of systematization" only when he is "resolutely unsystematic" and dramatizes this insoluble conflict in the strategies of his writing (*MF*, 63).

At the end of *The Prison-House of Language* (1972), Jameson reformulates his historical, dialectical, and critical project in response to the revision of our understanding of history and language by French structuralism.[2] In *The Political Unconscious* (1981), he turns the attack of poststructuralism on Western, including Marxist, "humanism," "hermeneutics," and "historical thinking" into a reaffirmation of his own dialectical political hermeneutics and Marxist historicism.[3] He works out the dialectic of ideology and utopia, the key role of narrative as a socially symbolic act, the notion of a political unconscious in order to restore the political dimension of the texts, the "primacy of history itself," and the stages and the dynamics of an act of interpretation that claims the "priority of a Marxist interpretive framework in terms of semantic richness" (*MF*, 64).

Clearly, Jameson's elaboration of a Marxist hermeneutic is intended less as a contribution to the discipline of literary criticism than as a project of radical cultural criticism that privileges the interpretation of cultural texts as "social acts, at once disguised and transparent" (*MF*, xiv–xv). He gives a historical reason for the privileged status of cultural critique today that, at the same time, marks a paradox crucial to any understanding of the crisis as well as the new potential of contemporary radical criticism. In a critical reassessment of Marcuse's notion of "affirmative culture" and of an adversarial culture, Jameson writes:

> What we must now ask ourselves is whether it is not precisely this "semi-autonomy" of the cultural sphere which has been destroyed by the logic of late capitalism. Yet to argue that culture is today no longer endowed with the relative autonomy it once enjoyed as one level among others in earlier moments of capitalism (let alone in pre-capitalist societies) is not necessarily to imply its disappearance or extinction. On the contrary: we must go on to affirm that the dissolution of an autonomous sphere of culture is rather to be imagined in terms of an explosion: a prodigious expansion of culture throughout the social realm, to the point at which everything in our social life—from economic value and state power to practices and to the very structure of the psyche itself—can be said to have become "cultural" in some original and as yet untheorized sense. [*MF*, 65]

In a "culture of the spectacle," in "consumer capitalism today," "everything is mediated by culture, to the point where even the political and the ideological 'levels' have initially to be disentangled from their primary mode of representation which is cultural" (*MF*, 65).

This *redefinition of culture*, the "omnipresence of culture in this society," and the "dissolution" of the fabric of traditional cohesive groups have two important consequences for the objectives and forms of radical cultural criticism today. On the one hand, Jameson places the radical deconstruction of the Western philosophical tradition and its reigning dichotomies, the uncovering, in cultural discourse, of the strategies of exclusion and marginalization of the "other(s)," in their concrete social and historical perspective. As he puts it in his important essay, "Reification and Utopia in Mass Culture" (1979):

> The only authentic cultural production today has seemed to be that which can draw on the collective experience of marginal pockets and the social life of the world system: black literature and blues, British working-class rock, women's literature, gay literature, the *roman québécois*, the literature

> of the Third World; and this production is possible only to the degree to which these forms of collective life or collective solidarity have not yet been fully penetrated by the market and by the commodity system.[4]

If this reaffirmation of a politically evaluative concept of "culture" ("authentic," "collective experience") finds its referents only in pockets of social life in Western countries that have defended or discovered "intentions and acts" alternative to the social system (in an argument similar to Christopher Lasch's in "Mass Culture Reconsidered"), it also points to the collective experience and the different lifestyles of non-Western cultures and societies that have been exploited economically and culturally but have also been "marginalized" as "the Other" by Western discourse. One should add, however, that these pockets of social life are marginal, the Other, and can be lumped together in the arbitrary way Jameson does only when seen from the ethnocentric and white male center of the dominant culture. In a decentered view, they also embody, in different ways, traditions, values, and cultural and communal forms *of their own* that are not only oppositional to but alternative to the "logic" of Western bourgeois society and the conventions of modernism. Only if we realize the different functions specific historical forms and strategies in art have in the cultural productions of oppositional groups can we escape the easy dismissal of their work as outmoded or second-rate. As Stanley Aronowitz has pointed out: "When we insist upon the historical and social specificity of the production of art and when the judgments [on the cultural productions of the social groups] are understood as ideologies restricted within contexts that are in no way universal, the art of the oppressed is explained as counterhegemonic, a series of discursive practices that adopt the abandoned modes of bourgeois art in order to oppose bourgeois domination."[5]

But we have to be very careful in our celebration of counterdiscourse or the discourse of others, as radical critics themselves all too quickly have absorbed dissenting minorities into the dominant white male First World culture that assigns them a strategic place in the general radical discourse. They are rewritten, as Craig Owens has shown, in terms of a "master narrative" (Jameson) and assimilated as parts of a long list of "liberation or self-determination movements," of "a vast, undifferentiated category, 'Difference.'"[6] As Gayatri Spivak, writing from the "point of view [of] a Third World feminist," has put it in her critique of Terry Eagleton's quest for a paradigm of "revolutionary literary criticism": "Just as Eagleton earlier accommodates deconstruction as a property of the dialectic, so does he accommodate feminism as a movement within the evolution of Marxist criticism. . . . Having praised feminist criticism . . . for its revolutionary-Marxist potential, Eagleton proceeds to trash it in three paragraphs: his main contention, feminism is theoretically thin, or separatist. Girls, shape up!"[7] The politics of inclusion, then, can lead to results similar to the politics of exclusion, particularly if the discourse of others is turned into a homogeneous, more or less monolithic theoretical or ideological construct such as "feminist criticism." Equally, as Spivak argues concerning women, "women's voice is not one voice to be added to the orchestra; *every* voice is inhabited by the sexual differential" ("*PI*," 277). With other groups, such as black Americans and Third World cultures, the dialectic of the politics of exclusion and inclusion in the prevalent tradition of radical cultural criticism takes on different forms.

On the other hand, the "increasing interpenetration of high and mass culture" in consumer capitalism provides an opportunity to overcome the traditional opposition of modernist high art and mass culture and to understand them, in Jameson's words, as different artistic/cultural transformations of "social and political anxieties and fantasies." With the historical advent of "modernism" two distinct "cultural spaces" developed, that of "high" culture and that of mass culture. Jameson summarizes this process in *The Political Unconscious:*

> Schematically, it may be described as a structural breakdown of the older realisms, from which emerges not modernism alone, but rather two literary and cultural structures, dialectically interrelated and necessarily presupposing each other for any adequate analysis: these now find themselves positioned in the distinct and generally incompatible spaces of the institutions of high literature and what the Frankfurt School conveniently termed the "culture industry," that is, the apparatuses for the production of "popular" or mass culture. [*PU*, 70]

If the two "literary and cultural structures" are dialectically interrelated, they cannot be cleanly opposed to each other in terms of utopia and ideology. In reappropriating Adorno's assessment of the adversarial and utopian dimension of (high) modernist art for the analysis of mass culture, Jameson suggests:

> Works of mass culture cannot be ideological without at one and the same time being implicitly or explicitly Utopian as well: they cannot manipulate unless they offer some genuine shred of content as a fantasy bribe to the public about to be so manipulated. . . . [A]ll contemporary works of art—

> whether those of high culture and modernism or of mass culture and commercial culture—have as their underlying impulse—albeit in what is often distorted and repressed, unconscious form—our deepest fantasies about the nature of social life, both as we live it now, and as we feel in our bones it ought rather to be lived. [*PU*, 71]

Jameson's persistent effort, since *Marxism and Form*, to retrieve the utopian impulse in radical cultural criticism, "the utopian principle as a hermeneutic or technique of decipherment, in opposition to the examination of the content of individual visions," has helped to reopen the discussion of the "Marxist perspective on the future" (in Ernst Bloch's sense), as it is no longer possible for Marxism to look for "a glimpse of the healthier, socially functional art of the past" (*MF*, xvi). But it must *not* be understood as the discovery of some kind of peaceful coexistence of ideology and utopia in all cultural productions in capitalist society. At the very end of *The Political Unconscious*, Jameson writes:

> Benjamin's formulation [that "there is no document of civilization which is not at one and the same time a document of barbarism"] comes, finally, as an appropriate corrective to the doctrine of the political unconscious which has been developed in these pages, reasserting the undiminished power of ideological distortion that persists even within the restored Utopian meaning of cultural artifacts, and reminding us that within the symbolic power of art and culture the will to dominate perseveres intact. It is only at this price—that of the simultaneous recognition of the ideological and Utopian functions of the artistic text—that a Marxist cultural study can hope to play its part in political praxis, which remains, of course, what Marxism is all about. [*PU*, 299]

Jameson's elaboration of the dual nature of the hermeneutic process, both of the "historically original form of negative dialectic in Marxism—whether ideology is in it grasped as mere 'false consciousness,' or, more comprehensively, as structural limitation" and of the various Marxist versions of a "positive hermeneutic"—"Ernst Bloch's ideal of hope or of the Utopian impulse; Mikhail Bakhtin's notion of the dialogical as a rupture of the one-dimensional text of bourgeois narrative, as a carnivalesque dispersal of the hegemonic order of a dominant culture; the Frankfurt School's conception of strong memory as the trace of gratification, of the revolutionary power of that *promesse de bonheur* most immediately inscribed in the aesthetic text"—entails the critical awareness that "the work of art does not so much express ideology as, by endowing the latter with aesthetic re-presentation and figuration, it ends up enacting the latter's own virtual unmasking and self-criticism" (*PU*, 73).

This political reformulation of the deconstructionist critics' thesis that (literary) texts "deconstruct themselves" has important implications for understanding the possible forms and functions of the traditions of radical cultural critique. It may contribute to a revision of the expectations recent critics of cultural radicalism have brought to the interpretation of the "radical" potential of cultural productions. Their radical "meaning," then, consists both in the "virtual unmasking and self-criticism" of the *forms* of ideology *and* in the *suspension* of the laws and structures governing everyday political reality and social experience, a suspension that can open up the world of the work of art and its reception to alternative, not exclusively oppositional, values, forms of interaction, and community (*PU*, 73).

I think that anthropologist Victor Turner's studies of societies as processes, as performances that always comprise both "social structure" and "communitas" and are characterized by continuity as well as by discontinuity, by the pervasive power of the social structure and norms as well as by their suspension in ritual places and periods of utopian communitas, can help us to work out a theory of radical traditions of discontinuity that locates such radicalism in the historical process and does justice to their oppositional, utopian, alternative potential without enclosing them in a myth of origin or a teleological view of history. In modern industrialized societies, the potentially revolutionary vision and experience of communitas finds its place, its expression in what Turner calls "liminoid" genres and media such as theater, literature, art, music, film, popular culture, sports, and games. Turner distinguishes the liminoid from the "liminal," a term he uses for ritualized practices in preindustrial cultures such as initiation rites (*rites de passages*). Although often historically traceable to such liminal rites, liminoid genres are institutionalized forms that mediate between the individual and community ("communitas").[8] Writers as "exceptionally liminal thinkers" dramatize in their works the potential of communitas of their specific society without "reflecting" or "expressing" its "social structure." If we grasp the discontinuous character of the suspension of social structure in liminoid forms of culture and the fact that they do *not* offer models or programs that can *directly* be applied to revolutionizing society, the widespread frustration about the "failure" of a radical cultural critique (and of "radical" art) and the viability of its traditions can be seen in a different light (*PU*, 74).

Jameson's project of a radically historicized Marxist hermeneutic that explores the "ideology of form," the "political unconscious" in cultural productions, and reads all literature as a "symbolic meditation on the destiny of community" has disclosed new perspectives for a radical historical cultural criticism. When he talks about "History" and the "political perspective" as "the absolute horizon of all reading and interpretation," he does not, I believe, see history as a master code or a "grand Narrative" (Jean-François Lyotard) that, in the end, subsumes all heterogeneity and discontinuity. Rather, he grasps history in "dialectical thought" as an "anticipation of the logic of a collectivity which has not yet come into being," as the horizon and perspective of a "concrete collective life of an achieved Utopia or classless society" that will never be a fixed state of society where men and women can rely on final certainties. Jameson also takes up the challenge of the recent emphasis in historical theory on "narrativity" and "textuality" in historiography, on the processes of "meaning production" (*PU*, 82ff.). He shares Hayden White's assertion that, from a semiological perspective, "the form of the text is the place where it does its ideologically significant work."[9] But he refuses to obliterate the difference between the modes of literature and history by simply regarding them as "nothing but texts." In *The Political Unconscious* he writes: "We would therefore propose the following revised formulation: that history is *not* a text, not a narrative, master or otherwise, but that, as an absent cause, it is inaccessible to us except in textual form, and that our approach to it and to the Real itself necessarily passes through its prior textualization, its narrativization in the political unconscious" (*PU*, 75).

If history is a narrative, it is one without a telos, representing a never-ending conflict, class struggle, *and* dialogue. In this reading of "class discourse" as "essentially dialogical in structure," as Jameson alludes to Bakhtin, "History" provides a perspective, or "solution," that allows the Marxist critic to claim that "*all* class consciousness—or in other words, all ideology in the strongest sense, including the most exclusive forms of ruling-class consciousness just as much as that of oppositional or oppressed classes—is in its very nature Utopian" (*PU*, 75).

If these claims, however, are to be more than purely formal and thus socially and historically empty conceptions that everything is historical or political and that ideology always implies utopia, Jameson must concretize and historicize them in a dialectical analysis of specific forms and constellations of culture and society and of their critical and utopian potential. He has tried to do this in many of his publications, often in a sketchy way, but in greater detail in the 1980s in his essay "Periodizing the 60s" in *The 60s Without Apology* (1984), in his foreword (1984) to

Jean-François Lyotard's *The Postmodern Condition*, and in his long article on the aesthetics and politics of an "oppositional postmodernism," "Postmodernism, or the Cultural Logic of Late Capitalism" (1984), which would become the first chapter of *Postmodernism, Or, The Cultural Logic of Late Capitalism* (1991).[10]

Jameson conceives of his use of a notion of unity, of synthesis, as one of determinate negation, in Adorno's sense, as both the "explosion of the unified text into a host of clashing and contradictory elements" and the "reunification" of this multiplicity "at the level of its process of production" (*PU*, 76). Nevertheless, we also find in his work passages where History with a capital "H" is understood less as "horizon" of understanding and interpretation, as a dialectical and dialogical process, than as "ultimate ground," as the "unity of a single great collective story," as the "experience of Necessity." Jameson strongly argues that this notion of "unity of a single great collective story" is to be understood not in terms of the myth of origin or of teleology, but in a "reflexive," "dialectical" way, "registering difference as well as identity," and that "Necessity" is not a "type of content, but rather the inexorable *form* of events." But he does not always escape the danger, or temptation, to use his key terms in a substantive manner in order to refute the claims of competing critical systems and philosophies, of turning the "textualization or narrative (re-)construction" of History as "an absent cause" into manifestations of "a total synchronic structure."[11]

It is remarkable how Jameson has taken up in his books and his work on the politics of postmodernism all major philosophical, social, and cultural approaches and forms of discourse and their traditions, analyzed them in a critical historical and political perspective, and made them productive in his own cultural theory and criticism. More than any other critic he has tried to do justice to the inherent strengths of all kinds of "critical operations," from historicism, European Marxism, psychoanalysis, structuralism, poststructuralism to postmodernism. Instead of dismissing most of them as misguided or ideological, he has dialectically worked out their power, but he is not content with describing a plurality of incommensurable interpretive approaches. Instead, he has attempted to read them as voices in a polylogue and *agon* of cultural interpretations that can find in Marxism their "final horizon": "In the spirit of a more authentic dialectical tradition, Marxism is here conceived as that 'untranscendable horizon' that subsumes such apparently antagonistic or incommensurable critical operations, assigning them an undoubted sectoral validity within itself, and thus at once cancelling and preserving them" (*PU*, 77).

In his essay "Criticism in History" (1976), Jameson had argued that "if you prolong any of these methods even on its own terms—you always reemerge into the historical dimension itself, which thus comes as an implicit or explicit completion of all literary analysis or interpretation."[12] If this emphasizes again the inescapable awareness of historical consciousness and the historical process, later in the same essay he claims that in the United States, in the mid-1970s, "Marxism has once again seemed to many to provide the only intellectually coherent and fully satisfying historical and economic explanation for the things that have been happening to us. It is a total explanation, and this is its formal superiority over all the other partial kinds of accounts" ("*CH*," 46). Again, this claim of the unique privileged status of Marxism, of its power as a "total explanation," in some important sense tries to retrieve Lukács's notion of "totality" from its explicit dismissal by poststructuralist philosophy. Jameson understands it, with Hegel, not as "a place of truth" but as "a perspective and a method whereby the 'false' and the ideological can be unmasked and made visible" ("*CH*," 46). Yet this "negative and methodological status of the concept of 'totality'" in Jameson's argument for the priority of Marxism, at the same time, by being defended as "an ultimate *semantic* precondition for the intelligibility of literary and cultural texts," for its "semantic richness," can all too quickly result in the homogenization and incorporation of all expressions of radical difference and discontinuity ("*CH*," 46). In his essay "Periodizing the 60s," Jameson offers a "unified field theory" of the decade, arguing in terms of "a series of significant homologies," explicitly distinguishing his approach from "some proposition about the organic unity of the 60s on all its levels," but he nevertheless leaves the impression that somehow he sees everything corresponding with everything else on a world scale ("*PS*," 78).

It is important to point out and criticize the hidden historical implications and political consequences of poststructuralist thought, but it is premature to reinterpret its insistence on the difference between deconstruction and dialectical thinking as only *apparent* and to be easily rewritten in the interpretive framework of the Marxist dialectic. It is equally important to reread the work of the Frankfurt school in the light of deconstruction and postmodernism, as Michael Ryan and other critics have done, but it is misleading and historically counterproductive to reinterpret the difference between Adorno's negative dialectics and Derrida's deconstruction as only "apparently antagonistic and incommensurable" (*PS*, 79). Jameson's own subtle analyses of cultural processes, of discursive practices, of criticism in history and his emphasis on a world-historical perspective beyond Western ethnocentrism reveal that cultures and societies have to be reconstructed and criticized both in terms of a historical, dialectical hermeneutic *and* in terms of heterogeneity, discontinuity, and decenteredness. Radical cultural criticism today finds its most powerful rationale in working through, in a double sense, the tensions and radical differences in contemporary society and culture. The dialectic of a negative and a positive hermeneutic as it applies to the complex structures and processes of Western capitalist societies and cultures must be complemented and revised by a decentered approach to and from non-Western, nondominant discursive practices that cannot be integrated into an all-encompassing synthesis.

For radical cultural critique in the United States this means, finally, that the very notion of politics has to be reconsidered. In *Marxism and Form*, Jameson had raised this question when he asked what radical politics can mean in "postindustrial monopoly capitalism" in a postmodern age:

> In such a situation, within the United States itself, there is no tactical or political question which is not first and foremost theoretical, no form of action which is not inextricably entangled in the sticky cobwebs of the false and unreal culture itself, with its ideological mystification on every level. Not whether the street fighter or urban guerilla can win against the weapons and technology of the modern state, but rather precisely where the street *is* in the superstate, and, indeed, whether the old-fashioned street as such still exists in the first place in that seamless web of marketing and automated production which makes up the new state. Such are the theoretical problems of Marxism today, at least in what might be termed the overdeveloped countries. (*MF*, 80)

In his subsequent work, Jameson has consistently tried to elaborate these problems and contribute to their solutions, but the difficulty in knowing "where the street is" for the radical intellectual has not prevented some critics from accusing him of political passivity, abstractness, or idealism. Jameson himself defined his position on these matters. At the beginning of the 1970s, he wrote in his essay "Marxism and Teaching": "To create a Marxist culture in this country, to make Marxism an unavoidable presence and a distinct, original and unmistakable voice in American social, cultural and intellectual life, in short, to form an American Marxist intelligentsia for the struggles of the future—this seems to me the supreme mission of a Marxist pedagogy and a radical intellectual life today."[13]

In the 1980s, particularly in *The Political Unconscious*, Jameson carefully redefined traditional key concepts such as "modes of production," "class consciousness," "ideology," "utopia," "discourse," and "historicism," and explored their contemporary social and political repercussions, supplemented them with concepts such as the "political unconscious," and reflected on the institutional contexts in which the radical intellectual works. And against the "historical amnesia—a repression both of past and of imaginable future"—that he finds especially prevalent in the United States, he has given more of his attention to a rediscovery of the "great radical traditions" in America that "have been stamped out in almost every generation" and reassessed their radical potential (*PU*, 10). The rediscovery of these radical traditions in the United States and their utopian potential, however, can contribute to advancing the political project of radical cultural critique only if the historical distance and conceptual *difference* of the discursive practices of earlier critics is acknowledged.

The Radical Intellectual, Poststructuralism, and Postcolonial Discourse: Edward W. Said

In the preface to *Intellectuals in Power: A Genealogy of Critical Humanism* (1986), Paul A. Bové writes: "Edward Said has produced the most powerful model of oppositional critical practice within the American literary academy. In large part, Said's project results from his organic relationship to an oppressed and homeless people. . . . Said, therefore, appears frequently in this book because his position reveals what a critical humanism is capable of when it sets out to fulfill its progressive secular potential."[14] Bové's assessment of Said's achievement gives some indication of what I consider the most consequential objectives of Said's critical project and the crucial questions his work as a "radical intellectual" has raised: How can oppositional critical practice in the United States reconstitute itself after the poststructuralist deconstruction of the Western humanist tradition and the crisis of radical literary and cultural criticism at home? To what extent does the common institutional context of the American intellectual in a university enable, accommodate, or depoliticize the radical scholar's work? If it is one of the major problems for the critical intellectual today to situate his or her work and relate it to a clearly defined constituency, Edward W. Said, as a Palestinian in Western exile, seems to be in a particularly difficult, but also productive and challenging position. But what does Bové's "organic relationship" actually mean? Can it or should it overcome the experience and the intercultural construction of "otherness" and "difference"? How can Said succeed in combining, or negotiating, his Western avant-garde work as a radical literary and cultural critic with his political commitment to and his active interventions in the Palestinians' fight for national recognition, regional independence, and cultural enunciation? In what sense can a "critical" and "secular" humanism reaffirm the moral dimension of critical cultural work after Foucault's discourse analysis, which had suspended the category of the "subject," without reestablishing the radical critic as a new or old culture hero? And how can the radical Western intellectual and the postcolonial intellectual define the formal strategies of their critical discourse?

Said has been recognized widely among American literary and cultural critics as one of the most prominent figures of oppositional critical practice today, but the reactions to his work have been very divergent. He has been widely attacked and denounced by mainstream critics and "Orientalist" scholars for transgressing the boundaries of literary and cultural criticism, for his idiosyncratic critical vocabulary, and for his commitment to radical scholarship and to political activism in the name of the Palestinian people.[15] Critics from the Left have criticized his theoretical work for lacking clarity and consequence in terms of Marxist theory and have found his engagement with French poststructuralist thought less than satisfactory. Some American critics, such as Paul Bové and Jim Merod, who have acknowledged the profound impact of Said's work on their own redefinitions of oppositional criticism and the role of the humanist intellectual, have expressed reservations concerning the political thrust of Said's critical practice. Bové emphasizes Said's specific "organic relationship" to an oppressed people, which seems to make him a natural model of the Gramscian ideal of an "organic intellectual" with the kind of real constituency for which radical Western intellectuals have been looking. Nevertheless, Bové charges Said with reintroducing in his revisionary reading of Foucault's discourse analysis and theory of power the ideal of the intellectual as hero who continues to work with "those enabling figures basic to the origins and perpetuation of the dynastic discourses against which the oppositional critic always struggles" (*IP*, 31). In his wide-ranging study, *The Political Responsibility of the Critic* (1987), Merod takes exception to Bové's rather single-minded defense of Foucault against Said. In his exposition of the problem, Merod critically reexamines Said's theory and practice as elaborations of Foucault's "transgressive intellectual."[16] As we will see, Said's work raises a number of questions, and critics such as Bové and Merod have carefully investigated important issues. What is amazing, however, in all these critical, but sympathetic responses to Said's critical practice is that almost all of them focus exclusively on his explicit contributions to literary theory or redefinitions of Western humanities and ignore, or only mention in passing, his work on Orientalism and the politics, culture, and discursive formations of the world of Islam. If they refer to *Orientalism*, they discuss the book mainly as the prime example of an American (revisionary) Foucauldian analysis of discourse and power, but they fail to take up the challenge of cultural (and intercultural) otherness and difference indicated in the book and further developed in Said's subsequent work on the world of Islam and postcolonial discourse and to explore the repercussions of these reflections on Said's project of oppositional, interventionist criticism "at home."

The essays in *The World, the Text, and the Critic* (1983) explicitly and self-critically define and elaborate Said's project of oppositional cultural practice and its specific critical strategies. His notion of a secular, "interventionary" criticism that resists the dominant culture and remains rigorously skeptical grows out of his commitment to a fundamental reconstitution of American literary criticism vis-à-vis French poststructuralism, an increasingly radical questioning of the ethnocentrism of Western discourses, and a reformulation of the moral responsibilities of a politically active intellectual.

Said situates his critique in a powerful reassessment of contemporary European literary and cultural theory and a reconstruction of American Left literary criticism, past and present. He responds to the radical philosophical propositions of French poststructuralism (Derrida, Foucault) and criticizes its depoliticization in American literary deconstructive criticism, which in his view has displaced poststructuralism's critical potential and philosophical thrust by isolating "textuality" and the "self-deconstruction" of literary language. Ironically, American avant-garde literary criticism has canonized deconstruction as a new theoretical system or master discourse. Said also points out the failure of American "leftist" criticism to draw on "the American radical movement that ended with the McCarthy period" and to work out an oppositional, revisionist, historical critique of the hegemonic power of contemporary culture.[17] In his "Reflections on American 'Left' Literary Criticism," first published in 1979, he writes:

> No one would have any trouble finding a Left in American culture between the twenties and the fifties. . . . To [F. O.] Matthiessen . . . literature and criticism are nourished by the very same experiences out of which economics,

> material history, and social conflict are generated. . . . The problem is to see how he spoke so passionately and politically of the critic's responsibilities and why, twenty-odd years later, critics like de Man (whose current influence is very estimable) direct their attention to the impossibilities of political and social responsibility. [*WTC*, 162]

Said does not answer this question, even though he does complain about a "relative absence of the historical dimension" in literary studies since the 1960s, "even in their Marxist variety" (*WTC*, 165). He knows that "the transition from the notion of the Left in politics to the Left in literary criticism [is] a difficult one to make" (*WTC*, 160) and that history has destroyed some of the foundations of Matthiessen's radical criticism and subverted the meaning of the very terms "Left" and "Right":

> So far as I have been able to tell, the kind of Marxism practised or announced in university literary departments owes very little to the American radical movement that ended with the McCarthy period. The new Marxism came to this country partly as a result of the interest in French criticism and later the Frankfurt School, partly because of the general wave of antiwar agitation on the campuses. It did so in the form of sudden discovery and just as sudden application to literary problems. Its main weaknesses were the comparative absence of a continuous native Marxist theoretical tradition or culture to back it up and its relative isolation from any concrete political struggle. [*WTC*, 166]

In Said's view, this unmediated adoption of European "theory," this relative "absence of the historical dimension," and this "isolation from any concrete political struggle" have led to a form of academic literary studies on the left that, "far from producing work to challenge or revise prevailing values, institutions, and definitions, have in fact gone too long a way in confirming them" (*WTC*, 168). Or they have, in restricting their domain to "something called literature," as Gerald Graff and Christopher Lasch have also argued, "effectively confirm[ed] the culture and the society enforcing those restrictions" (*WTC*, 175).

In his essay, Said briefly discusses the internal and external challenges to the dominance of New Critical literary criticism during the late 1960s and the often unmediated search for relevance and new interdisciplinary programs. But he does not reconstruct in more detail the specific historical processes that led to the "comparative absence of a continuous native Marxist theoretical tradition or culture" in the United States or alternative forms of radical literary criticism (*WTC*, 168). Obviously, there cannot be a body of works or movements that constitute something like a "radical tradition" the cultural critic could simply hold onto or recover. If there is an indigenous radical tradition in the United States, it is, in Theodor W. Adorno's words, a "tradition of the anti-traditional," of discontinuity, of the critique and questioning of the form of tradition that has been institutionalized as ideology, "affirmative culture" (Herbert Marcuse), or the "politics of Culture" (Alan Trachtenberg). It is a tradition of social critique as well as of countercultures, sustaining alternative ways of life that have to be discovered, "wrested away from conformism" (Walter Benjamin), and redefined and reconstituted ever again.

If Said does not provide a genealogy of American Left literary criticism, he pursues instead the question how under these circumstances effective strategies of an oppositional literary and cultural criticism in advanced capitalist societies in the West can be developed, how problems of power, authority, and cultural formations can be critically addressed and worked out. What most American literary and cultural critics have failed to realize and to explore consciously is the fact that all intellectual and cultural work is enmeshed in relations of power in history and society and "occurs somewhere, at some time, on some very precisely mapped-out and permissible terrain, which is ultimately contained by the State" (*WTC*, 169). Drawing on Antonio Gramsci's analysis of hegemony and the complex functioning of culture and cultural pluralism in sustaining the power and authority of the "modern Western State" as well as on Raymond Williams's notion of "cultural materialism," Said poses the question of the role of the radical intellectual today, of "modern critical consciousness, of oppositional criticism" (*WTC*, 174). He briefly characterizes his explicitly secular concept of affiliation as providing the focus for a genuinely historical and politically oppositional understanding of cultural formations, defining "affiliation" as "that implicit network of peculiarly cultural associations between forms, statements, and other aesthetic elaborations on the one hand and, on the other, institutions, agencies, classes, and amorphous social forces" (*WTC*, 174).

In other essays in *The World, the Text, and the Critic*, Said offers a more detailed analysis of these affiliations in an oppositional discourse on literature and culture. The critic's responsibility is, as he writes in his "Introduction: Secular Criticism," to face not only the "text" but also the "world," to "affirm the connection between texts and the existential actualities of human life, politics, societies, and events" (*WTC*, 5). For Said this does not mean to relate the literary text to some kind of environment or background, but to rediscover that the text itself is a dynamic field, that texts always "are in the world, and hence worldly," that texts "to some degree . . . are events, and, even when they appear to deny it, they are nevertheless part of a social world, human life, and of course the historical moments in which they are located and interpreted" (*WTC*, 4). Texts have to be studied in a "worldly" and "historical" way. Critics have to determine "the social and external constraints upon production, as well as the discursive and cultural (that is, internal) systems that provoke and assimilate literary production." In being in the world, being worldly, "texts are fundamentally facts of power, not of democratic exchange," as the discursive situation, "far from being a type of conversation between equals, . . . is more usually like the unequal relation between colonizer and colonized, oppressor and oppressed" (*WTC*, 48).

If texts are worldly and facts of power and if the discursive situation is inherently political, then criticism as well, or literary theory, is always embedded and reconstituted in institutional contexts, is "always situated: it is skeptical, secular, reflectively open to its own failings" (*WTC*, 26). It cannot simply be transferred from one period, place, or discursive formation to another without undergoing crucial transformations. In his essay "Traveling Theory," Said sketches, as we have seen, a general framework for historically analyzing the patterns of influence or interaction between theories of different countries or times that transcends the common debate, or polemic, of the accommodation and appropriation of European social and cultural thought by American critics. The historical transfer of ideas and theories, therefore, *necessarily* entails *transformation* of their forms and functions, which the critic of traveling theory has to reconstruct and explore in its political implications.

Nevertheless, Said in his essay focuses exclusively on examples of an "appropriation" of "revolutionary" theories that have robbed them of their "insurrectionary quality" and have led to "impoverishment" or "rarefaction," without pursuing the question in what sense these European theories may have in their transformation, in the crucially *different* academic, cultural, and political situation in the United States, effectively contributed to repoliticizing and rehistoricizing American literary criticism. This hesitation may find its explanation in his rigorously tentative, skeptical, and self-reflexive notion of a "secular criticism" that he sets out to locate "between culture and system" (the title of one of the key essays in his book). Said defines "culture" as closure, as "a system of discrimination and evaluation," as "a system of exclusions legislated from above but enacted throughout its polity, by which such things as anarchy, disorder, irrationality, inferiority, bad taste, and immorality are identified, then deposited outside the culture and kept there by the power of the State and its institutions" (*WTC*, 11). In his analysis, the institutions of culture perform their hegemonic function through a process of constant redefinition and rearticulation of difference: "The dialectic of self-fortification and self-confirmation by which culture achieves its hegemony over society and the State is based on a constantly practised differentiation of itself from what it believes to be not itself" (*WTC*, 12). On the other side, the critic has to beware of "system," of the "impersonal system of disciplines and methods," of the domestication of oppositional, "interventionary movements"—such as French poststructuralism—into a theoretical system abstracted from "the events, the physical senses that made it possible and render it intelligible as the result of human work" (*WTC*, 4). It has to prevent critical thought from being absorbed by "the ethic of professionalism" (*WTC*, 4).

If criticism wants to overcome "the overall compliance of the intellectual class to which critics belong" and to subvert "the regulated, not to say calculated, irrelevance of criticism" (*WTC*, 25), not excluding Left criticism, it must keep distance and situate itself between the dominant culture and the totalizing forms of critical systems, place itself "skeptically between culture as a massive body of self-congratulating ideas and system or method, anything resembling a sovereign technique that claims to be free of history, subjectivity, or circumstance" (*WTC*, 202). Only by working at this critical "nodal point" can it be true to the dialectic at work in "affirmative culture" (Herbert Marcuse) or "hegemony" (Antonio Gramsci), which in turning "culture" into ideology, power, and systems of exclusion and oppression has *at the same time* produced their very opposites, namely a powerful resistance to domination and domestication and enabling forms of cultural critique. Said writes, "If culture exerts the kinds of pressure I have mentioned, and if it creates the environment and the community that allows people to feel they belong, then it must be true that resistance to the culture has always been present" (*WTC*, 14). Intellectuals have often contributed to the working of hegemony, but they have also "stood for values, ideas, and activities that transcend and deliberately interfere with the collective weight imposed by the nation-state and the national culture" (*WTC*, 14).

Said's "oppositional criticism," then, constitutes itself through the awareness and unrelenting discursive dramatization of *distance* and *difference*: "If criticism is reducible neither to a doctrine nor to a political position on a particular question, and if it is to be in the world and self-aware simultaneously, then its identity is its difference from other cultural activities and from systems of thought or of method" (*WTC*, 29). It is only through this identity in difference that for Said oppositional criticism can pursue its *positive* goal, "noncoercive knowledge produced in the interests of human freedom" (*WTC*, 29).

This description of the oppositional quality and dynamic of criticism has far-reaching implications. How does Said's commitment to the "project of modernity," the ideas and ideals of the enlightenment, and the responsibility of the intellectual relate to his critical reception of the attack on the humanist tradition in French poststructuralism, especially in Derrida and Foucault? How does he situate his oppositional criticism in the intellectual and social worlds? Said, first of all, emphasizes the *individual moral* commitment of the intellectual, the "individual consciousness placed at a sensitive nodal point" (*WTC*, 15). But he knows that contemporary literary criticism has achieved its methodological independence only "by forfeiting an active situation in the world," by celebrating modernist alienation and "homelessness," that it has replaced a concern with the "relations of power at work in history and society" by a "rhetorical enthusiasm for buzz words like scandal, rupture, transgression, and discontinuity" (*WTC*, 173). Said, therefore, argues that the individual critical mind must be very much aware of "the *collective* whole, context, or situation in which it finds itself" (*WTC*, 15, my emphasis) and must combine this "worldly self-situating," this "sensitive response to the dominant culture" with the knowledge that the individual consciousness is a historical and social actor in the world. That is, the critical intellectual must—and here Said quotes Raymond Williams—"act on behalf of those alternative acts and alternative intentions whose advancement is a fundamental human and intellectual obligation" (*WTC*, 30).

This commitment to enlightenment, to noncoercive knowledge in the interest of human freedom, and to solidarity with the oppressed and alternative acts and intentions returns Said to the question of what the "between" in his project of oppositional "criticism between culture and system" actually means, how key terms such as "text," "discourse," and "world" can mediate between the individual critical consciousness and the collective context and social responsibility without collapsing the difference.

Said pursues these problems in a lengthy discussion of the works of Jacques Derrida and Michel Foucault in his essay "Criticism between Culture and System." In his comparison of Derrida and Foucault, he finds that both—in spite of their divergent views on criticism—"consciously attempt to take revisionist positions toward a reigning cultural hegemony" and that they are "aware of the danger that what they do might turn itself into a critical orthodoxy, an unthinking system of thought impervious to change and insensitive to its own problems" (*WTC*, 208). Both produce criticism in Said's sense, but in contrasting their critical strategies Said finds Foucault more challenging to contemporary "insular and scholastic" American criticism than Derrida, as he not only "moves us into the text," but "in and out," reading the inscriptions of power in the text as its claim on actuality (*WTC*, 183). Derrida's definition of a text concentrates on its deconstruction, on its self-difference, on the imperceptibility of the text that always "hides" from the first glance "the law of its composition and the rules of its game" (*WTC*, 184). In his more recent work, Derrida has radicalized his deconstructive work on hybrid texts at the boundaries of disciplinary discourses by experimenting with alternative forms of writing, by exploring, as Said puts it, quoting Derrida, an "*écriture double*, one half of which provokes an inversion of the cultural domination Derrida everywhere identifies with metaphysics and its hierarchies, the other half of which 'allows the detonation of writing in the very interior of the word, thus disrupting the entire given order and taking over the field'" (*WTC*, 185). But Said accuses Derrida's "reading method" of being "unable to get hold of the local material density and power of ideas as historical actuality," of collapsing the difference between the text and the world: "The search *within* a text for the conditions of textuality will falter at the very point where the text's historical presentation to the reader is put into question and made an issue for the critic" (*WTC*, 212). Derrida explicitly distinguishes his notion of deconstruction from dialectical thinking—Said quotes from *Disseminations*, in which Derrida says of his "anticoncepts, antinames, counterideas" that reveal textuality: "'These points of indefinite pivoting . . . mark the spots of what can never be mediated, mastered, sublated, or dialecticized through any *Erinnerung* or *Aufhebung*'" (*WTC*, 206). Yet Derrida's balancing act in his (intertextual) deconstructive readings between a philosophical critique of the complicitous use of language and his tentative projection of alternative terms is characterized by a strong ascesis that directs its "dedefinitional energies" on the undecidability and indeterminacy in a text and not on its effective historical power. Derrida's "programmatic hesitation toward his historical situation, toward his work's affiliation with certain types of work and not with others" has kept him from a pronounced historically specific deconstructive critique of social formations, institutions, and manifestations of power (*WTC*, 210).

Foucault also stressed the difference of his notion of discourse from dialectical thinking, as Said pointed out in his review essay on *The Archeology of Knowledge* in *Diacritics* (1974) and in his book *Beginnings* (1974).[18] "Archeology" is the "retrieval of the archive" as the "place of discourse," discourse being "an historically and particularly apprehensible order where a statement occurs" ("Ethics," 29). Discursive practices take place within an *épistème*, a "system of distances," "a set of moving constraints that establish an outer limit of knowledge" ("Ethics," 34) at a given moment in history. "The filled, activated space of a given epoch," Said writes in *Beginnings*, "Foucault calls an *épistème*; the filling is *discourse*, a body that has temporal duration and is comprised of *énoncés* (statements)" (*B*, 295). For Foucault, "discourse is not dialectical" ("Ethics," 34), but characterized by "difference," by "reversibility," "discontinuity," "specificity," and "exteriority," as Said emphasizes in his exposition of *L'ordre du discours* (1971) in *Beginnings* (*B*, 297–313). The method is "postnarrative," because Foucault no longer understands history as linear, as a narrative sequence, but as *genealogy*, "decentered," a break of the present and the past, shaped by "dispersion," "displacement," "transformation," "discontinuity," "coincidence" (*B*, 282). As Foucault defined the concept in an interview in 1977, "[Genealogy] is a form of history which can account for the constitution of knowledges, discourses, domains of objects etc., without having to make reference to a subject which is either transcendental in relation to the field of events or runs in its empty sameness throughout the course of history."[19] In *Beginnings*, Said mentions Foucault's argument that Hegel's dialectic "so compelled thought into continuities that any radical philosopher since Hegel has to think against Hegel" (*B*, 296). Foucault set himself the task of including elements of "chance, discontinuity, and materiality" into thought and of elaborating a "theory of discontinuous systematizations" (Foucault, *L'ordre du discours*, as quoted in *B*, 296). His understanding of discourse tries critically to uncover the power of texts by reading them as integral to the "social processes of differentiation, exclusion, incorporation, and rule" (*WTC*, 212). As Said concludes in his essay "Criticism between Culture and System":

> Foucault's greatest intellectual contribution is to an understanding of how the will to exercise dominant control in society and history has also discovered a way to clothe, disguise, rarefy, and wrap itself systematically in the language of truth, discipline, rationality, utilitarian value, and knowledge. And this language, in its naturalness, authority, professionalism, assertiveness, and antitheoretical directness, is what Foucault has called *discourse*. The difference between discourse and such coarser yet no less significant fields of social combat as the class struggle is that discourse works its productions,

> discriminations, censorship, interdictions, and invalidations on the intellectual, at the level of base not of superstructure. The power of discourse is that it is at once the object of struggle and the tool by which the struggle is conducted. [*WTC*, 216]

For Foucault, the master discourse of society became "invisible" sometime near the end of the eighteenth century when it began to hide the "systematic rules of its formations and its concrete affiliations with power" (*WTC*, 217). Language was dispersed into special disciplinary discourses, in the plural, that in their institutionalization in the culture obscured their interrelationships as well as their uses as means of social control. This process in the history of culture, of knowledge, defines the intellectual's political task: he or she has to read the text and the network of intertextuality as social practice and make the discourses visible again. Said writes:

> Foucault's interest in textuality is to present the text stripped of its esoteric or hermetic elements, and to do this by making the text assume its affiliations with institutions, offices, agencies, classes, academies, corporations, groups, guilds, ideologically defined parties and professions. Foucault's descriptions of a text or discourse attempts by the detail and subtlety of the description to *resemanticize* and forcibly to redefine and reidentify the particular interests that all texts serve. [*WTC*, 212]

If the "master discourse" of society works as "power," as systematic "exclusion" and "incorporation," the critic's own discourse serves as a "counter-memory for the text" and has to function as a counterdiscourse (*WTC*, 184). It is at this point that Said considers Foucault's work to be lacking in consequence. He acknowledges that Foucault "has written his books in solidarity with society's silent victims, to make visible the actuality of discourses and to make audible the repressed voices of its subjects" (*WTC*, 216). And he emphasizes a major shift in Foucault's work after 1968, when Foucault began to analyze the function of discourses—no longer Discourse with a capital "D"—and the genealogy of knowledge less "in terms of types of consciousness, modes of perception and forms of ideology [than] in terms of tactics and strategies of power," as Foucault put it in an interview in 1976 (Foucault as quoted in *WTC*, 219). Yet Said criticizes Foucault for being "unable to deal with, or provide an account of, historical change" (*WTC*, 152), as he does not seem to be interested in investigating the *causes* of the development of "discourses" and "takes a curiously passive and sterile view not so much of the uses of power, but of how and why power is gained, used, and held onto" (*WTC*, 221).

Said does not accept the theoretical and political consequences of Foucault's critique of the concept (and critique) of ideology as delimited by its opposition to "something like truth," by presupposing "something of the order of a subject," and by depending on "the infrastructure or economic or material determinant for it" (*P/K*, 118). Said explains the reason for Foucault's "passive and sterile view" of the omnipresence of power as his "disagreement with Marxism," in Foucault's truncated understanding and use of the dimension of historical change, of "the central dialectic of opposed forces that still underlies modern society" (*WTC*, 221). In "Traveling Theory" he writes, "In human history there is always something beyond the reach of dominating systems, no matter how deeply they saturate society, and this is obviously what makes change possible" (*WTC*, 246). The lack of self-reflexivity in Foucault's theory of power that is a consequence of the suspension of the notion of a subject as a historical agent has a price Said is not willing to pay: "In short, power can be made analogous neither to a spider's web without the spider nor to a smoothly functioning flow diagram; a great deal of power remains in such coarse items as the relationships and tensions between rulers and ruled, wealth and privilege, monopolies of coercion, and the central state apparatus" (*WTC*, 212).

In Said's view, the limitations of Foucault's theory of power become even more glaringly evident if we situate it in the wider context of the postcolonial world. Neither Derrida nor Foucault has been particularly committed to questioning the presuppositions and the procedures of his own work in the Western, or French, *ethnocentrism* both have criticized in general political terms. Foucault does not seem interested in the fact, Said writes in *The World, the Text, and the Critic*, that

> history is not a homogeneous French-speaking territory but a complex interaction between uneven economies, societies, and ideologies. Much of what he has studied in his work makes greatest sense not as an ethnocentric model of how power is exercised in modern society, but as part of a much larger picture involving, for example, the relationship between Europe and the rest of the world. He seems unaware of the extent to which the ideas of discourse and discipline are assertively European and how, along with the use of discipline to employ masses of detail (and human beings), discipline was used also to administer, study, and reconstruct—then subsequently to occupy, rule, and exploit—almost the whole of the non-European world. [*WTC*, 222]

Near the end of his key essay "Criticism between Culture and System," Said confronts the consequences of his scholarly historical and critical work on Orientalism, his political engagement in Near Eastern politics, and of the Islamic world's representation in the West. He argues that the very notion of the West, the superiority of Western society and culture, was constituted, and has repeatedly been reconstituted, by processes of exclusion, by essentializing "the Orient" as the West's inferior "Other." What we consider the meaning of "our" culture has always been constructed in a process of *intercultural* production. Said refers to his book *Orientalism* (1978), in which he offers a genealogy of the Western discourse of (mainly British and French) "Orientalism" (of the Islamic Near East) and its transformations from the early efforts of "knowing the Orient" during the eighteenth century to its secularization, professionalization, and institutionalization in universities and public discourse in the century after Napoleon's occupation of Egypt.[20] The final part of the book analyzes the system of ideological fictions and political institutions in the wake of British and French late-nineteenth- and early-twentieth-century imperialism, its crisis and reformulation in the service of the American bid for control of the whole area, and as a reaction to the resurgence of political and cultural strength among the peoples in the Near East. What had been a "fundamentally philological discipline and a vaguely general apprehension of the Orient" has been turned in the post–World War II era into "a social science speciality" of "area studies" policy experts supporting American economic and political interests (O, 290). What has *not* changed, however, is the powerful totalizing construction of the Orient by the West as its inferior Other, a construction that has *never* been challenged or tested by the reality of the Near East, as "the Orient" in the Western mind is arrested ontologically, outside history, at a more primitive stage of humankind and can never change and never "represent itself" (O, 70, 322).

For Said, then, Orientalism is not a system of ideas or of simple lies and distortions of the truth that could easily be corrected, but an "integral part of European *material* civilization and culture," which Orientalism expresses and represents "culturally and even ideologically as a mode of discourse with supporting institutions, vocabulary, scholarship, imagery, doctrines, even colonial bureaucracies and colonial styles" (O, 2). He explicitly conceived *Orientalism* as a case study in Foucauldian "discourse analysis," as a study of a total network of interests, of power, of domination, complemented by a Gramscian emphasis on hegemony and on the constraining as well as enabling productive effects of culture (O,

6, 14). Said does not accept in his analysis of the "anonymous collective body of texts constituting a discursive formation like Orientalism" Foucault's elimination of the notion of the historical subject. He emphasizes instead the *dialectic* "between individual text or writer and the complex collective formation to which his work is a contribution" (O, 23, 24). The questions he raises are:

> What is the meaning of originality, of continuity, of individuality, in this context? How does Orientalism transmit or reproduce itself from one epoch to another? In fine, how can we treat the cultural, historical phenomenon of Orientalism as a kind of *willed human work*—not of mere unconditioned ratiocination—in all its historical complexity, detail, and worth without at the same time losing sight of the alliance between cultural work, political tendencies, the state, and the specific realities of domination? [O, 15]

These questions concerning the interrelations of politics and culture can be answered only in the specific historical circumstances of the individual study. In the case of Orientalism two consequences are crucial for Said's book. First, *Orientalism* is characterized methodologically by a broadly historical and anthropological "hybrid perspective" that makes it possible to combine a genealogical analysis in terms of Foucault's "discursive formation" with a hermeneutic interpretation of individuals' intentions and their moral responsibility as expressed in texts (O, 23). The "antihuman," oppressive, and devastating effects of the discourse of Orientalism in all its political and institutional repercussions on the peoples of the Near East—to whom Said as a Palestinian exile belongs himself—ask for an approach that can also clearly assign causes and responsibility where they belong and that can specify the role and task for the critical intellectual who wants to see things changed. Even though Said points out in a Foucauldian move that he does not want to talk about the "truth" of Orientalism vis-à-vis Near Eastern "reality," but about the powerful effects of the internal consistency of Orientalism and its ideas about the Orient, he feels bound to ask how we can "undertake studies in contemporary alternatives to Orientalism" (O, 6).

This also indicates the second aspect, the fact that Orientalism is an expression of Western ethnocentrism, so that a study of Orientalism necessarily brings up the question of how "we" can "represent" *other cultures* or, particularly, how they can *represent themselves*. Said does *not* opt for a pure "insider" perspective, as if only a Palestinian could write about Palestinians or a black American about black Americans (O, 322), but for something like an *intercultural dialogue* that might help to transcend the constraints and limitations of power in "our" understanding of non-Western cultures and societies without constructing their "difference" as a way of controlling them. Yet in *Orientalism* Said tends to recover and define the "alternatives to Orientalism" too much within the boundaries of the Western discourse he sets out to dismantle. As John Carlos Rowe writes in his brilliant critique of *Orientalism*: "Said must conceive of this tradition to be a sort of 'anti-tradition,' or 'counter-culture,' which marginalizes itself with respect to the dominant culture. And yet this process of marginalization is mythologized by Said himself until it clusters into a single, albeit complex, image of a margin inhabited by: the avant-garde artist, the Orient, Woman, the 'third world,' and the genealogical critic himself."[21]

Said pursues these questions in his next two books. *The Question of Palestine* (1979) sets before the American reader a picture of the specific Palestinian experience in history, its "traumatic national encounter with Zionism," which has systematically been excluded from public knowledge by "the hypocrisy of Western (and certainly liberal Zionist) journalism and intellectual discourse."[22] Said considers it his moral duty to penetrate this ideological smokescreen and to show things as "*they actually are* for Palestinians and for Arabs," to expose their historical reality (whatever the epistemological status of "reality" might be) (*QP*, 214). What is most important in this undertaking is not to be held captive by thinking in terms of simple oppositions of good and bad. Several times in his book, Said points to the unique historical experience of the Holocaust for the Jews, which to a large extent explains Israel's fear and uncompromising attitude toward the Palestinians (*QP*, 60, 231). He writes:

> We Palestinians are clearly struggling for our self-determination but for the fact that we have no place, no agreed-upon and available physical terrain on which to conduct our struggle. We are clearly anticolonialist and antiracist in our struggle but for the fact that our opponents are the greatest victims of racism in history, and perhaps our struggle is waged at an awkward, postcolonial period in the modern world's history. [*QP*, 122]

This also means that the main objective of his book is not primarily to elaborate the victimization of Palestinians by Zionism, but to show and contribute to the Palestinian people's collective fight for constructing and representing a national cultural identity and political consciousness of their own: "It must not be forgotten that the Palestinian was not simply a function of Zionism. His life, culture, and politics have their own dynamic and ultimately their own authenticity" (*QP*, 114). In his historical experience of always "*being represented*, never able to speak for [himself or herself]" (*QP*, 25), the Palestinian turns out to be "at once a representative and an outcast" (*QP*, 154). In fact, as an "outcast, as transnational extra-territorial being, [or] as oppressed nonentity inside Israel," the Palestinian is "central to, or at the core of, the Middle East problem" (*QP*, 169). And, we could add, the Palestinians in their homelessness seem to be the collective incorporation of, as well as a radical challenge to, the modern Western intellectual's constitutive "homelessness."

Said's project demands a specific historical method and a vision of historical change. He quite clearly points out that "Zionism" in its effects can be studied only *genealogically* "in the framework provided by imperialism" but, at the same time, also as a practical system "for *accumulation* (of power, land, ideological legitimacy) and *displacement* (of people, other ideas, prior legitimacy)" (*QP*, 57, 73). Only through this methodological move could Said transcend the study of ideas of individual authors as well as of anonymous political and ideological traditions. Only this dual approach could provide a perspective that would make it possible to see Palestinians and Jews within a common historical perspective, a common "self-conscious rational struggle conducted in the interests of human community" (*QP*, 235), a struggle based on fundamental human rights such as self-determination, being allowed to "live free from fear, insecurity, terror and oppression, free also from the possibilities of exercising unequal or unjust domination over others" (*QP*, 53), and also of having a home you can call your own. Said's openly utopian vision is not a reaffirmation or reestablishment of the traditional, ethnically more or less homogeneous national state (or one dominated by the largest national group). It is not a return to "origins," to an original "place," but is "utopian"—Said uses the term "nonplace" (*QP*, 124)—in the sense that it explicitly acknowledges the "unstable identity," the "dispersion and exile," and the "cubistic form of Palestinian existence" (*QP*, 162) in his tentative idea of a "secular democratic state in Palestine for Arabs and Jews" (*QP*, 220), an idea he has actively supported as a member of the Palestinian National Council.

Said's next book, *Covering Islam* (1981), takes up the problems of understanding and (mis)representing other cultures in the *American* context in a study of how the media and the experts controlled the way Americans should perceive and interpret the world of "Islam," particularly the Iranian revolution and the Teheran Embassy hostage crisis.[23] The "consensus on 'Islam' as a kind of scapegoat for everything [the Americans] do not like about the world's new political, social, and economic patterns"

(*CI*, xv) led to a widely distorted and reductive picture of the Islamic world, which in the age of U.S.-dominated mass media may be said even "to be learning *about itself* by means of images, histories, and information manufactured in the West" (*CI*, 52). Ironically, the strong Western commitment to the idea of a monolithic, unchanging, backward state of "Islam" prevented Americans from realizing the political and social processes at work in contemporary Muslim societies that were directed against the autocratic, "medieval" traditions the West continued to identify with the world of "Islam" (*CI*, 64, 94). Yet this powerful and devastating "ideology of difference" has also bred its own "counteralternative practices," as Said elaborates in his essay "An Ideology of Difference" (1985). Therefore, what Said focuses on in *Covering Islam* is the question of how we can get beyond these pervasive long-standing misrepresentations of "the Orient" or "Islam," how we as Americans or Europeans can really understand the Muslims' *own interpretations* of the complex societies of Islam and their internal developments, how we can understand a non-Western culture—which means, at the same time, how we can understand our own Western culture in a less homogeneous and exclusionary way. This seems to be a particularly formidable task in a country like the United States, which has been characterized by a totalizing, transhistorical nationalist consensus and myth of "America."

Near the end of *Orientalism*, Said had pointedly raised the general theoretical questions "How does one *represent* other cultures? What is *another* culture? Is the notion of a distinct culture (or race, or religion, or civilization) a useful one, or does it always get involved either in self-congratulation (when one discusses one's own) or hostility and aggression (when one discusses the 'other')?" (O, 325). If "culture" is a "hegemonic system," if a culture is always trying to appropriate other cultures, how can we "study other cultures and people from a libertarian, or nonrepressive and nonmanipulative, perspective?" (O, 24). How can we understand and accept the genuine differences among human cultures if there can be no "true representation," if all representations, "because they *are* representations, are imbedded first in the language and then in the culture, institutions, and political ambience of the representer?" (O, 272). In *Orientalism* these questions mean "what of some alternative to Orientalism? Is the book an argument only *against* something, and not *for* something?" (O, 325). How could an oppositional critical consciousness work out alternatives to Orientalism? At the time he wrote *Orientalism*, Said's as yet undeveloped "theory of culture as a differentiating and expressive ensemble rather than as simply hegemonic and disciplinary," as James Clifford put it in his review essay on *Orientalism*, does not permit Said to take into account any national oppositional movements, but allows him only to indicate how individual Western scholars such as Louis Massignon or, even more impressively, individual writers such as Gérard de Nerval and Gustave Flaubert (*O*, 181–90) somehow succeeded in transcending or subverting the "power" of "Orientalism."[24] In theoretical terms, Said could only briefly suggest ways out of the totalizing system of Orientalism through reflexive "methodological self-consciousness," a "continual self-examination of . . . methodology and practice," and a "direct sensitivity to the material before them," qualities he found in the works of some individual scholars working on the margins of institutions or on the boundaries of disciplines (*O*, 326). Yet these remarks remain more or less moral appeals and do not provide convincing arguments for alternative ways of knowledge and practice.

A few years later, in *Covering Islam*, Said discusses the possibility of understanding another culture more extensively, referring to the debate in anthropology over the "complicity between imperialism and ethnology" (*CI*, 131). He defines two conditions that must be fulfilled if we want to achieve a knowledge, however tentative that may be, of another culture: first, "uncoercive contact with an alien culture through real exchange" and, second, "self-consciousness about the interpretative project itself" (*CI*, 142) or the awareness that this knowledge is a "social activity and inextricably tied to the situation out of which it arose" (*CI*, 156). Said also takes a first step in overcoming the failure he accuses Western scholarship on Islam of, namely that it never has systematically dealt with *Islamic* writing on Islam, Islamic writing that may be *different* in its strategies from what the West regards as scholarship. Still, when he comes to characterizing the "*antithetical knowledge*" (*CI*, 149) of Islam that we have, he mentions three groups of scholars and intellectuals who have worked as outsiders and radicals *in the West*, giving Islamic scholars only a minor voice in this endeavor. Instead of exploring in more detail the problems and prospects of *intercultural knowledge* in general or of the double status of being a Palestinian by birth and an intellectual educated in the West, an experience he shares with quite a number of other Palestinians, Said again emphasizes the critical stance and position the *Western oppositional intellectual* has to achieve. It remains, finally, a *moral decision* of *individuals*, even though the individual is now seen as supported by an intellectual *community*. As he writes in the final paragraph of *Covering Islam*, "Underlying every interpretation of other cultures—especially of Islam—is the choice facing the individual scholar or intellectual: whether to put intellect at the service of power or at the service of criticism, community, and moral sense" (*CI*, 164).

It is this tension between a radical systematic critique of Western discourses on "other" cultures and the enabling articulations of other cultures representing themselves, between intercultural dialogues and Western antithetical or oppositional knowledge, and between the community of intellectuals and the people, on the one hand, and the precarious positioning of a homeless scholar who is always in exile, on the other, that Said pursues in his work in the early 1980s. In his essay "Opponents, Audiences, Constituencies, and Community" (1982), Said addresses directly the role of a "politics of interpretation and the politics of culture" in "the Age of Reagan."[25] Oppositional criticism has to uncover and expose the "actual *affiliations* that exist between the world of ideas and scholarship, on the one hand, and the world of brute politics, corporate and state power, and military force, on the other" ("Opp," 2). Said traces again the "depoliticization" of American literary criticism and the "sustained self-purification of humanists" and interprets them as an "integral part of the historical moment presided over by Reaganism" ("Opp," 19). He proposes to counter the noninterference demanded by the academy, the government, and the corporate elites with a "program of interference" that crosses "borders and obstacles," reopens "the blocked social processes ceding objective representation (hence power) of the world to a small coterie of experts and their clients," and acknowledges that "the audience for literacy is not a closed circle of three thousand professional critics but the community of human beings in society" ("Opp," 24).

Clearly, this "program of interference"—which Said, again, defines as a "dialectical response" ("Opp," 24)—expresses his hope of finally overcoming, or at least mastering, the tensions between his own work as an avant-garde literary critic and intellectual in the West, especially his books *Beginnings* and *The World, the Text, and the Critic*, and as a political intellectual and activist involved in Near East political affairs, multiculturalism, and postcolonialism in the so-called Third World, especially in his books *The Question of Palestine* and *Covering Islam*. It is, finally, to comprise *both* "Western cultural radicalism" *and* the "radical nationalism of the non-Western world," as he had written at the end of his early review essay on Foucault ("Ethics," 37). But his agenda for an oppositional "politics of culture" and "politics of interpretation," as he applies it to the politics, society, and culture in the *United States*, is in danger of emptying cultural criticism and the "world of ideas and scholarship" too radically of a political potential of their own, when he confronts the critic too directly with the "world of brute politics" in the Age of Reagan. He situates his critical, rigorously secular exposure of the politics of culture and of literature in Reagan's America in an analysis of the peculiar "configuration of constituencies and interpretive communities" ("Opp," 17) in order to find a perspective for change: "How can interpretation be interpreted as having a secular, political force in an age determined to deny interpretation anything but a role as mystification?" ("Opp," 19). Yet the crucial difference of cultural criticism from the world of political organizations and structures, as well as the political implications of the literary and cultural critic's work he had elaborated in his critical reading of Derrida's and Foucault's work and in his studies of Orientalism and the world of Islam, are impatiently put aside when he confronts a question posed in Terry Eagleton's critique of Fredric Jameson's *The Political Unconscious:* "How is a Marxist-structuralist analysis of a minor novel of Balzac to help shake the foundations of capitalism?" (Eagleton as quoted in "Opp," 15). Said concedes that obviously "the answer to this question is that such readings won't" ("Opp," 15), but he also attacks Eagleton for failing to provide an alternative of his own. I think Said's own polemical conclusions, permeated by his longing for community or constituency and for politically meaningful, effective cultural work, are somewhat premature, or rather mistaken, when he agrees with Eagleton that Jameson's and Frank Lentricchia's works are characterized by "their political 'unclarity,' their lingering pragmatism, eclecticism" and even by "the relationship of their hermeneutic criticism to Reagan's ascendancy" ("Opp," 15). It is too easy to charge Jameson and Lentricchia with "marginality and vestigial idealism" and an "apolitical content and methodology" that simply accepts the "cloistral seclusion" of "literature" and "Marxism" ("Opp," 15) if we grant the importance Said in other contexts gives to the radical dismantling of Western discourses, the "distance" and "difference" of oppositional criticism, and the working out of counterdiscourses.

Radical cultural critique, therefore, must assume a complex and wide-ranging political significance in the social and cultural process. "Interpretation always makes a difference," as Lentricchia put it in his response to Eagleton and Said in his book *Criticism and Social Change* (1983).[26] But we also have to accept the limited political role and impact of cultural criticism, of cultural productions, and have to acknowledge the different, discontinuous forms of expression and communication it has worked out if we want to grasp the political potential it may have. If the "paradoxical" identity of "oppositional criticism," as Said puts it in *The World, the*

Text, and the Critic, is defined by the "social goals . . . [of] noncoercive knowledge produced in the interest of human freedom," this is not just an empty hope or abstract utopia, but can find some "potential space inside civil [capitalist] society" (*WTC*, 29). Twice in this book Said quotes Raymond Williams's statement that "however dominant a social system may be, the very meaning of its domination involves a limitation or selection of the activities it covers, so that by definition it cannot exhaust all social experience, which therefore always potentially contains space for alternative acts and alternative intentions which are not yet articulated as a social institution or even project" (Williams as quoted in *WTC*, 29, 240). Yet in *The World, the Text, and the Critic*, Said has not fully brought this insight to bear on American literature and culture, which he tends to portray in too generalized and homogeneous a manner, a portrait that necessarily focuses on isolated oppositional intellectuals and writers at the expense of the potential of ethnic, minority, or other oppositional sub- or countercultures. If we understand discourse as a form of social action, as a form of power and desire, the radical cultural critic has to uncover and expose the power game of master discourses and institutions, of Discourse, of Culture, of History, and of Tradition, all with capital letters. But he or she has also to articulate and project the alternative discursive practices, the alternative histories, traditions, and counterdiscourses, in the plural, within Western capitalist societies *and* to face and respond to the "discourses" and "histories" of "others," of the societies and cultures of the so-called Third World. It is in this sense that American cultural criticism as "discourse theory" must transcend and redefine its traditional boundaries, acknowledge the heterogeneous and multicultural character of culture(s) in the United States, and become radical *cultural studies*.

In his essay "Orientalism Reconsidered" (1985), Said briefly discusses quite a number of "interventionary" analyses and theoretical projects in American (and English) cultural and literary studies.[27] He succeeds in providing a much more complex and convincing account of the *common endeavor* of these oppositional intellectuals that explicitly accepts *plurality*, *difference*, and *unstability* in their work without renouncing the claim to attaining the social and political goal of "noncoercive knowledge in the interest of human freedom." He strongly reaffirms the "consciously secular, marginal, and oppositional" character of these practices with reference to the dominant culture and authoritative systems they want to dismantle and to replace ("*OR*," 106). His emphasis, however, is now less on systematic comprehensiveness than on "local" knowledge and political practice in a common project of alternative critical work:

"We note a plurality of audiences . . . , a plurality of terrains, multiple experiences, and different constituencies, each with its admitted (as opposed to denied) interest, political desiderata, disciplinary goals. All these efforts work out of what might be called a decentered consciousness, not less reflective and critical for being decentered, for the most part non- and in some cases anti-totalizing and anti-systematic" ("*OR*," 105–106). Said briefly mentions the importance of the intellectual and political work done in the United States by "subaltern groups—women, blacks, and so on," but warns against any form of "possessive exclusionism" some representatives of these groups may favor, claims that, if we take them seriously, would make any inter- or intracultural understanding impossible ("*OR*," 106). Said finds equally dangerous the quest for a new "grand synthesis" that could too easily "wipe out both the gains and the oppositional consciousness provided hitherto by these counter-knowledges" ("*OR*," 107). He does not elaborate, however, how these counterknowledges could help rearticulate his own understanding of the oppositional potential for change within American culture and society at large.

Said discovers most of the kind of oppositional work he proposes in recent American anthropology. In his critical essay, "Representing the Colonized: Anthropology's Interlocutors" (1989), he discusses books by Marxists, feminists, anthropologists of praxis, and other politically committed individuals and schools.[28] He also mentions the programs of postmodern anthropologists who have been heavily influenced in their critique of the traditional ethnocentric ethnographic work of their discipline and in their own discursive strategies by poststructuralist literary and cultural theory, anthropologists such as James Clifford, George Marcus, and Michael M. J. Fischer. Nevertheless, Said finds "a genuine malaise about the sociopolitical status of anthropology as a whole" ("*RC*," 208), namely its complicity as a discipline with imperialism and colonialism, a complicity the new oppositional schools in his mind do not seem to have overcome:

> In fact, there is no way that I know of apprehending the world from within our culture (a culture by the way with a whole history of extermination and incorporation behind it) without also apprehending the imperial contest itself. And this I would say is a cultural fact of extraordinary political as well as interpretive importance, because it is the true defining horizon, and to some extent, the enabling condition, of such otherwise abstract and groundless concepts like 'otherness' and 'difference.' The real problem remains to haunt us: the relationship between anthropology as an ongoing

> enterprise and, on the other hand, empire as an ongoing concern. ["*RC*," 217]

Said attacks in a polemical manner the pervasive "fetishization" of "difference" and "otherness" in Western ethnographic and critical discourse in general and the "textualization" of other cultures and societies in postmodern anthropology ("*RC*," 213), as they tend to ignore, or obfuscate, the problem of how "the colonized represent themselves," or, in Gayatri Spivak's words, "how the subaltern can speak."[29] Said's objections raise crucial questions concerning the practice and theory of anthropology today, but he much too quickly dismisses the work "postmodern" anthropologists such as George Marcus, Michael M. J. Fischer, and Paul Rabinow have done.

Again, *how* can the "other" cultures "represent themselves," *how* can they speak? How can they become "interlocutors" in an intercultural dialogue and not remain "native informants" "constructed" by Western anthropology and colonialism? How can the key concept of culture be redefined in a way that it does not fall victim to the totalizations of the institutions of culture in the West or the "anthropologizing" of "other" cultures or dissolve into a set of arbitrary signs and expressions of collective human behavior? How can *they* develop indigenous cultural textual strategies in a situation of a neocolonial encounter? How can the *anthropologist* or a *Palestinian-Western critic* "between cultures," such as Said, negotiate and tentatively project critical textual strategies that could communicate and testify to the critical, reflective, decentered consciousness traversing a plurality of terrains, multiple experiences, and different constituencies Said had envisioned in his essay "Orientalism Reconsidered"?

In *The World, the Text, and the Critic*, Said had claimed the *form of the essay* as a "radically skeptical form" for his secular criticism (*WTC*, 26). More than anything the "essential formal incompleteness" of the essay and its specifically literary strategies enable the oppositional critic to escape "closure" and to decode the text's "dialectic of engagement in time and the senses," without relinquishing "the essay's consciousness of its marginality" to the (apparent) formal completeness of the text it analyzes (*WTC*, 50). "The central problematic of the essay as a form is its *place*, by which I mean a series of . . . ways the essay has of being the form critics take, and locate themselves in, to do their work" (*WTC*, 50). Said stresses the reflective, exploratory, as well as committed character of the essay, its "ironic" mode that makes it an expression of "willed homelessness," as Said puts it in another context (*WTC*, 7).

In *Orientalism*, Said had pointed out that history and narrative could be used as powerful counterstrategies against the totalizing, essentializing "permanence of vision" of Orientalism, provided they are conceived and "written" in a radically secular, demystified way that opens up human institutions and actualities to change: "Narrative, in short, introduces an opposing point of view, perspective, consciousness to the unitary web of vision: it violates the supreme Apollonian fictions asserted by visions" (*O*, 240). In his later essay, "Representing the Colonized," he takes up the recent wide-ranging theoretical discussion of narrativity and reclaims the political power of *narrative*, namely the disruptive and culturally enabling emerging counternarratives of non-Western peoples' fight for national liberation and cultural articulation, against Jean-François Lyotard's postmodernist dismissal of the two great narratives of emancipation and enlightenment in favor of smaller local narratives of performativity. Here the self-reflective, experimental, open textual strategies of postmodern anthropologists—and writers, of course—*can* be very helpful to the oppositional cultural critic who faces his or her own dilemma as an intellectual as well as the challenges of the "unrepresentability" of "subaltern" experiences and consciousness. Postmodernism in this sense, however, is not the reductive version as an "aesthetic of quotation, nostalgia, and indifferentiation" that Said offers, but "situates itself" in a post- or neocolonial world that demands, and makes possible, an intercultural dialogue, or polylogue, of the de- and reconstructive forms of more recent Western writing and the various cultural representations of the so-called Third World in their distinctive "otherness" ("*RC*," 222).

After we have become aware of the intimate interconnections of modernism and colonialism, of their historical dialectic, different political readings of many of the great modern writers as well as new forms of articulations by postcolonial cultures beyond the fixed and essentializing notions of nativism and cultural nationalism have become possible (see Said's essay "Yeats and Decolonization," 1989). As Said writes in "Intellectuals in the Post-Colonial World" (1985), "Many of the post-colonial writers bear their past within them—as scars of humiliating wounds, as instigation for different practices, as potentially revised visions of the past tending towards a future, as urgently re-interpretable and re-deployable experiences in which the formerly silent native speaks and acts on territory taken back from the colonialist" (54f.).[30] Both for the Western oppositional intellectual and the postcolonial intellectual, though in different ways, the dream of finding a *stable identity* by situating theory politically or of *overcoming* the "difference," the tensions between Western and non-Western cultures, within our (or their) own culture(s) as well as between cultural criticism and political activism, must be relinquished. Yet these tensions, these differences, these interactions *can be* illuminated, explored, and negotiated in a secular perspective and represented in "experimental" forms of cultural practice and "counternarrative" forms of writing that tell a different story and tell the story differently.

At the end of "Representing the Colonized," Said writes, "Exile, immigration, and the crossing of boundaries are experiences that can therefore provide us with new narrative forms or, in John Berger's phrase, with *other* ways of telling" ("*RC*," 225). One important and productive alternative is a form of genuine *intercultural dialogue*, such as the study by the postmodernist anthropologist Michael M. J. Fischer and the native anthropologist Mehdi Abedi, *Debating Muslims: Cultural Dialogues in Postmodernity and Tradition* (1990), which in its ambiguous title plays upon the dialogues, multiple discursive positionings, contestations, and polyphony among Muslims, between Muslims and non-Muslims, and between the two authors, one a Muslim insider and one a non-Muslim outsider, each drawing not merely upon their individual opinions but upon the several cultural traditions that have constructed each of them.[31]

Said's *After the Last Sky: Palestinian Lives* (1986), a text with photographs by the Swiss photographer Jean Mohr, can be taken as another powerful model that dramatizes and exploits Said's positioning "between" Western and non-Western cultures. Said's text succeeds in responding to the photographs of Palestinian "everyday" life (and suffering) and in capturing a complex, highly charged political and cultural reality and the confusing experiences of his fellow Palestinians in various places of exile in "essentially unconventional, hybrid, and fragmentary forms of expression" and in "alternative modes of expression."[32] It is a "personal rendering of the Palestinians as a dispersed national community," a "multi-faceted" portrayal informed by a "double vision" (*LS*, 6). It is a book that sets out to find the scattered traces of Palestinian lives in their discontinuity, in autobiographical memories, in cultural traditions, in oral narratives, and in Palestinian literature. It is at the same time a story of the quest for origins and homes lost in the ordeal of history *and* a utopian construction, or creation, of a people in their fight for national representation and liberation. Said writes:

> Since our history is forbidden, narratives are rare; the story of origins, of home, of nation is underground. When it appears it is broken, often wayward and meandering in the extreme, always coded, usually in outrageous

> forms—mock-epics, satires, sardonic parables, absurd rituals—that make little sense to an outsider. Thus Palestinian life is scattered, discontinuous, marked by the artificial and imposed arrangements of interrupted or confined space, by the dislocations and unsynchronized rhythms of disturbed time. [*LS*, 20]

After the Last Sky is a very tentative, meditative, and fragmentary book, free of Said's often sharp polemical attacks in his political statements and writings. It is characterized by "formal instability," a "broken narrative, fragmentary composition, and self-consciously staged testimonials" (*LS*, 38), and it is permeated by Said's experience of being an insider and an outsider at the same time, a distinction, however, that the Palestinian experience has confused: "For Palestinian culture, the odd thing is that its own identity is more frequently than not perceived as 'other.' 'Palestine' is so charged with significance for others that Palestinians cannot perceive it as intimately theirs without a simultaneous sense of its urgent importance for others as well" (*LS*, 40).

> "Ours" but not yet fully "ours." . . . Thus the insider becomes the outsider. Not only have the interpositions between us and Palestine grown more formidable over time, but, to make matters worse, most of us pass our lives separated from each other. Yet we live in comradely communication despite the barriers. Today the Palestinian genius expresses itself in crossings-over, in clearing hurdles, activities that do not lessen the alienation, discontinuity, and dispossession, but that dramatize and clarify them instead. [*LS*, 40]

After the Last Sky is a testimony to Said's own dispersed identity that finds, or posits, its "center," however, in his strong moral commitment to noncoercive forms of knowledge and of living together.

[5]

POSTMODERN ANTHROPOLOGY, MULTICULTURAL CRITIQUE, AND AMERICAN CULTURE STUDIES

Postmodern Anthropology and the Concept of American (Multi)culture

When Henry Nash Smith defined American Studies in 1957 as "the study of American culture past and present, as a whole," he summarized more than two decades of a wide-ranging and self-conscious *critical* analysis of culture in the United States and, at the same time, initiated the search for the *unified* or holistic "method" through which American Studies would, finally, achieve maturity as an (interdisciplinary) discipline. The 1930s were the decade when, as Warren Susman pointed out years ago, the complexity of American culture as well as the culture concept were discovered and discussed in the wider public. We think of the work of cultural anthropology, of the studies in cultural relativism by Margaret Mead or of patterns of culture by Ruth Benedict that emphasized the unity of cultures and often were written with a self-critical look at American culture in mind. What was, however, even more important was the fact that during the 1930s American culture manifested itself as a *multiculture*, as a culture that was characterized even more by variety, heterogeneity, tensions, and alternative traditions than by the strong drive toward national identity and consensus. Cultural anthropologists, critics, and "documentary" writers, such as "native anthropologist" Zora Neale Hurston, Constance Rourke, and James Agee (with photographer Walker Evans, in *Let Us Now Praise Famous Men*), worked out radical new methods and strategies of cultural *critique* and ethnographic *writing* in the study of plural American cultures. Thus historian Caroline F. Ware, writing for the American Historical Association in *The Cultural Approach to History*, could argue in 1940 that the "total cultural approach" by no means implies that American culture is something like an organic unity, but that

"American culture" is exactly the *multiplicity* of regional, ethnic, and class cultures and the interactions of these cultures in terms of rhetoric as well as of power, *not* some "common pattern" or the Anglo-Saxon tradition to which these "other" groups have "contributed."[1]

During World War II and the postwar decade, notions of unity and consensus and functionalist models and structural analyses dominated discussions of American culture and society. Insofar as nondominant groups and cultures received any attention, they were judged according to the "contribution" model. In anthropology, Alfred L. Kroeber and Clyde Kluckhohn collected hundreds of definitions of "culture" in their monograph *Culture: A Critical Review of Concepts and Definitions* (1952) and offered some kind of overall synthesis. Six years later Alfred L. Kroeber and Talcott Parsons, the most influential sociologist of the time, published a joint statement, "The Concepts of Culture and of Social System," in the *American Sociological Review* that testified to their agreement on a common "structural" theoretical model and analytically distinguished the areas and problems to be studied by anthropology and sociology respectively.[2] This also meant that the critical potential of cultural anthropology as a project of understanding the dynamic process of a culture as a whole, including social structure, was lost, even though the way mainstream American cultural anthropologists had conceived of a culture as a whole had focused on "common patterns" and neglected intra- and intercultural differences. Among scholars in American Studies, some of this critical potential was rediscovered, although treated in a reductive manner, during the following decade by John William Ward, who, in his essay "History and the Concept of Culture" (1965), defined history as "the study of the consciousness of men in the past" and culture as "the organization of social experience in the consciousness of men made manifest in symbolic action," which easily led him to the definition of the historian as a "retrospective cultural anthropologist."[3]

It is obvious how little of the radical work done during the 1930s in the context, often at the margins, of cultural anthropology and cultural criticism on the complexity, heterogeneity, and materiality of cultures in the United States remains in Ward's overall definitions. It therefore does not come as a surprise that during the crisis of American Studies of the late 1960s and the 1970s the culture concept of cultural anthropology, or what was taken as its culture concept, was rejected for political and theoretical reasons. American Studies was dispersed into numerous group- or problem-oriented interdisciplinary studies programs, such as Black Studies, Women's Studies, Ethnic Studies, Popular Culture Studies, and Urban Studies.[4]

In the late 1970s, however, scholars in American Culture Studies (a term introduced by Robert Sklar, Robert Merideth, Jay Mechling, and David Wilson) began to look again to anthropology for models that would enable them to relate the various programs to each other and to develop methods of analysis and strategies of critical discourse that would reconstruct something like American culture as a common frame of reference. Even though the discipline of anthropology was also confronting a serious crisis, as the essays edited by Dell Hymes in *Reinventing Anthropology* (1972) indicate, it seemed to offer new models for the study of American culture as a whole.[5] Jay Mechling and John L. Caughey carefully took up (and adapted) the "cognitive anthropology" or "New Ethnography" of Anthony F. C. Wallace, Stephen A. Tyler, and others as the new "paradigm (or disciplinary matrix) for American Culture Studies" (Mechling). To them, the New Ethnography made possible a more rigorous analysis of the "deep cognitive structures which in their patterns of occurrence, constitute modern American culture" (Mechling), the "ethnography of everyday life" (Caughey), and "Popular Culture Studies" (Mechling) and, more generally, "introspective," "reflexive culture studies" (Caughey, Mechling).[6]

In spite of the interesting and innovative work done by adherents of the New Ethnography, however, this new paradigm for American Studies seemed too abstract and limited in its focus on cognitive patterns and rules and on componential analysis. The different versions of "symbolic anthropology" by Victor Turner and Clifford Geertz provided a more challenging understanding of culture in terms of "process, system, and symbol" and "process, indeterminacy, reflexivity" (Turner). Turner's studies of the symbolic dimensions of a culture, of the tensions between social structure and communitas, in terms of contested *public* dramas, rituals, and guiding metaphors, which he reads as a "reflexive metacommentary on society and history," offered a critical reading of cultural symbology and of the social work of fiction, culture, and ideology. Geertz's "interpretive anthropology" or "semiotic theory of culture" focuses on the "production" of "shared and *public* meanings," on the interpretations of the "*texts* of *social action*" to be reconstructed as "local knowledge" of the "other" subjects in a closely argued "thick description." Both Turner and Geertz had a strong impact on American Studies during the 1980s.[7] Their works were adopted too often, however, in an unmediated manner, without regard for different contexts, such as those of oral and print cultures. In addition, they were not really implicated in a socially situated analysis of the heterogeneity of American culture, and they were sometimes used as little more than ritual scholarly references. In the end, scholars in American Studies were left with the very difficult task of developing new ways of describing, interpreting, and writing about the extraordinarily complex urbanized, postindustrial multiculture permeated by cultural differences that demand cross-cultural and comparative modes of analysis.

These questions about the role and the expressive forms of "otherness" and "difference" in the comparative analysis of cultures, about the implications of writing ethnography, about cultural criticism as forms of discourse on and of "difference" were at the center of debates in anthropology as well as in literary theory and criticism in the 1970s and 1980s. The urgent call for reinscribing and resituating ethnographic work as well as cultural and literary critique as social and cultural practices in the relations of power in contemporary postindustrial and post- or neocolonial societies created a new constellation of critical perspectives and discursive strategies that promised to be very productive for work in American Culture Studies.

Postmodern anthropologists, who recognized major changes in the global social and cultural processes of the late twentieth century, had to distinguish their methods from their nineteenth- and early-twentieth-century precursors, to read the crisis of the humanities and social sciences as a crisis of "representation" that affects all the dimensions of traditional ethnography in a fundamental manner: the ethnographic authority of the anthropologist, his or her perspectival legitimation, the analytic patterns and interpretive models in understanding an "other" culture, the understanding of his or her own culture, the relations of language and reality, and particularly the communication of ethnographic fieldwork in the medium of language. One of the crucial insights postmodern anthropology pursues is, in James Clifford's words, that "ethnography is from beginning to end enmeshed in writing," or, as Stephen A. Tyler put it, is a "complex intertextual activity."[8] The presuppositions and the implications and consequences of postmodern anthropology are cogently discussed in a collection of essays edited by James Clifford and George E. Marcus that in the ambiguity of its title, *Writing Culture* (1986), indicates both the key theoretical problem of writing (and reading) culture and the social and linguistic context of our "literate," "writing culture." The subtitle of the book, *The Poetics and Politics of Ethnography*, moreover, suggests that it is in the *writing* of ethnography that the *political* meanings and consequences of anthropology will manifest themselves. To postmodern anthropologists, language is not an "objective," "neutral" medium that could ever make possible a direct or an objective representation of "reality." To them, power and history are always already inscribed in language as discourse, modes and traces of inscription the ethnographer can never fully control or "eliminate" (*WC*, 7).

Therefore, postmodern anthropology finds one of its most powerful manifestations in a radical demystification and deconstruction of the political implications and consequences of the research models and writing strategies of traditional anthropology that go well beyond the earlier attack on "anthropology and the colonial encounter."[9] What postmodern anthropologists deconstruct are the forms of "allegorization," of "coherent ethnographic fictions" that have traditionally been used in Western culture to domesticate, appropriate, and colonize "other" cultures in order to "define" our own culture. "The maker . . . of ethnographic texts," writes James Clifford in the introduction to *Writing Culture*, "cannot avoid expressive tropes, figures, and allegories that select and impose meaning as they translate it . . . all constructed truths are made possible by powerful 'lies' of exclusion and rhetoric" (*WC*, 7). In his essay "On Ethnographic Allegory" (1986), Clifford not only shows that ethnography, scholarly and otherwise, has always "emplotted" certain Western "allegories," "stories" or "narratives," "readings," or guiding "metaphors" into the representation of other cultures in order to appropriate them, but claims that "the very activity of ethnographic writing—seen as inscription or textualization—enacts a redemptive Western allegory" (*WC*, 99). The very mode of textualization has always contained what Clifford calls the "ethnographic pastoral" or the "allegory of salvage"—that is, the legitimizing strategy that through the written representation of an oral culture a "primitive," preliterate, and "original" culture in the very moment of its historically preordained disappearance is "saved in the text" (*WC*, 112).

In the 1980s, the basic assumptions of this allegory of salvage were, however, seriously challenged. It was no longer possible to hold onto the clean distinction between oral and literate cultures, the notion of a progressive passage from oral to literate culture, or the understanding of ethnographic textualization as a process that "saves" a "disintegrating" (oral) culture at the price of a loss of "authenticity" of unmediated experience. Derrida has cogently criticized Western logocentrism and the primacy of speech over writing ("writing as corruption"). Foucault has dismantled Western humanism and the myth of an objective science that, since the seventeenth century, has tried to eliminate all traces of rhetoric, tropes, and fictionality from scientific discourse and to relegate them to the realms of literature and art. He has shown how this mode of scientific discourse has, however, always been permeated, and perverted, by the unacknowledged and hidden "subjectivist" traces of power and history. Clifford takes up this philosophical critique of Western humanism and enlightenment and applies it to a critical analysis of ethnographic research methods and modes of scientific discourse that uncovers the contradictions inherent in its claims of providing an objective description or interpretation of another culture.[10]

To Clifford, the subversion of the "disciplinary matrix" of cultural anthropology by no means entails an evasive move to indeterminacy or irresponsibility. New paradigms are in the making. As he puts it in his essay "On Ethnographic Authority" (1983), "Paradigms of experience and interpretation are yielding to paradigms of discourse, of dialogue and polyphony."[11] In "On Ethnographic Allegory," he asks us to "open ourselves to different histories" and to conceive of the ethnographic text as a "palimpsest" in which "different allegorical registers" are inscribed, distinguished, and dramatized. If all ethnographic texts are "allegorical," the ethnographer must take responsibility for his or her "construction" of another culture or of his or her own culture. This process will (re)immerse the work in history, in the contested area of the range of "allegories," or readings of the culture that are possible, residual as well as emergent, in this particular historical context.[12]

The question of the responsibility of the ethnographer facing the "postmodern condition" (Lyotard) in which all the old foundations of knowledge and the "grand narratives" of the Western tradition have been eroded is discussed in its complexity in another important work of postmodern anthropology, George E. Marcus and Michael M. J. Fischer's *Anthropology as Culture Critique: An Experimental Moment in the Human Sciences* (1986). The authors consider their situation of methodological and disciplinary self-criticism an important opportunity to reaffirm and radically reformulate the traditional "Janus-faced character" of work in anthropology.[13] They critically reconstruct the forms this dialectic between understanding the "difference" or "otherness" of other cultures and the critique of our own culture has taken on in the history of American and English anthropology since its professionalization in the early decades of the twentieth century. They define the contemporary crisis in the human sciences as involving the "adequate" "description" of social "reality" that cannot be solved by the institutionalization of new paradigms. Marcus and Fischer suggest instead that the belief in total theoretical systems be replaced by a projection and practical application of multiple, experimental forms of cultural critique of other cultures as well as of our own. In their book, they discuss various models of cultural critique in recent anthropology and convincingly show their achievements and limitations.

In this context of the analysis of innovative, experimental modes of ethnographic discourse, Marcus and Fischer explicitly open up anthropology or ethnography as a "Janus-faced discourse" to developments in the "discipline" of *cultural criticism*. They call this process the "repatriation of anthropology as cultural critique" (*ACC*, 113) and criticize their colleagues for ignoring the "idea of cultural critique," as it was explored during the first half of the twentieth century by the Frankfurt school, in the line of French surrealism, exemplified by the works of Michel Leiris and Georges Bataille, and by American cultural criticism of the 1920s, in the documentary modes of the 1930s, and in sociology by the Chicago school of urban ethnography.[14] Moreover, they also refer their colleagues to contemporary forms of cultural and social criticism in the United States, to critics such as David Riesman, Philip Rieff, Richard Sennett, Daniel Bell, and Christopher Lasch.

Marcus and Fischer offer some critical remarks, but do not really engage in a serious critical discussion of the glaring differences between these various critical movements and their sometimes precarious historical positioning; rather, they read them in a general way as exemplifying two traditional techniques of cultural critique that "bring ethnographic research abroad to bear on cultural issues at home." "Epistemological critique" defamiliarizes and demystifies our common ways of thinking and conceptualization by seeing our society and culture from its margins and from multiple locations, by strategies of ideology critique, by a self-critical reflection on the social and cultural determinants of the critic's role and positioning. "Cross-cultural juxtaposition" confronts our society and culture with other, alternative ways of life, often with so-called primitive cultures, and normally takes on the form of utopianism (*ACC*, 133, 137).

Marcus and Fischer know, however, that these two "basic styles of cultural critique" cannot simply be taken up again and "repatriated" in anthropology today. Ideology critique too often continues to cling to a clear-cut opposition of ideology as deception and to the "real" laws and dynamic of society as a whole, established by a scientific analysis. Cross-cultural critique, on the other hand, has tended to romanticize more "primitive," "exotic" cultures, past and present, as more fulfilling and organic ways of life and to oppose them in its rhetoric *directly* to the negative picture of our own literate, industrialized, and urbanized culture. "What matters, then," Marcus and Fischer conclude, "is not ideal life elsewhere, or in another time, but the discovery of new recombinant possibilities and meanings in the process of daily living anywhere. Alternatives, then, must be suggested within the bounds of situations and lifestyles that are the objects of cultural criticism" (*ACC*, 115).

A critical postmodern anthropology must *reflect* and *enact* the ambiguity, the double-consciousness of its position and research in its discursive practices. The critique of Western civilization and of the world of science must not tempt the anthropologist into "radicalizing" the goal "to improve accounts of the long-sought-after native point of view" in an "ethnography of experience" in versions of "going native" (*ACC*, 43). As Gisela Welz points out: "In Action Anthropology, 'going native' is supposed to make the anthropologist more responsive to the needs of the people he or she is studying. Yet another type of 'going native' is in search of other cultures more conducive to self-growth and spiritual awareness."[15] These forms of "going native" eliminate the productive and inescapable intercultural tension in ethnographic work. By celebrating a non-Western, "nonrational" culture and the (seemingly) complete stepping out of the context of one's own culture, the process of going native reifies the "otherness" of the other culture and ignores its own unavoidable intercultural dimensions.

Anthropology as cultural critique has to realize that "alternative" ways of life must be uncovered in the multiplicity of tendencies and potential difference that coexist in every cultural situation and context, tendencies and forces that oppose, or adapt to, dominant culture or are incommensurable with it. It has to understand that the description and interpretation of *every* cultural situation and context is inherently *intercultural*. As Marcus and Fischer point out:

> For anthropology, the issue is how to conduct critical ethnography at home by making use of its cross-cultural perspective, but without falling prey to overly romantic or idealized representations of the exotic in order to pose a direct alternative to domestic conditions. A distinctly anthropological cultural critique must find ways to explore equally the possibilities for alternatives in both situations—the domestic and the cross-cultural—using the juxtaposition of cases (derived from ethnography's built-in Janus-faced perspective) to generate critical questions from one society to probe the other. [*ACC*, 117]

"Difference" and "otherness" are finally rediscovered in the cultures of the West and dramatized in ethnographic discourse as inherent to the process of (inter)cultural understanding. Marcus and Fischer briefly indicate some of these "differences within and alternatives to mainstream American life," these "other domains already exist[ing] within our own social world," such as in the debates on "gender differences," on the "differences between black and white, lives of the poor and the middle class, gay lives and straight," or on "mass-cultural forms," "popular culture, and the foundation of public consciousness" (*ACC*, 135, 153).

Clearly, this project of a "critical ethnography at home" requires and implies a radically new understanding of culture, unless it is just another version of cultural pluralism. James Clifford indicates the new directions in his introduction to *Writing Culture*: "If 'culture' is not an object to be described, neither is it a unified corpus of symbols and meanings that can be definitely interpreted. Culture is contested, temporal, and emergent" (*WC*, 19). Postmodern anthropologists do not conceive of any culture as a singular "system," "structure," or "pattern" of values, attitudes, or behavior that can be analyzed objectively. They also object to the concept of culture as a "text" or an ensemble of "dramas" and "ritual events"—key terms in the interpretive and symbolic anthropology of Clifford Geertz and Victor Turner—as long as this implies that the anthropologist can decipher and read them in an authoritative, fundamentally monological interpretation. To postmodern anthropologists, culture is a polyvocal, contested, complex process of the construction and deconstruction of meanings and identities, full of contradictions and changes. It is in and through this dialectical process, through the interactions and relations of power among the members and groups of a society as well as in the forms of expression and communication, or, equally, the "ruptures of communication," between the anthropologist (or cultural critic) and the "informants" of another culture (or of his or her own culture) that the "liminal world" of a network of "shared symbols" is "mutually constructed" and this particular "culture" and its conceptual model is "realized," "invented," or "re-encoded."[16] In his book *The Invention of Culture* (1981), Roy Wagner comments on the experience of doing fieldwork: "Before this [the anthropologist] had no culture, as we might say, since the culture in which one grows up is never really 'visible'—it is taken for granted, and its assumptions are felt to be self-evident. It is only through 'inventions' of this kind that the abstract significance of culture (and of many another concept) can be grasped and only through the experienced contrast that his own culture becomes 'visible.' In the act of inventing another culture, the anthropologist invents his own, and in fact he reinvents the notion of culture itself."[17]

If the potential meaning of culture is invented and realized in social practices, in processes of defamiliarization, of interaction and confrontation with manifestations, or expressive forms, of "other" cultures and if in our literate, highly self-conscious culture "the study of culture is culture," in Roy Wagner's phrase (*IC*, 16), postmodern anthropologists must transcend, or subvert, the boundaries of scientific discourse, hermeneutic interpretations, and intertextuality in a narrow sense and create new modes of ethnographic discourse. James Clifford makes us aware of one of the fundamental decisions in the Western tradition that has predetermined our dominant notion of cognition, of the representation of knowledge, and of our ways of writing about culture that postmodern ethnography has to revise: "Once cultures are no longer prefigured visually—as objects, theaters, texts—it becomes possible to think of a cultural poetics that is an interplay of voices, of positioned utterances. In a discursive rather than a visual paradigm, the dominant metaphors for ethnography shift away from the observing eye and toward expressive speech (and gesture)" (*WC*, 12).

Because culture, in the context of this discursive paradigm of ethnography, is not something that can be defined through observation, description, or interpretation, but something that is always polyvocal, contested, temporal, open-ended, and emergent, cultural anthropology has to give up the old program and ideal of understanding a "culture as a whole," as a total system. Instead, it has to negotiate and produce "positioned utterances" and to grasp and communicate their social and cultural status and meaning. As it studies "utterances" and is itself always already immersed in language, is itself a positioned utterance, postmodern ethnography is a "hybrid textual activity" that "traverses genres and disciplines and experiments" with new modes of discourse, new ways of "writing culture" (*WC*, 12).

Among these, the "dialogic mode," "polyvocality," and "co-operative texts" have drawn most attention (*ACC*, 30f., 69–71).[18] The ethnographer writing in the dialogic mode tries to "let the subjects speak for themselves," gives a detailed account of the communicative situation, and reflects on his or her own experience, research interests, and cultural prejudices. American folklore studies and the oral history projects in the 1970s and 1980s have developed sophisticated procedures that have overcome the often crude and biased methods of the documentaries and Works Progress Administration slave narratives and folk interviews of the 1930s. However, the difficulty of letting "other" people, "other" cultures speak for themselves, of grasping and communicating "indigenous discourse" persists. Moreover, it is still the ethnographer who asks the questions, pursues the research project, and composes the final ethnographic text as a whole. Some postmodern anthropologists such as Stephen A. Tyler have, therefore, devised and portrayed in a great rhetorical sweep the possibilities of more radically "polyvocal" or "co-operative" texts of a "dispersed authority" or "dispersed authorship" and open forms that do not set out to present" or represent something. Instead, they want to "evoke" in the reader a constructive effort that "makes available through absence what can be conceived but not presented" and that produces the—or one—meaning of the text.[19]

Undoubtedly, the "experimental moment" in American anthropology, the project of "anthropologizing the West" (Paul Rabinow), has produced stimulating new ways of understanding culture, or cultures, of writing about culture, of cultural critique. Yet much still seems to be openly programmatic and demanding further—cooperative—clarification.

The strong emphasis on problems of textualization and cross-cultural differences in postmodern ethnography had grown out of a self-critical reflection on the work, the failures of communication, and the ambiguous social and political position of the Western anthropologist doing fieldwork in another (non-Western) culture, as Paul Rabinow's *Reflections on Fieldwork in Morocco* (1977) and Vincent Crapanzano's *Tuhami: Portrait of a Moroccan* (1980) powerfully show. The particular strength of these critical "postmodern"—and postcolonial—reflections in most contributions to *Writing Culture* and in *Anthropology as Cultural Critique*, namely their direct engagement with and critique of the social and cultural experience of difference, a "distinctive type of cultural activity," of a "culturally mediated and historically situated self which finds itself in a continuously changing world of meaning" (Paul Rabinow), and their radical questioning of the presuppositions of Western culture, the practice of ethnological research work, and ethnocentrism in general has too often been misread and reduced in later debates to questions of postmodern "style" or postmodern literary strategies of "textualization."[20]

Yet critical self-reflexivity and the concept of ethnocentrism have to be challenged and complemented by non-Western perspectives and discursive practices. Whereas anthropology has widely been implicated from its beginning as an academic discipline in Western colonialism and imperialism, postmodern ethnography as cultural critique must be reconstituted as a critique of colonialist and post- or neocolonialist discourse. The self-critical and highly sophisticated postmodern ethnographic strategies in writing "about" other cultures should, however, not only self-reflexively be directed at the Western anthropologist's own difficulties in composing his or her text. The critique of Western ethnocentrism radically questions and subverts the foundations and categories of the discipline of anthropology, but as an internal critique it necessarily is comparative only in a one-sided way, and it tends to reinterpret basic forms of difference, especially of race or (post)colonial politics, in terms of its project of cross-cultural understanding. Henrietta L. Moore puts it succinctly in *Feminism and Anthropology* (1988): "[In the critique of ethnocentrism] the authority of the anthropological discourse itself is never challenged. It is still the dominant Western discourse—albeit purified—which is going to define what is anthropology and what is not anthropology, what is ethnocentric and what is not. Other agendas, other anthropologies, are not going to be heard."[21] Postmodern anthropologists have to confront the problems of how "the colonized represent themselves" (Edward W. Said) or how "the subaltern can speak" (Gayatri Spivak), problems that cannot be solved simply by "textualizing" the other culture in "polyvocal" texts of "dispersed authority" that "evoke" a "new kind of holism."[22]

The postmodern celebration of the "end" of the "grand narratives" of history and its emphasis on otherness and difference in cultural poetics must be careful not to forget the devastating impact of Western history on other, colonized cultures and their increasingly powerful articulation of their own role in a global history no longer conceived solely in Western terms. As Edward Said writes in his critical assessment of the "malaise about the sociopolitical status of [current] anthropology as a whole," in his essay "Representing the Colonized: Anthropology's Interlocutors" (1989): "In fact, there is no way that I know of apprehending the world from within our culture (a culture by the way with a whole history of exterminism and incorporation behind it) without also apprehending the imperial contest itself. And this I would say is a cultural fact of extraordinary importance, because it is the true defining horizon, and to some extent, the enabling condition, of such otherwise abstract and groundless concepts like 'otherness' and 'difference.' The real problem remains to haunt us: the relationship between anthropology as an ongoing enterprise and, on the other hand, empire as an ongoing concern."[23] It is the "disruptive articulation" of the "subaltern" (Said) that Gayatri Spivak pursues in detail in her essays, "Subaltern Studies," on the "unrepresentability" of "subaltern consciousness" and "expressive subjectivity" in the context of the Western critique of humanism and on the reinscription of a "*positive* subject-position for the subaltern . . . as a strategy of our times."[24]

Many of these problems are particularly pronounced when we turn to a self-reflexive, intercultural understanding of *American* culture(s) and the strategies of "ethnographic" writing of and in American cultural critique. If every culture is always "contested" and inherently "intercultural"—and this perhaps applies even more to American culture than to any other, and if culture is always, as James Clifford puts it, an "inscription of communicative processes that exist historically between subjects in relation to power" (*WC*, 15), a more rigorous analysis of the specific role of cultural mediation and of the "power" of discourse and (inter)textuality in the context of the changing social and cultural formations in the United States is necessary.

Also, the cultural perspectives and critical voices, the "native" critical discourses of the various ethnic groups, particularly of black Americans, have only very tentatively been acknowledged, much less incorporated into any postmodern anthropological study of American culture. Admittedly, the many powerful forms of a feminist cultural critique have hardly found a place in *Writing Culture*, as they did not seem to have contributed, as Clifford claims, to the "theoretical analysis of ethnographies as texts" as pursued by (male) postmodern anthropologists (*WC*, 20). Yet Clifford and Rabinow strongly support a critical dialogue between postmodern and feminist anthropology, a dialogue that, in fact, has produced important insights.

Henrietta L. Moore's powerful and wide-ranging book, *Feminism and Anthropology* (1988), distinguishes "feminist anthropology" from "the study of women" or the "addition" of women's concerns to work in anthropology. She defines it instead as a fundamental revision of the theory and practice of the discipline itself that focuses on "the study of gender, of the interrelations between women and men, and of the role of gender in structuring human societies, their histories, ideologies, economic systems and political structures." If it is impossible "to pursue any sort of social science without a concept of gender," a successful reconstitution of anthropology in terms of gender would seem to make the project of a specific "feminist" anthropology redundant. But Moore shows not only how much anthropology has neglected explicitly to take into account the dimension of gender, but also how little it is prepared to adequately conceptualize "difference" in terms of gender (or race). She also finds this theoretical dilemma in versions of feminist theory that essentialize the category "woman" and fail to explore the real local historical differences among women themselves, in a single culture as well as between different cultures. Moore's complex, politically conscious theoretical model of feminist anthropology emphasizes the multiple and often conflicting constellations of "differences"—in terms of gender, class, race—and explores the interrelationship of feminist anthropology and of feminism as a political movement. In the final chapter of her book, she mentions the "current radicalism in anthropology [that] experiments with forms of ethnographic writing" (Clifford, Marcus, Fischer), which has not yet received the serious critique it deserves. But when she argues that "this new approach" has "strong continuities with the traditional anthropological approach to cultural difference," a notion she extensively criticizes in the course of her book for its theoretical limitations, it becomes evident that she has in mind the more limited concept of culture in British social anthropology, whereas postmodern anthropology in the United States is critically indebted to its more inclusive, more complex, though often more diffuse understanding in American cultural anthropology.[25]

Marilyn Strathern, another British social anthropologist, has also carefully examined the social constitution of feminist and anthropological practice. She defines their relationship as an "awkward" one, as they are "differently structured in the way they organize knowledge and draw boundaries, in short, in terms of the social relations that define their scholarly communities." But they also should critically engage each other, as feminism "mocks the anthropological pretension of creating a product in some ways jointly authored" and anthropology deconstructs feminists' pretension that "they can ever really achieve that separation from an antithetical Other which they desire."[26] In another long essay, "Out of Context: The Persuasive Fictions of Anthropology," published in 1987, Strathern takes up the revisionary reassessment of the "modernist epoch" in British social anthropology (Malinowski's functionalist approach) that was begun by her colleagues E. W. Ardener and M. Crick for a critical reading of American postmodern anthropology. Occasionally, Strathern refers to the understanding of postmodernism as an experimental writing strategy of "scrambling" or "jumping contexts" or as "provocation for its own sake," but she is careful to point out—drawing on the work of Fredric Jameson, Craig Owens, and Hal Foster—that anthropologists such as Clifford, Marcus, and Rabinow do not merely celebrate a relativistic and pluralistic notion that all positions in culture and politics are now open and equal (Foster). Instead, they make use of and develop postmodernist discursive strategies not to "blur" genres or to "flatten" historical differences among and within cultures by turning everything into problems of "textuality," but in order to juxtapose, confront, and negotiate different social and cultural contexts, different literary and ethnographic productions. It is at this point that Strathern raises questions about the precise social contexts and relationships in which postmodern anthropology is situated and to which it speaks and that she proposes feminist discourse as a more successful alternative. To her, contemporary feminism is postmodern in the sense that it is constructed as an inherently polyvocal, dialogic, and deliberately transdisciplinary enterprise, and feminists know precisely "on whose behalf and to what end [they] write," being located in the politics of the feminist movement.[27] Clearly, feminist discourse can clarify and help redefine the objectives and strategies of postmodern anthropology. Still, the relationship between contemporary feminism and postmodern anthropology seems to be more complicated or "awkward" in reality, as feminist critique and feminist movement are more contested, dispersed, and permeated by differences than Strathern's picture suggests. Also, the exploration of cross-cultural differences and discourses of other cultures in experimental ethnography certainly addresses dimensions of a (counter)cultural discourse in the United States insufficiently articulated in her feminist anthropology.

The essay by Frances E. Mascia-Lees, Patricia Sharpe, and Colleen Ballerino Cohen, "The Postmodern Turn in Anthropology: Cautions from a Feminist Perspective" (1989), is an extensive and direct feminist critique of American postmodern anthropology. It discusses many of the same questions and issues Marilyn Strathern has raised, critically analyzes a wide range of recent work in anthropology, feminist criticism, and postmodern theory, and exposes in a particularly penetrating way the political implications of the new (male Western) approaches and strategies. When the three American feminist scholars quite concisely conclude that "those anthropologists sensitive to the power relations in the ethnographic enterprise who wish to discover ways of confronting them ethically would do better to turn to feminist theory and practice than to postmodernism," we have, however, to qualify their rejection of "postmodern anthropology" somewhat. In spite of some more balanced remarks, they finally base their polemic on a reductive conception of postmodernism as "an aesthetic view of the world as a global shopping center," as an "ideology that sustains the global economic system," focusing on "free play," "style," and "form," a version of postmodernism certainly not advocated in the work of Clifford, Marcus, Fischer, or Rabinow.[28]

Multicultural Critique in the United States

It is at this point that postmodern anthropology encounters the recent developments in American literary and cultural critique. Marcus and

Fischer point out that the issues of new textual strategies have been "explored most trenchantly by philosophical and literary theories of interpretation," and they mention "postmodernism in literature and art, poststructuralism in . . . literary criticism" (*ACC*, 5, 7f, 9). But they do not elaborate these suggestions in their book in more detail, even though Marcus had discussed the "numerous alternative frameworks in contemporary literary criticism" and the "new rhetoric," especially of Hayden White, in the research report "Ethnographies as Texts," which he wrote with Dick Cushman in 1982.[29] In *Writing Culture*, James Clifford makes a similar observation: "Ethnography is moving into areas long occupied by sociology, the novel, or avant-garde cultural critique . . . , rediscovering otherness and difference within the cultures of the West" (*WC*, 23) In the introduction to his collection of essays, *The Predicament of Culture: Twentieth Century Ethnography, Literature, and Art* (1988), Clifford again addresses the question of ethnography as radical cultural critique in relation to avant-garde literature and art: "Ethnography is an explicit form of cultural critique sharing radical perspectives with dada and surrealism. Instead of acquiescing in the separation of avant-garde experiment from disciplinary science, I reopen the frontier, suggesting that the modern division of art and ethnography into distinct institutions has restricted the former's analytic power and the latter's subversive vocation."[30]

This reevaluation of art, fiction, literature, and the critical avant-garde does not mean, however, that postmodern ethnography can find the solutions to its problems of textualization by simply appropriating strategies worked out in those fields, as those traditional terms and institutions have themselves come under attack. Also, the widespread commitment to the deconstruction of literary discourse and textuality as such would seem only to enhance postmodern anthropology's precarious position. Nevertheless, it is obvious that in the context of the rehistoricization of criticism, of resituating textuality, the powerful discourses of "difference" and the new experimental forms of writing in critical postmodernism can in many ways help to clarify and to situate the utterances of postmodern anthropology as American cultural critique. Anthropology will have to confront both the expressive forms and theoretical reflections of the "otherness" of marginalized or oppressed groups in the multiculture of the United States and the reconstruction of critical "differences" within the institutions and formations of dominant culture itself.

The recent forms of radical cultural critique among oppositional critics and in minority discourses in the United States find, on the other hand, in the concept of culture carefully and cogently redefined by postmodern anthropology through its self-reflexive, cross-cultural perspective, its intercultural understanding of cultural practices, and its constitution and reconstitution of cultural identities in terms of difference and polyvocalism a powerful challenge and resource that can help us to reconceive American Culture Studies as multicultural critique. The widespread political questioning of the very existence of anthropology as a scholarly discipline can remind American Culture Studies that "America" is not only a "rhetorical battle-ground," but also a contested intercultural "reality."[31] The interest in a theoretical reformulation of the objectives and strategies of American Studies provides the context for combining a radically cross- and intercultural perspective with a new awareness of the dynamics of alternative cultures and visions in America.

Under the conditions of postmodernity, the extraordinarily heterogeneous and dynamic multiculture of the United States has attained a crucial position in contemporary debates, as it has for a long time been characterized by a continuous revision and renegotiation of boundaries in cultural conflicts, shocks of recognition, and states and areas of liminality in which cultural knowledge is produced. As James Clifford recognizes in a remark on an essay by Michael M. J. Fischer: "Postmodernism . . . is . . . a general condition of multicultural life demanding new forms of inventiveness and subtlety from a fully reflexive ethnography" (*WC*, 22). What to postmodern anthropologists characterizes cultural *poiesis* and politics has also been a particularly *American* experience, "the constant reconstitution of selves and others through specific exclusions, conventions, and discursive practices" (*WC*, 24).

The project of working out mutually challenging and productive interactions in the context of American Culture Studies between self-reflexive, historical modes of cultural and literary criticism that are "attuned to the power of language no less than the language of power," as Sacvan Bercovitch puts it, and new forms of a fully reflexive, intercultural ethnography must not be understood, however, as another effort to finally achieve the scholarly paradigm of a comprehensive synthesis and total analytical "method" of the study of American culture as a whole.[32] The recent critical reflections in anthropology as well as in literary and cultural criticism make any attempt to interpret a culture, particularly American culture, "as a whole" a futile and politically very dubious undertaking, if by "unity" and "wholeness" we still have in mind something like a consistent structure or even a dialectical unity. Obviously, any culture in the comprehensive sense is politically unified through processes of power and hegemony and—this applies to American culture particularly well—through national myths and common resources and representations of the mass media. And in any culture a utopian desire for unity and wholeness, toward Victor Turner's communitas, is at work. Yet the old notion of the unity of a national culture as constituted and sanctioned by a clearly marked territory of its own, by a more or less ethnically homogeneous population, and by a tradition of its own has never adequately described the culture of the United States and is even less useful at a time of postindustrialism, postmodernism, and multiculturalism. We must ask if it is not rather through processes of self-reflection, self-differentiation, alternative visions and expressive forms, discontinuity, and displacements that American culture continually reconstitutes itself as always contested and emergent. The new understanding of culture in postmodern anthropology and in the intercultural critique of American radical and minority discourses suggests ways for American Culture Studies to grasp and conceptualize the heterogeneity, multiplicity, and dynamics in and of American cultures, past and present, beyond pluralist diversity, without falling for the temptations of a new "synthesis," hastily moving "beyond" ethnicity, or dissolving cultural conflict and difference in the rhetorics of circulating "social energy" in a "speculative" culture in the United States.[33]

In applying the revisionary understanding and representations of the culture concept in postmodern anthropology to American culture, as cultural critics we must become aware of a crucial *doubleness* or *ambiguity* in the use of the term "culture." On the one hand, we are asked to see the various realms of a "culture" or "society," such as the social, economic, political, and cultural realms, in a common focus or, better, to address their interrelations, their tensions, their differences as a network of complex and often conflicting interactions, and not limit our analysis to the work of the traditional sphere of "culture" in the limited sense. On the other hand, it is exactly the seeming omnipresence of these processes of cultural mediation and the increasing economic, social, political, and public role they have acquired in American and Western societies over the past decades in the context of the post-Fordist economy of postindustrialism and postmodernity that ask for a reassertion of distinctions and differences and a careful analysis of the specific modes of representation at work in the cultural sphere and of their social, political, and economic repercussions. These more specifically cultural processes should not simply be confused with society or culture at large or with the totalizing culture concept of the New Historicism. If we want to move beyond the common understanding of postmodernism as a playful eclectic pluralism of dehistoricized cultural forms of the "anything goes" variety or as a purely formalized version of (white male) "self-reflexive fiction," we have to historicize the discourse on postmodernity as well as the New American Studies and become aware of the specific historical dynamics of postmodernity and postmodernism in the United States, as explored in David Harvey's *The Condition of Postmodernity* (1989), Fredric Jameson's *Postmodernism, Or, The Cultural Logic of Late Capitalism* (1991), and Mark Poster's *The Mode of Information: Poststructuralism and Social Context* (1990).[34]

In his recent work, Mark Poster reconstructs critical social theory beyond the Marxist "mode of production" paradigm at the point of intersection between the new communication phenomena of an increasingly electronically mediated society in the United States and poststructuralist theory. Poster explores the different configurations of communication, of symbolic exchange in an information society that have changed significantly the network of social relations and the constitution of the subject. These transformations deeply affect the modes of cultural production and the role of the media and of "intertextuality" in what John Carlos Rowe terms an "immaterial economy."[35]

In *The Condition of Postmodernity*, David Harvey has situated the cultural forms of postmodernism in a wide-ranging analysis of the economic, social, and cultural changes of Western capitalism since the early 1970s that have fundamentally changed the cultural representation of time and space and transformed a Fordist economic system into an economy and society characterized by processes of more flexible accumulation and a complex interplay of centralizing and decentralizing movements. Harvey's admittedly tentative account and evaluation of the postmodern condition(s) most convincingly works with architecture and urban design. In his brief discussion of the aesthetic and cultural meanings of postmodern literature and of the more experimental modes of representation, however, he emphasizes too much the "affirmation" of "flatness," "fragmentation," "ephemerality," "eclecticism," and "anarchy" in postmodern culture, an understanding of postmodernism that certainly does not apply to a wide range of cultural production, particularly by minorities and subcultures (*CP*, 44, 350).

In a preliminary assessment of postmodernism, Harvey emphasizes its concern for "differences, for the difficulties of communication, for the complexity and nuances of interests, cultures, places, and the like," in contradistinction to the rather generalizing "meta-languages, meta-theories, and meta-narratives of modernism" (*CP*, 113). He fully endorses Andreas Huyssen's argument that the radical, oppositional power of postmodernism lies in its focus on "the multiple forms of otherness as they emerge from differences in subjectivity, gender and sexuality, race and class, temporal (configurations of sensibility) and spatial geographic locations and dislocations."[36] In his book, Harvey explores the reflections of the social and economic practices and relations in the expressive forms of postmodernism, complex interactions that he defines as "conjoining . . . mimesis and aesthetic intervention" (*CP*, 115) Yet he also rejects much of postmodern artistic practice and aesthetic and cultural theory as "tak[ing] matters too far," as "bordering on nihilism" (*CP*, 116). This reductive view of postmodern cultural productions ignores their cultural dynamics and political potential effects. Harvey blames postmodern artists and critics for "actively celebrating the activity of masking and cover-up, all the fetishisms of locality, place, or social grouping, while denying that kind of meta-theory which can grasp the political-economic processes (money flows, international divisions of labour, financial markets, and the like) that are becoming ever more universalizing in their depth, intensity, reach and power over daily life" (*CP*, 117). In a generalizing move against the fashionable use of "difference" and "otherness" he writes: "Worst of all, while it opens up a radical prospect by acknowledging the authenticity of other voices, postmodernist thinking immediately shuts off those other voices from access to more universal sources of power by ghettoizing them within an opaque otherness, the specificity of this or that language game. It thereby disempowers those voices (of women, ethnic and racial minorities, colonized peoples, the unemployed, youth, etc.) in a world of lop-sided power relations" (*CP*, 117). This warning is well taken and highlights important weaknesses in some widely publicized versions of postmodernism. Yet Harvey's emphasis on the continuing need for metatheory seems to have led him in the remaining three parts of his book to neglect the potential and the cultural dynamics of these "other voices" of difference, of postmodernisms in the plural. When he does refer to them, he does so mainly as examples of the commodification of "oppositional and subcultural" expressive forms in "flexible collages" for the cultural consumer market (*CP*, 301). All too easily, his project of defining the condition of postmodernity turns into elevating the practices to a predominantly white- and male-directed economy, society, and cultural formation as a normative frame that conceives of oppositional and alternative social and cultural movements and their discourses as wholly complicitous with (not just implicated in) the structures of power or as manifestations of difference somehow external to the generalizing vision of the condition of postmodernity.

Fredric Jameson's magisterial *Postmodernism, Or, The Cultural Logic of Late Capitalism* (1991) also relates American and Western postmodernist culture (and its reorganization of time and space) to transformations in capitalist economy and society. Jameson devotes most of his attention to a critical exploration of the phenomenology and dynamics of postmodern culture, its aesthetic modes of representation, its communicative processes and new media, and the social repercussions of a restructuring of the very scope and meaning of culture and the public sphere. However, in his long postscript, he explicitly addresses the question of the necessity and the implications of a critical approach to postmodernism that attempts to situate it in the total context of a new stage or period of Western capitalism at large, which Harvey covers in much more detail. In responding to critics of his earlier publication of the first chapter of the book, who attacked him for his "totalizing" approach, Jameson distinguishes the philosophical concept of "totality" as a "total system" from a form of cultural critique in terms of "totalizing" as a "praxis," an "operation," of "pointing to the hidden power relations behind our humanist and positivist systems of unifying disparate materials," and of theorizing the "cultural production" of late capitalism (*P*, 198, 203–4, 208–9, 331–33, 399–413). Jameson writes, "[I]f the word *totality* sometimes seems to suggest that some privileged bird's-eye view of the whole is available, which is also the Truth, then the project of totalization implies exactly the opposite and takes as its premise the impossibility for individual and biological human subjects to conceive of such a position, let alone to adopt or achieve it" (*P*, 332).

For Jameson, the concept of postmodernism is "not merely contested, it is also internally conflicted and contradictory" (*P*, xxii). Still, in spite of his emphasis on open dialectical thinking, on the "impurity" of "postmodernism theory" as a new discursive genre, and on the self-reflexive, tentative status of the "mode of production" model, the totalizing approach to postmodernism and postmodernity we find in Jameson seems to face a systematic problem (*P*, 391, 394). Jameson quite explicitly acknowledges the "resistant and heterogeneous forces" in postmodernism:

> [T]he totalizing account of the postmodern always included a space for various forms of oppositional culture: those of marginal groups, those of radically distinct residual or emergent cultural languages, their existence being already predicated by the necessarily uneven development of late capitalism, whose First World produces a Third World within itself by its own inner dynamic. In this sense postmodernism is 'merely' a cultural dominant.

> To describe it in terms of cultural hegemony is not to suggest some massive and uniform cultural homogeneity of the social field but very precisely to imply its coexistence with other resistant and heterogeneous forces which it has a vocation to subdue and incorporate. [*P*, 159]

Yet as Jameson's notion of the postmodern depends on a critical account of a dominant "mode of production" of white hegemonic First World culture and their more recent crises and transformations, it tends to interpret the "new" social movements and alternative modes of representation of ethnic or racial minorities as well as of women in the United States and the social and cultural practices of the so-called Third World primarily in terms of their opposition to and negation of the culturally dominant "structures of feeling" or "structures in domination" (*P*, xx–xxi). Jameson views such minority discourses as responses to the global processes of the flexible development of multinational capitalism (*P*, xvi, xviii, 159, 319, 406). What his approach often fails to recognize is that as long as we reduce the practices or discourses of "difference" and "otherness" in the culture of postmodernity to rhetorical gestures, a pure and random play of signifiers, pleas for liberal tolerance, fashionable commodities of cultural capital, or simply the reverse side of dominant ideological notions, we reenact a kind of thinking in dichotomies that does not conceive of the construction, deconstruction, and reconstruction of difference as historically inscribed in all the cultural processes and signifying practices of American society (*P*, 159, 340–43, 96, 144, 272, 372). If postmodernity is to be understood as something like a period concept and postmodern culture as the multiple representations of a highly conflictual and inherently "impure" stage in social and economic development, then the heterogeneity, the various manifestations of difference as well as the mediated homologies of contemporary culture and society must be approached from an explicitly intercultural point of view that attempts to reconstruct the dimension of historical agency from competing perspectives in an interplay or confrontation with different voices and discourses.

If my critical account of the new concept of culture, intercultural understanding, and cultural critique in postmodern anthropology calls for situating its revisionary project in the U.S. context, the problems with Harvey's and Jameson's totalizing studies of postmodernism and the conditions of postmodernity have revealed how challenging it is to theorize differences and differentiation as constitutive of the dynamics of American multiculture. We have to beware of falling for what Jameson criticizes as a dehistoricized "absolute and absolutely random pluralism" or for a periodizing and totalizing abstraction that appropriates the power of alternative and heterogeneous cultural practices in an all-encompassing, centralizing model (*P*, 372). A critical concept of postmodern culture in the United States takes up the challenges to Western ethnocentrism and explores the multiple interactions and the doubleness of its cultural representations and practices. It articulates the dialogical, but also antagonistic or asymmetrical relationship between, on the one hand, the radical self-reflectiveness and self-criticism in terms of ethnocentrism, gender, race, ethnicity, or class in recent forms of cultural critique and, on the other hand, the alternative manifestations of countercultural perspectives and their complex interplay in the "native" discourses of racial and ethnic minorities and feminist discourses. The radical discourses of cultural difference in American culture, society, and politics, developed by literary and cultural critics such as Sacvan Bercovitch, Alan Trachtenberg, Carolyn Porter, Edward Said, John Carlos Rowe, and Fredric Jameson, often precariously mediate text and context, explore the tribulations and promises of pluralism, and pursue in their critical textual strategies the experience of the heterogeneity, the historical tensions, and the polyvocality of American culture(s), which have always subverted the ideological drive as well as the utopian quest for unity.

Feminist and minority discourses dramatize the dialectic of accommodation and resistance and reinvigoration of a culture of difference in the American multiculture and the double-consciousness and double-voicedness of their indigenous and vernacular discourses. In situating their theoretical and practical work in the power relations of the politics of culture(s) in contemporary America, postmodernism does not mean for them an exhaustion of traditional literary forms and genres or demand a decentering of the subject. They can draw on rich resources of expressive culture and alternative traditions; they have always been decentered in American culture and society and struggled hard to create and renegotiate identities out of double-consciousness and difference in cultures that continue to be emergent.

Mapping sexual and racial difference implicates feminist thought in a critical debate on the strategies and objectives of a postmodern theory of culture. The feminist writer and critic does not so much set out to rediscover a nourishing tradition or a community of past meanings as "stage[ ] a conflict with the past, complicating notions of history and simultaneously demonstrating a commitment to its very absences."[37] Feminist cultural critique calls for dialogue, for sustaining what Elizabeth Meese terms "multi-voiced contra/dictions," for the intersubjective construction of new meanings and identities, and for developing what Tania Modleski calls "more interactive, mutually implicating methods of cultural inquiry."[38] For the black feminist critic Hazel V. Carby, a politically conscious feminist theory and practice is situated in the project of materialist, critical cultural studies that stresses the tentative, exploratory, dialogic nature of its discourse, demanding that "black feminist criticism be regarded critically as a problem, not a solution, as a sign that should be interrogated, a locus of contradictions."[39] It is in this context of rearticulating her "fully politicized feminist criticism" in patriarchical capitalist society that Modleski critically relates its performative, utopian power to the notion of "enunciation," the "enunciation of cultural difference" (as distinguished from "cultural diversity"), as it has been defined by Homi Bhabha in his analysis of the dialectics and "ambivalence" of colonialist discourse, the psychosocial dynamics of colonialization and racism, and the functions and forms of a committed critical perspective characterized by the "cultural and historical hybridity of the post-colonial world."[40]

The difference and otherness inscribed in black criticism is inherently social and historical as well as indigenous to its mode of critical discourse, as it has always been a "discourse about itself."[41] It exposes the conflicts of different voices and traditions in American culture and claims something like a separate space and voice in the culture at large. As native or indigenous writers and ethnographers, members of ethnic or marginalized groups reaffirm alternative modes of knowledge and cultural critique that resist a politics of inclusion, mere reversal, binary opposites, a recourse to essentialism, as well as the temptations of pluralism. Moreover, black criticism as double-voiced, as African American discourse has produced powerful new forms of cross-cultural analysis and experimental de- and reconstructions of cultural identities of difference and otherness. As African-American criticism, it has started to become critically engaged in the interactions between the analysis of the "ambivalence" of the discourse of colonialism, provocatively expounded by Homi Bhabha, of the projects of postcolonial discourse in the "new" literatures in English (or english) in Africa, the Caribbean, India, Australia, Canada, and other countries, and the construction of "minority discourse" in the United States, of the "epistemological, political, and cultural consequences which the struggle [of minorities] with the hegemonic culture entails," as Abdul JanMohamed and David Lloyd have put it.[42]

At the same time, these minority discourses as well as feminist criticism transcend their separate spaces and voices by rearticulating culture, history, and cultural critique in the United States in general. They show that "race," "ethnicity," "gender" *qua* "difference" are not "essentialist" terms that can or should be turned into representations of alterity but are cultural and social constructions inherent in *every* discourse.

Obviously, if I take up the notion of multiculturalism—a much-abused term in 1980s political debates on the future of the American educational and political system—to characterize American culture, this is not meant as a covering term for all aspects of diversity in U.S. culture and society. In my argument the multicultural dynamics of American society are seen neither as a revolutionary threat to the American liberal consensus in political culture nor as a celebration of a so-called postmodern playful eclecticism nor simply as the vision of a new, more inclusive democracy. Since the 1970s, fundamental social, political, and demographic changes have strengthened the multicultural features and articulations of American society, a development that undoubtedly asks for a new political and educational philosophy or program.[43] However, as the discussion of postmodern cultural practices and of postmodernism theory has shown, we cannot adequately grasp these representations of American culture as a multiculture by negotiating their position on a continuous scale between the two extremes of fragmentation and synthesis and then try to steer some kind of middle-of-the-road course. In spite of many important clarifications and critical insights of Arthur Schlesinger, Jr.'s *The Disuniting of America: Reflections on a Multicultural Society* (1991) and, in a different manner, Elizabeth Fox-Genovese's *Feminism without Illusions: A Critique of Individualism* (1991), both works clearly reveal the limitations of the fragmentation versus synthesis approach.

What is often lacking in the current emotionally charged discussions is any theoretical effort to define the term "multiculture" or "multiculturalism" in its specific dimensions, workings, and dynamics in the context of the United States today. Often the term is used as a different translation of "cultural pluralism" or as exclusively relating to the existence, visibility, and political claims of various national or ethnic groups. If we want to work out something like a theory of the American multiculture and the contours of a rehistoricized multicultural critique in American Culture Studies, we have to clarify much more cogently the dimensions and implications of the very concept of multiculture in the American context. It is here that the doubleness and ambiguity of the term "culture" finds its most confusing and, at the same time, most productive articulation.

First of all, multiculturalism as a critical discourse does not refer to an ensemble of ethnic, racial, or regional cultures that are conceived as more or less complete or independent entities with membership, territories, and traditions of their own. Instead, it tries to register the fact that this traditional understanding of the coherence of cultures has become highly questionable and that cultural identities are continually constructed and revised in processes of intra- *and* intercultural interactions. These "cultures" or groups do not have a stable identity and are not to be seen as more or less homogeneous, but are themselves characterized by heterogeneity and by complex and often antagonistic relations to other groups and the dominant culture. So-called large ethnic groups such as Asian Americans and Latin Americans turn out to be defined by the dominant culture and to comprise very different groups in terms of national origin, race, gender, class, and, in some cases, religion. They often draw sharp boundaries between themselves in order to negotiate their own identities. This implies that the concept of multiculturalism, or, perhaps better, multiculturality, as applied to the United States, refers to a number of very different phenomena and sets of problems in American culture at large. The various dimensions of the American multiculture such as gender, race, class, religion, ethnicity, regionalism, high versus folk, popular, or mass culture, and language are cultural and social constructs that draw and negotiate the boundaries of sociocultural identities in different, often conflicting ways, as the controversies among feminist critics, in African American critics, and in ethnic studies have made evident.

This quite clearly shows that in important ways all modern and, particularly, all postmodern societies are multicultural, that multiculturalism, or multiculturality, is nothing unique to the United States and is not another version of American exceptionalism, but that it exposes cultural critique to its intercultural and comparative perspectives. Historically, the dynamics of multiculturalism in the United States have been especially challenging, and their political, social, and cultural repercussions have been repeatedly addressed. American multicultural critique can be productive as a concept, or research program, only if it marks and explores the conflicts, asymmetry, ruptures, and differences within a culture and between these differently constructed subcultures and, at the same time, tries to engage cultural studies in an analysis of their interrelations in terms of cultural representations and discourses of power. It will always be *im*plicated in the dominant formations of power, but not necessarily *com*plicitous with them. The models of sociocultural identity and meaning produced and offered by these cultures of difference may, to some extent, be "created" by the dominant culture in order to legitimate its hegemony and to diffuse opposition. But in their heterogeneity, complexity, and hybridity they are also used and re-encoded by the various groups and communities to delegitimize the structures of power and to project alternative and enabling models of social organization and cultural representation.

In this sense, multicultural critique can also help us see the discursive consequences of the different dimensions and fault lines in the American multiculture from an intercultural, historical perspective. If the general public discovery of an American culture and of the culture concept during the 1930s often led to cultural chauvinism or a shallow Americanism, it also opened up cultural critique to an understanding of American culture as a multiculture of manifold differences, of competing ethnic and marginalized groups, of subcultures and alternative traditions in a society characterized by a strong consensus as well as unequaled heterogeneity. The critical use of the culture concept led to the rediscovery of many new areas and expressive forms and deeply changed our view of American culture and our way of writing about it. The crisis of the humanities and social sciences during the years of the Depression and World War II also led to the first efforts of conceiving interdisciplinary American Studies programs. Over the following decades each of the various dimensions of multicultural discourse at one time moved to the center of debates in the public culture and in American Cultural Studies. The proponents of the various dimensions (such as region, race, ethnicity, and gender) offered new readings of American culture at large in terms of the political situation and cultural experience of the groups with which they identify. Seeing American culture from the perspective of one of its fault lines, these critics redefined the other multicultural dimensions and often displaced their respective constructions of cultural difference and identity in a way similar to the displacement of the dimension of class in the debates on the political implications of multiculturalism or Afrocentrism.

In response to these changes in American society and culture, the American Studies movement provided a public forum for dialogues and controversies for many of these increasingly visible critical articulations of dissenting and marginalized groups. Obviously, these multicultural articulations were in some ways contained and appropriated in institutional contexts. Yet American Studies were also transformed by them, challenged them to redefine their critical cultural functions by confronting their culturalist approach to the wider dynamics of material processes of the society at large, and helped to create and acknowledge new critical and dissenting forms of cultural analysis inside and outside academia.

The institutionalization of the different interdisciplinary cultural studies programs such as Women's Studies, African American Studies, or Ethnic

Studies since the 1960s has had ambiguous effects. It certainly resulted in a strong emphasis on separateness and fragmentation. But instead of looking for a new synthesis beyond the exploration of the social and cultural functions of the dimensions of multiculture in the United States, we should realize that in some of these oppositional interdisciplinary programs, particularly in Women's Studies and African American Studies, new intercultural perspectives and strategies of a transdisciplinary American multicultural critique have been worked out that transcend and transfigure old oppositions and polarities, such as fragmentation or synthesis, as well as the fixation on particularism. American multicultural critique must respond to the "blurring of genres" observed by Clifford Geertz in contemporary cultural and social sciences not by moving beyond differences, but by exposing and redefining the multiple interrelations between the approaches and strategies of the various discourses and disciplines and by engaging cultural critique in the exploration of American culture at large as a force field of sociocultural differences and identities. We cannot construct the unity of the American multiculture in a time of postindustrialism and postmodernity by stubbornly holding onto the saving grace of the liberal consensus or by mistaking the emphasis on society as spectacle, on the omnipresent circulation of social energy in postmodern or New Historicist discourse that engages all the traditional "realms" of modern societies, as the overcoming and transcendence of differences or divisions of labor and social organization in reality. It is the specific historical manifestations and the critical articulations of multicultural differences and their intra- and intercultural interactions that constitute and, at the same time, situate a critical concept of American culture, postmodernity, and multicultural studies in the United States.

[6]

CULTURAL HYBRIDITY AND DIASPORA IN AFRICAN AMERICAN LITERATURE AND CRITICISM: FICTIONS OF A POSTMODERN MULTICULTURALISM

Postmodernism, Multiculturalism, and Minority Discourses

The notions and theories of postmodernism and multiculturalism were for a long time rejected, or at least regarded with deep suspicion, and often still are, by writers and critics from minority groups as well as by women writers and feminist theorists in the United States. Postmodernism in its early phase was seen as an aestheticist celebration of the "anything goes" variety or as an expression of self-doubt, self-pity, and/or self-reflective language games of the "literature of exhaustion" (John Barth) by white late modernist male writers who could afford to neglect the more urgent cultural and political issues at the center of minority and feminist discourses. Where postmodernism was permeated by the American version of what was called "French poststructuralist thought," the proclamations of the death of the subject and the end of history were seen as a sophisticated ideological ploy by white dominant patriarchal culture to declare key concepts of Western philosophy outmoded or defunct at the very moment when feminists and minority critics had begun to powerfully reclaim their own histories and to (re)construct and represent their own subjectivities. Even a large-scale theory of the cultural logic of postmodernism as a new stage in the history of world capitalism as proposed by Fredric Jameson, who identified the cultural work of minorities and other underprivileged groups as the most promising sites and forms of resistance and cultural revolution produced in the gaps and ruptures of capitalism, was criticized as once again assigning a strategic place to minority and feminist discourses in a totalizing theory instead of giving them an equal opportunity to define their own objectives and speak in their own voices. Similarly with multiculturalism. "Multiculturalism" was seen as a retranslation of the earlier term "cultural pluralism," still based on a plurality of more or less self-contained, stable, and homogeneous ethnic groups whose cultural forms and rituals of representation were publicly acknowledged and turned into exotic consumer goods without changing or even explicitly addressing the traditional, white-male-dominated power structure in American society. Or "multiculturalism" was rejected as a highly questionable blanket term for ethnic absolutism or essentialism that refused to see the inherent and incontestable heterogeneity of American culture and of all cultural groups in the United States in order to pursue straight interest-group politics. Therefore, if leading black intellectuals such as Cornel West and Hazel Carby have called for a move "beyond multiculturalism," they discard widely propagated, yet reductive versions of multiculturalism that ignore the crucial redefinitions of the concepts of culture, identity, and community worked out in recent (cultural) anthropology and in minority and feminist discourses.

Obviously, the critical, often polemical reaction of minority or feminist critics to the popularized notions of postmodernism and multiculturalism has been justified, but this is only part of the story. I think it important to remember that the very term "multiculturalism" was introduced into debates on the specific meaning and achievements of American culture not so much by educators, cultural brokers in politics, or sales managers as by the black writer Ishmael Reed, who was the only black writer, other than Clarence Major, who was frequently seen by white avant-garde critics as a representative of literary postmodernism. In the early 1970s, Reed began employing the term "multiculturalism" in order to transcend the limitations of his own version of a black aesthetic, of what he had called "Neo-HooDooism." Neo-HooDooism had been in itself a remarkably syncretist theory of black culture, but he gave the term up in order to respond creatively to the ethnic and racial mixture in the cultures of California, characterized by cultural heterogeneity and hybridity.

The genealogy and conflicting uses of the terms "multiculturalism" and "postmodernism" indicate that neither concept has fixed theoretical and political implications and neither is necessarily an ideologically obfuscating or reductive notion that minority and feminist critics should not engage in. On the contrary, such critics' own theoretical and political projects have articulated and elaborated, in their reaction to the pressures of the public debate on postmodernism and multiculturalism, crucial terms and strategies of the analysis of the intercultural and transnational dynamics of American culture(s). Minority discourses have transcended their sometimes essentializing "cultural nationalist" focus on exclusively reclaiming their own particular indigenous traditions and on establishing specific, unique forms of advanced "vernacular" or "native" theory in order to reengage in the exploration and articulation of the tensions and complexities of the *interrelationships* among different cultures and subcultures and of a heterogeneous American culture at large from a postcolonial perspective. On the other hand, feminist theorists, realizing that they often had too quickly identified feminism with the experience and the theoretical objectives of white (middle-class) women, opened up to a dialogue with the feminist contributions of women of color and to a cultural critique in terms of "eccentric" subject positions and nonstable communities, to use the words of Teresa de Lauretis, who has argued that feminist theory came into its own in the "post-colonial mode."[1]

Therefore, if the concepts of postmodernism and multiculturalism are to be used in a critical vein in contemporary American cultural studies, they have to be theorized in terms of an understanding of culture(s) as always inherently heterogeneous, unstable, intercultural, and hybrid. Versions of this theory of culture have been elaborated in anthropology in its self-reflective critique of ethnographic appropriations of "other" cultures in "colonialist" encounters, in postcolonialist criticism, in the work of postnational "new" Americanists, and, with all their rich and conflictual repercussions, in the border discourses of minority critics from different backgrounds and different locations. If postmodernism, in this sense, sets out to reconstruct and project alternative modes of historical thinking, of representation, and of writing in a postcolonial, globalizing as well as relocalizing world and if a critical multiculturalism engages in the complex interplay of various, not just ethnic, dimensions of cultural difference and social heterogeneity, a multicultural postmodernism manifests itself in the constitution, reconstitution, and representation of multiple, intercultural identities, of unstable, and conflicting forms of (often transnational) communities, and of multiple modes of rewriting cultures and histories in a world characterized by disjunction and discontinuity. It has found complex expression in literary texts in the widest sense, in fictions that reconstruct and redefine "history" and "memory" not as counternarratives of truth, but as actively engaging in the struggles and negotiations of complex intercultural and intertextual dynamics, and that envision, explore, and provoke alternative modes of cultural work without reifying or essentializing them.[2] The strategies of writing of a multicultural postmodernism can be read in terms of key concepts of intercultural analysis as they have been articulated (and theorized) in the border discourses in texts by minority writers, by writers and critics of marginalized groups, positioned and/or positioning themselves at the borders and boundaries of cultures. These border discourses of transculturation, creolization, hybridity, border cultures/crossings, *mestizaje*, and diaspora are activated by the fiction projects of writers of a multicultural postmodernism and energize them in turn. But they also provide the enabling visions for the articulation of critical theories of a postmodern multiculturalism, as terms like "double-consciousness," "signifying," "dialogics," and "cultural translation" indicate.[3]

For contemporary *African American fiction* the critical notions of "cultural hybridity" and "diaspora" seem to be crucial for understanding the specific cultural dynamic and power at work in its texts, as they open up African American criticism to its transcultural or, to use Homi Bhabha's terms, "transnational and translational" dimensions. The concepts of cultural hybridity and diaspora, both of which have to be read in a spatial *and* a temporal way, have had a long history in African American thought, from W. E. B. DuBois's "double-consciousness" and Pan-Africanism to the more recent provocative work of black British critics such as Stuart Hall, Paul Gilroy, and Kobena Mercer or of a Caribbean-U.S. American migratory intellectual such as Carole Boyce Davies. These concepts enable critics to map the force field of the complex intercultural or cross-cultural interactions of the (multi)cultures of Africa, Europe, the Caribbean, and North America, as they are represented and enacted in the dramatization of cultural identities, communities, and histories in African American novels, autobiographies, and other texts.

Thus, in our context, these terms have to be explored in their various and specific manifestations in contemporary African American literature written in the United States, in contradistinction to their uses in other cultural contexts. Therefore, in the following section of my essay I also address the question of how the novels by Ishmael Reed, Alice Walker, Toni Morrison, Gloria Naylor, Sherley Anne Williams, Charles Johnson, John Edgar Wideman, and Paule Marshall that I have selected for analysis rearticulate and "transculturate" (Mary Louise Pratt) the border discourses of hybridity and diaspora in their fictional strategies. The next section pursues the question of how African American literary and cultural theorists have responded to the explorations of multicultural postmodernism in African American fiction and proposed their versions of a radical (feminist) black postmodernism (bell hooks, Wahneema Lubiano, Cornel West) or of a critical multiculturalism beyond essentialism and reductive "culturalism" (Henry Louis Gates, Jr.). In the concluding section I widen the scope of the debate and indicate the intricate interrelationships between African American multicultural postmodernism and the respective versions of other "minority literatures" and redefine the discourses of multicultural postmodernism of "minority cultures" as voices and representations of an *intercultural, transnational American literature and culture at large.*

Multicultural Postmodernism: Contemporary African American Fictions

Ishmael Reed's complex, multivoiced, and self-reflective novels of the late 1960s and 1970s were seen as innovative contributions not only to the critical Black Arts Movement, but also to early literary postmodernism. They are characterized by a fragmenting of the text, a multiplicity of discourses and intertextual references, and black "signifyin(g)" (Henry Louis Gates, Jr.). They question the key role of "writing culture" by confronting in a complex collage various written discourses with oral culture, music, film, and photography. Reed's novels deconstruct dominant history and historiography and myths and reclaim or rearticulate counterhistories and alternative myths such as the Egyptian Osiris–Seth–Horus myth and its transformations in African American cultures, in voodoo or hoodoo practices, in black music and folk culture. They rewrite black history as well as distinctive genres of American and, more specifically, of African American literary history, such as the slave narratives in *Flight to Canada* (1976), without claiming any essentialized past on which something like a stable black culture and community could be built. If Reed called for "making our own future texts," these texts are not something simply to hold onto, but are expressions of an open, ever to be renewed creative and collective effort, an intertextual and intermedia project, as *Mumbo Jumbo* (1972) makes clear, that is not national in scope, but intercultural and diasporic in a global sense. Therefore, his founding of the Before Columbus Foundation and his call for the recognition of multiculturalism as "a new phase in American writing" and the publication of several journals of multicultural writing since the 1970s from *Yardbird Reader* and *Y'Bird* to *Quilt* and *Konch*, often coedited with Al Young, were a logical move beyond his earlier syncretist, intercultural black Neo-HooDooism.[4] Reed claimed, "Voodoo is the perfect metaphor for the multiculture," even though American literary and cultural criticism was hardly ready at the time to follow up the consequences of his pioneering work (*SONO*, 232).

From a very different background, the novels of Alice Walker can be read as indigenous "ethnographies" of black America in the medium of fiction, as fictions that dramatize the questions and projects of a "native anthropology"—for example, of oral culture, narrative voice, (inter) cultural otherness and difference, ethnographic authority, the possibility of subaltern speech, life histories, or indigenous forms of writing—and deconstruct them as modes of literary writing in an era of postmodernity. Her novel *The Color Purple* (1982) gives voice to the demanding struggle of a black woman in the American South to (re-)create African Americans' own history, fiction, and narrative voice. Walker shows how Celie slowly attains control over her life and re-creates the crossed-out written "I am" from the beginning of her narrative by writing letters (as she had been strictly forbidden to speak to anybody about having been raped), first to God, then to her sister Nettie in Africa (letters never mailed). Thus she seems to reverse the generally celebrated priority of the oral tradition in the African American tradition. Yet Celie's "life history" is authorized and authored in a way of writing or telling in which the novelist has given up her privilege of "inventing lives" and, instead, opens up her work to listening to her characters, trying to let them tell their own stories. However, Walker does not relinquish her responsibility as an author—the book is called "a novel," but her authorship *qua* "respons(e)ibilty," her identity as a writer, is plural, multivoiced, and self-different rather than unified. At the same time, in Nettie's letters from Africa, Walker dismantles Western missionary colonial discourse in Africa as well as the allegory of salvage promoted by Western anthropology. She also dramatizes the intercultural differences between African Americans and Africans who do not feel any common "black nationalist" bonds with "their brothers and sisters sold to America," as the black missionaries had expected. Yet the disillusionment about the "common goal: the uplift of black people everywhere," the recognition of intercultural differences also clears the space for a new, open-minded exploration of the historical interrelations of Africans and African Americans and for envisioning richer, truly cross-cultural identities and forms of community. If it has been objected that the all-encompassing happy ending of *The Color Purple* is a fairy tale solution, of "sameness without difference" beyond society and history, we should realize that the utopian closure is not offered as a realistic solution to social problems or intercultural conflicts. The abruptness of the celebration of harmony and unity at the end of the book, the shifting of codes, can be read as indicating the limits of the form of the "epistolary novel" and of the "modern" form of the African American novel, of the modern "fictional" history of African Americans, revealing the need to work out new models for realizing the project of finding and reconstituting voice, writing, history, and common identity.[5]

Alice Walker's next novel, *The Temple of My Familiar* (1989), is an ambitious effort to realize this goal in a kind of "magic realism" that suspends and transcends the common distinction between history and myth, individual and society, storytelling and writing, past, present, and future, Africa and African America, or black and white. The novel continues the story of *The Color Purple* but also extends and rewrites it, contrasts it with other characters and stories, vastly extending the geographic scope to include, in addition to the South and to West Africa, the eastern part of the United States, California, and South America and retracing the lives of the characters and of contemporary societies back to the beginning of human history. The main characters, Fanny Nzinga, Carlotta, Suwelo, and Arveyda, with very different backgrounds, are interrelated in the novel in manifold, sometimes confusing ways and are placed in a force field of ancestors, kin, and other "extended family" ties on several continents in which they have to situate and articulate themselves. In different ways, all of them have to unlearn the selves, the identities, including the sexual identities, they had constructed for themselves, to transcend the narrow confines of "their cultures," to go into "exile" in order to (re)discover "home." They have to give up the social roles and occupations and the "disciplinary" discourses they had acquired (e.g., as a historian or a teacher of women's studies) for more open, sensitive, communicative modes of feeling, thinking, teaching, creating art, and acting in an intercultural world always in process. If Ola, Fanny's father in Nigeria, a famous but also frequently attacked revolutionary hero and minister of culture and dramatist in an African country after independence from colonial rule, (re)acquaints Fanny not only with her African heritage, but also with the vicissitudes of living in a colonial and postcolonial world, it is Lizzie in Philadelphia who is the ancestral mother of African Americans. She tells Suwelo the story of (wo)mankind, deconstructs and reverses the common myths of society, and replaces them by the recovery of alternative, "fantastic" communal visions. Lizzie retells history in terms of a "dream memory" that goes deeper than the collective memory and, finally, "heals" him so that he can re-create himself as a spiritual being capable of establishing a new relationship with other persons, particularly women: "In the dream world of my memory, however, there is something. I do not remember this exactly, as I remember the other things of which I have told you. But the memory, like the mind, has the capacity to dream, and just as the memory exists at a deeper level of consciousness than thinking, so the dream world of the memory is at a deeper level still. I will tell you of the dream on which my memory, as well as my mind, rests. When I think of it I realize there was at least a peaceful foundation."[6]

The novel is narrated by a multiplicity of voices, from different perspectives, without hierarchization or "center"; the narrative is nonchronological, fragmented, jumping in place and time, from the present to the past or to the future, from fictional characters to historical figures, using different styles to create a spiritual wholeness and community. Walker once compared the experimental form of her novels, talking about *Meridian* (1976), to a literary "collage" à la Romare Bearden or a literary "crazy quilt" that attempts to express the complex interrelations between the black oral and literary traditions in a dynamic literary structure.[7] *The Temple of My Familiar* is a more radical version of this kind of collage or crazy quilt that seems to open up and transcend the boundaries of a black modernism. Bonnie Braendlin has quite rightly suggested that we read the novel as a form of postmodern "pastiche."[8] Obviously, it was Walker's aim not to obliterate all differences in favor of an all-encompassing "womanist" holistic vision of life, but to honor intercultural differences as well as differences in terms of race and gender. Still, the question must be raised whether the overambitious novel that over time strives to include virtually all contemporary issues and controversies does not too much lack the "edges," the "parodic" constellation of different styles and genres of writing that a black postmodern collage, crazy quilt, or pastiche requires, even if the latter, as a "parody of forms," is defined by Henry Louis Gates, Jr., in relation to Walker's use as "the absence of a negation" and a form of the "double-voiced" that "implies unity and resemblance."[9] Instead, *The Temple of My Familiar* often tends to fall into the trap of repeating worn-out cultural clichés without a difference, of endless preaching, of producing an uneasy mixture of reclaiming alternative myths and histories, and of displaying the scene and the offerings of new age promises of spiritual salvation.

If Ishmael Reed set out, in *Flight to Canada*, to deconstruct the foundational genre of the slave narratives and their black modernist versions produced in the vein of the Black Arts Movement and to explore the artistic potential of slavery as a metaphor for American culture, Toni Morrison, in her novel *Beloved* (1987), reopens the question of the meaning of slavery, of the importance of history as "rememory," of "fill[ing] in the blanks the slave narratives have left."[10] In her essay "The Site of Memory" (1990), she points out that "yet no slave society in the history of the world wrote more—or more thoughtfully—about its own enslavement" but that, nevertheless, "there was no mention of [the slaves'] interior life" ("SOM," 301–302). She sees her task as "ripp[ing] that veil drawn over 'proceedings too terrible to relate,'" a task that she finds as crucial for a "marginalized" group such as African Americans as it is difficult to accomplish, because historical research, her own memory, or recollections of others are not sufficient: "[M]emory and recollections won't give me total access to the unwritten interior life of these people. Only the act of imagination can help me" ("SOM," 302). This is an act of imagination as "a kind of literary archeology," based on a lot of information and knowledge and relying on images, on pictures (*not* "symbols") and "the feelings that accompany the picture," writing "from the image to the text. Not from the text to the image" ("SOM," 303).

Beloved is a "historical novel" in a sense, as it is based on the "historical" figure of Margaret Garner, but at the same time it explores the modes of the "fantastic."[11] It tries to bring back to consciousness, to rememory, and to make the black community finally acknowledge the interior life of slavery and its own involvement in the brutality of its experience and to recognize its African American identity as its *American* identity as something to be reappropriated. For Morrison, the novel is a medium for combining print and oral culture/literature, realism and the supernatural, and public and private lives.[12] *Beloved* transcends the form of Western thinking that is based on clear oppositions and dichotomies, of the self and the collective "we" that Sethe finally accepts. The book revises the meaning of "reality," recovers the reality of African spirituality, the reality of the supernatural, the fantastic, the magical, the living presence of ancestors. It also revises the notions of linear history and dramatizes the interrelations of the past, the present, and the future in an effort of "literary archeology," giving voice to the "disremembered and unaccounted for."[13]

How can this be done if the writing of history fails to reclaim the crucial formative experiences of the black American history of slavery? How can the traces of the repressed past be transfigured into a living truth? How can the novelist refigure and re-present the disfiguring effects of slavery? How can he or she read the scars, the traces of brutal violence in slavery, on Sethe's back? If *Beloved* tries to "fill in the blanks the slave narratives have left," this, ironically, can be achieved only if "the language [of the novel] has . . . holes, spaces, so that the reader can come in," realizing that what is left out is as important as what is there," writing and reading as acts of discovery and re-creation of meaning ("*R*," 341). *Beloved* is not a chronological story, portraying the development from slavery to freedom and literacy, as was typical of the (mostly male) slave narrative tradition.

The question of the black "self" remains an open one. The various levels of time, the reclaimed West African sense of time as well as the "hybrid" Euro-American visions and voices of history, constantly intermingle, as in a crazy quilt, and writing is a "working through [of the act of rememory] as an unending process." Sethe, for whom "the future was a matter of keeping the past at bay," must learn to represent the "unspeakable things unspoken" in the language of the imagination, to "read" herself, the traces of slavery, her body's "text," and to acknowledge that Beloved speaks for the "Sixty Million and more" lost during the Middle Passage (*B*, 42, epigraph).

Morrison had to find a literary form and kind of historical counternarrative in which she could embody these fragmentary images and rememories, both her sense of self as an individual (though not a "stable" self) and her imaginative recovery of black diasporic women's history and community (yet community, again, as something that has ever to reconstitute itself). If Morrison succeeds in filling in the blanks that slave narratives and the historiography of slavery have left and if she makes the reader gain access to the unwritten interior life of slaves and thus to their American history and identity, her literary act of imaginative recovery provides no closure, but reopens the quest for rememory and the tentative forms of community, as the enigmatic and multifaceted sentence repeatedly used near the end of the novel indicates: "It was" or "This is not a story to pass on." It is not a story of slavery and Reconstruction "reclaimed" that the reader now can hold onto and "pass on," in the double sense of to tell and to leave alone, but it, or complementary and competing versions of it, *have* been told, passed on in different individual and disembodied voices and de- and reconstructing modes of narrative and language the reader is asked to respond to and reenact, with signifying differences. However, if Morrison succeeds in this sense, she not only rememorizes and rearticulates something like "African American history," but fundamentally rewrites *American history and identity* in general as inherently hybrid in showing that the Middle Passage and slavery were foundational to the history of the American Republic from its very beginning (*B*, 210–17). She shows that the norm of "whiteness," seen as a noncolor and identified with universal enlightenment meanings, has always already been constituted by its muted reference to the enslavement of blacks and open or hidden racism, as the (negative) construction of blackness, of "Africanism, deployed as rawness and savagery, . . . provided the staging ground and arena for the elaboration of the quintessential American identity," as she writes in her *Playing in the Dark: Whiteness and the Literary Imagination.*[14]

Toni Morrison's literary project of rememory and history, of rewriting the slave narratives, of gaining access to the "interior life of slavery," of reconstructing and envisioning the diasporic complexity and heterogeneity of forms of African American identities and communities as American identities and communities, is pursued in complementary ways by other African American novelists such as Sherley Anne Williams, Gloria Naylor, and Charles Johnson. Sherley Anne Williams's novel *Dessa Rose* (1986) is based on historical incidents Williams had read about in the celebrated essay "Reflections on the Black Woman's Role in the Community of Slaves" by Angela Davis, who had found them in historian Herbert Aptheker's book *American Negro Slave Revolts* (1947).[15] The novel also revises Williams's own short story "Meditations on History" (1980) and rewrites William Styron's novel *The Confessions of Nat Turner* (1967), which was a rewriting, many argue also a misreading, of Thomas Gray's account of the black slave rebel Nat Turner's "Confessions" of 1831. As the intricate intertextual interrelations indicate,[16] the novel is about the meaning of history, about resistance to slavery, about a power struggle between blacks and whites, between a black slave and a white "master scribe," about historical memory and the writing of history. Therefore, it is particularly about the power of discourse and counterdiscourse, about the power and "authority" of fiction(s), about the white narrator's power to "frame," to "name," to define in language his black subjects as objects, as slaves. But it is even more about the process of the slow evolution of the slave Dessa's affirmative, vernacular language, which at the same time is a language of the community of slaves, a collective language. In the course of the novel, white discourse is more and more disrupted and deconstructed. Dessa achieves more control over her name, her language, her African heritage, and her actions: "I didn't have no words to make sense of what my eyes was seeing, much less what I'd been doing. I was someone I knowed and didn't know, living in a world I hadn't even knowed was out there" (*DR*, 197). Her struggle against slavery and her mistrust of white women, of the slave mistress Rufel, who saves her life and that of her child, slowly turn into a solidarity among women, black and white, and cause her to pass on her story—if these are the right words in view of Beloved—the memory that is hers, to her children and grandchildren. Yet, again, in *Dessa Rose* oral and written storytelling, different discourses, multiple narratives, and often indeterminate narrative voices continue to be employed in interaction as dramatizing the hybrid complexities of a white and black/African American society.

Gloria Naylor's *Mama Day* (1988) is a novel of black Africans in the diaspora, of the radical contrast between living in New York City and on an island in the Gullah Islands that is a liminal space, "another world," not belonging to any of the Southern states, set in a liminal time where the common distinctions of past and present do not apply.[17] In Willow Springs, African spirituality and community rituals as well as the divided and divisive legacy of slavery live on. If it offers George, who grew up in New York without any "history" or "ancestors," his first experience of community, it is portrayed less as a kind of pastoral idyll than as a place full of jealousy, hate, and secret rituals that George has to confront and that Cocoa and her aunts fail to control. The novel is narrated in a multiplicity of voices, individual and communal. It explicitly addresses the questions of the encounter of cultures, of geography and genealogy, of the failure of the ethnographic approach of understanding "other" cultures, even if it is your "own," and of the urgency and danger of exposing yourself to, and trying to reclaim, the power and spiritual legacy of African and African American women: "Reema's boy, . . . dragging his notebooks and tape recorder, . . . rattled on about 'ethnography,' 'unique speech patterns,' 'cultural preservation,' and whatever" (*MD*, 7). If Cocoa sets out to pass her experience and knowledge on to her children—the novel is set in the year 1999, and she talks to the dead George at his grave—in her case it is not a mere promise of solution, but the knowledge of the self-difference of individual and collective memory. In some sense, *Mama Day* is a reappropriation and reengendering of Shakespeare's colonial pastoral *The Tempest*, of Prospero and Caliban, but in its cultural counternarrative it also rewrites the powerful tradition of black women's novels from Zora Neale Hurston to Toni Morrison. If Willow Springs is a liminal, a "eu-topian" place in the literal sense, it is utopian as a promise only in the sense that it exists in the literary imagination as a challenge to African Americans, to Americans in general, to "really listen this time," to recognize and transform a complex and highly charged cultural memory (*MD*, 10).

Toni Morrison's epigraph to *Beloved* is "Sixty Million and more" (*B*, epigraph). This reference to the Middle Passage, the crucial experience of cultural rupture and change in African and African American history and the very site and symbol of the clash of cultures and processes of radical transculturation, is the horizon, subject, and formative principle of Charles Johnson's *Middle Passage* (1990). *Middle Passage* is a "novel of memory," a novel of what Paul Gilroy has called the "Black Atlantic," a novel of the black diaspora, a novel of cultural encounters of Africans, African Americans, and white Americans over history.[18] But it is also a novel that refigures *American* history, identity, and culture *at large* as a hybrid, diasporic culture that cannot be understood in terms of a neat opposition of whites and blacks. The name of the ship, on voyage on the Middle Passage, the *Republic*, indicates that Captain Ebenezer Falcon's fight with his multiethnic crew and the mutinous enslaved Africans, members of the (fictive) West African tribe of the Allmuseri, led by Ngonyama, a fight that he tries to write down, to account for, in his logbook, is a fight about the meaning of "America," of the American Republic. Captain Falcon, the "infamous . . . empire-builder, explorer, and imperialist," but also a "Western" intellectual, enters in his logbook a record of a voyage in 1830 on a slaver and of "mutiny and death," of "history."[19] Rutherford Calhoun, the young narrator of the novel, a "newly freed bondman" (*MP*, 1), a "marginalized American colored man" (*MP*, 169), is asked to continue this narrative on his own after Falcon's death (*MP*, 146).

Calhoun, who joined the crew in New Orleans, escaping the police and marriage, is isolated and suspended between the white sailors, who see in him a black man to be easily taken for a slave or one of the Africans kept on board, and the Allmuseri, who see in him another American crucially distinct from their tribal culture: "I felt culturally dizzy, so displaced by this decentered interior and the Africans' takeover" (*MP*, 142). Calhoun himself draws a clear line between himself as a (legally) free American citizen and the Africans: "Truth to tell, they were not even 'Negroes.' They were Allmuseri" (*MP*, 70). But when the Allmuseri leader, Ngonyama, tells Calhoun, after the successful revolt, that he will be safe because he is their "brother," the young black American feels his isolation from "their common bond": "Yes, I was black, as they were, but they had a common bond I could but marvel at" (*MP*, 132). However, his position of exclusion and in-betweenness also enables him to cross the boundaries of his "own" American culture (dominated by whites) and become aware of a reversal of the opposition of civilization and savagery: "They saw us as savages. In their mythology Europeans had once been members of their tribe—rulers, even, for a time—but fell into what was for these people the blackest of sins. The failure to experience the unity of Being everywhere was the Allmuseri vision of Hell. And that was where we lived: purgatory.

That was where we were taking them—into the madness of multiplicity—and the thought of it drove them wild" (*MP*, 65). In another context, Calhoun observes, "[Ngonyama's] people saw whites as Raw Barbarians and me (being a colored man) as a Cooked one" (*MP*, 75).

Calhoun acts—is forced to act—as an intermediary, or cultural translator, between Americans and Africans, between the *Republic*'s officers and crew and the mutinous Allmuseri, between Captain Falcon and the crew, between the world of the *Republic* and the world ashore in the United States. Even though the novel is written in the form of nine entries in the log of the *Republic*, ranging from June 14 to August 20, 1830, entries written retrospectively, Johnson does *not* try to reenact the experience and the language of the time, or the possible vision of a young black freed slave after his return from the African voyage of 1830. The novel, instead, in a complex and counterfactual manner de- and reconstructs histories and myths from conflicting perspectives and reappropriates and assigns new meaning to the discourses of history writing and historical fiction from the slave narratives to Melville's "Benito Cereno" and Faulkner. In Johnson's philosophy, language is always already intersubjective and intercultural: "in words we find the living presence of others, . . . language is not—nor has it ever been—a neutral medium for expressing things, but rather . . . intersubjectivity and cross-cultural experience are already embodied in the most microscopic datum of speech," as he writes in his philosophical study *Being and Race: Black Writing Since 1970* (*BAR*, 38).

Middle Passage is a very erudite, self-reflective, and demanding book that can be charged with overextending the patience of the reader. But it is a philosophical novel that explores and rearticulates the potential of both philosophical thinking and the writing of fiction. The book intermingles "truth" and "fictionalizing" (the "lies" of the narrator) as well as different discourses of history and intellectual and spiritual traditions, as the three epigraphs announce, not only the "Western" Christian and the black American, but also the tradition of Buddhism and other Eastern philosophies. In its philosophical and spiritual voyage and its wider ensemble of characters, it is modeled on the West African sacrificial kingship rituals of the Dogon and the Bambara and, like Reed's pioneering *Mumbo Jumbo*, on the Egyptian Osiris–Seth–Horus myth. The novel is not a reenactment of these myths, but a hybrid literary "repetition with a difference" in the world of Jacksonian (and our own) America. *Middle Passage* dramatizes the interplay and border crossings of what in the Western tradition are distinguished as different and competing realms of thought and modes of communication, such as the philosophical, the sacred, the secular, the political, the mythical, the spiritual, the symbolic, the aesthetic, and the literary. If the voyage, the Middle Passage from Africa on a slave ship, "had irreversibly changed my seeing, made me a cultural mongrel" (*MP*, 187), as the narrator writes near the end of the book, his notion of America has also undergone a radical change: "If this weird, upside-down caricature of a country called America, if this land of refugees and former indentured servants, religious heretics and half-breeds, whoresons and fugitives—this cauldron of mongrels from all parts of the compass—was all I rightly call *home*, . . . then aye: I was of it" (*MP*, 179). Calhoun finally realizes (and accepts) that the American Republic is, like the ship, the *Republic*, "a process" (*MP*, 36) and that he himself has no stable identity, but has to negotiate the hybridity of a diasporic culture: "In myself I found nothing I could rightly call Rutherford Calhoun, only pieces and fragments of all the people who had touched me, all the places I had seen, all the homes I had broken into. The 'I' that I was, was a mosaic of many countries, a patchwork of others and objects stretching backward to the beginning of time" (*MP*, 162–63). "Writing doesn't so much record an experience—or even imitate or represent it—as it *creates* that experience," Johnson writes (*BAR*, 5–6). In his "descent"—"for the find we have got below" (*MP*, 99)—into the underworld, the collective unconscious, into the hold of the *Republic*, where the "dangerous shape-shifting" Allmuseri god is kept, the god appears to Calhoun in a feverish vision as his own father, "the fugitive Riley Calhoun," whom he is forced, finally, to confront, despite having said earlier, "In a way, I have no past" (*MP*, 167, 160). In a *rite de passage* of symbolic death and rebirth, Calhoun is given the deeper insight that "identity was imagined; I had to listen harder to isolate him from the We that swelled each particle and pore of him, as if the (black) self was the greatest of all fictions; and then I could not find him at all. He seemed everywhere, his presence, and that of countless others, in me as well as the chamber, which had subtly changed." And, finally, Rutherford Calhoun is transformed: in the Allmuseri god he faces himself: "Suddenly I knew the god's name: Rutherford" (*MP*, 171).

Equally, "sexes and races [are] blurred," African and American cultural "identities" are dissolved, suspended, and changed—and held in a cross-cultural tension (*MP*, 145). The whole notion of race based on "biology" and the "rituals of color and caste" are deconstructed (*MP*, 113). What had seemed to be the "ageless culture" of the African Allmuseri turns out to be subject to change and transculturation and in itself a deeply "hybrid" culture (*MP*, 78). There is no pure, unified, and perfect

African, non-Western spirituality and philosophy that Rutherford Calhoun could embrace. As Ebenezer Falcon points out to young Rutherford, the "'African god [he had] captured'" has "'a thousand names'" and "'all things are its image,'" is "'immaterial'" as well as "'material,'" "'omnipotential'" and "'omnipresent,'" "'is the universe,'" but also has its "'limitations'" and "'contradictions,'" because "'a god can't know its own nature. For itself, it can't be an object of knowledge. D'you see the logic here? The Allmuseri god is everything, so the very knowing situation we mortals rely on—a separation between knower and known—never rises in its experience'" (*MP*, 100–102). To Calhoun, "None of this was clear. Aphasic, I nodded anyway. My brain had stopped functioning a full five sentences ago" (*MP*, 102). Back in his cabin, visions of the Apocalypse occupy his mind. Ironically, Calhoun has the vision, or nightmare, that the omnipresent, omnipotent, shape-shifting god of the Allmuseri, who has "its limitations" in the horizon of Western philosophical thinking, when "colonized" and kept prisoner in the West, in the Republic of the United States would bring "history, as we know it," to its "end" and the complete union of "the sacred and the secular" lost in Western history would be regained—but as "Apocalypse," an Apocalypse Calhoun is not interested in being part of (*MP*, 103). Instead, after all these dreams and visions of all-encompassing unity and fulfillment, he ends by reentering the world as it is, with all its contradictions and limitations, but with a newly recovered spiritual openness and awareness: "For my part, I wanted to live a little longer. I was only twenty-three years old. The Apocalypse would definitely put a crimp in my career plans. I needed the world as I knew it, as evil and flawed as it was, to *be* there for a while" (*MP*, 103). For Calhoun, the lone survivor after the sinking of the *Republic*, his return to New Orleans is the return of a man reborn who is prepared for reconciliation with his brother Jackson and for marriage with Isadora, whom he had fled at the beginning of his voyage. He is finally able to redefine for himself proper male and female sexual roles.

Calhoun realizes that the Allmuseri had indeed become part of "the world of multiplicity" (*MP*, 140) and the world of *hybridity* ("difference") and *diaspora* ("displacement"): "Nay, you could assume nothing with them. But of one thing I was sure: There was a difference in them. They were leagues from home—indeed, without a home—and in Ngonyama's eyes I saw a displacement, an emptiness like all of his brethren as he once knew them were dead." And Calhoun continues: "Stupidly, I had seen their lives and culture as timeless product, as a finished thing, pure essence or Parmenidean meaning I envied and wanted to embrace, when the truth was that they were process and Heraclitean change, like any men, not fixed but evolving and as vulnerable to metamorphosis as the body of the boy we'd thrown overboard. Ngonyama and maybe all the Africans, I realized, were not wholly Allmuseri anymore. We had changed them . . . No longer African, not yet Americans either. Then what? And of what were they now capable?" (*MP*, 124–25). If the Allmuseri are, as Ashraf Rushdy claims, "the theory . . . and symbol of the postmodern condition," then this kind of postmodern condition also strikingly differs from the common notion of (white) literary postmodernism as the aesthetic style of the "literature of exhaustion" and the breakdown of systems of values and meanings.[20] Also, in dramatizing difference, displacement, and homelessness in the Allmuseri, in Calhoun (who desperately wants to "go *home*," *MP*, 137), as well as in Falcon and the crew, Johnson's narrator defines the dialectics of the *colonial* experience that affects, in obviously different ways, both the colonizer and the colonized, as Homi Bhabha's theoretical reflections on hybridity have made clear. But in continuing, in his own way, the logbook, in *writing* the logbook (and the novel), Johnson's narrator claims agency and his own voice as a colonial subject *and* an American citizen: "Even though I'd tell the story . . . , it would be, first and foremost, as I saw it since my escape from New Orleans" (*MP*, 146). In so doing, Johnson articulates the *postcolonial* moment, as Brian Fagel has pointed out: "Johnson's postcolonial enactment arises out of our present modernity, interrupting time and space to *speak* in an overdetermined, multi-vocal manner."[21] Yet, to be sure, it is a multivocal articulation of the fate of difference and of spiritual power, African and non-African, that also challenges the common meaning of the political in postcolonial discourse.

John Wideman is a black writer whose more recent work has been explicitly linked to questions of a black postmodernism.[22] His novel *Reuben* (1987) addresses the problems of living in a contemporary urban black community.[23] It is set in the black Homewood section of Pittsburgh, where Wideman was born in 1941 and in which he has set most of his fiction. Reuben, the main character of the novel, is an aging, intelligent, slightly hunchbacked, short black man who lives in an old trailer, where he conducts his law business, acting as a go-between for blacks in Homewood who must deal with the authorities downtown, a "'kind of god or spirit' trying to 'hold this community together, prop people up, keep them going,'" as Wideman put it in an interview.[24] Reuben is nobody specific but, at the same time, takes on many disparate and contradictory "identities," a version of the ancient trickster figure, performing as some kind of translator of cultures, as "messenger, factotum, busybody, moron, spy, gossip, hustler, old dog tray, cuckold, cocksman, nothing, everyman, flunky, fool, mountebank, wizard, storyteller, mute. Yeah, that's him all right. That's who he is" (*R*, 132). The "identity" and "reality" he "has" is discontinuous: "No matter how many cameras, a different Reuben in each frame, a slightly altered pose, a separate reality. Amazing, isn't it? How protean the simplest gesture. And each pose real, definitive, if we possessed a means of capturing it. If we could see everything. If we bore God's eye in our foreheads. A paradox, an irony" (*R*, 127; cf. 172). Reuben embodies Homewood's "saving spirit," combining the roles of an intellectual and of an artist in the community. He knows that he "can change little or nothing," but he does "[his] best" (*R*, 198), standing between his clients and their problems, giving them the chance to tell their stories or, better, to make them realize that they, as individuals, actually *do* have their own stories. He listens to them, takes the weight, gives them a new confidence that things *can* be worked out.

Reuben also knows that the stories his clients tell, or his own stories, are never "true" in any strict sense, that they are all representations of a fluid reality, are always "fictions" or "illusions" that have to be read, interpreted, and reconstructed. Words can never fully capture experience and reality, but "experience" does not exist without language: "Two knocks. Knock. Knock. The sound of someone at the door represented as it is in novels, cartoons. Knock. Knock. A rapping at the door expressed by the word *knock*, printed twice upon the stillness as if Reuben's life were being written, not lived. An afterimage floats where the words had disappeared. His old eyes playing tricks. His ears being silly. People hear sounds, not words. Words are bred in books and newspapers. Chunks of alphabet with arbitrary meanings attached . . . words faltered on their last legs, *knock*, *knock*, desperate to keep their power, to be seen as well as heard, seen as real by weak creatures like himself who pretended they were the authors of the universe" (*R*, 60–61). As "reality" is never simply out there, but always mediated, the novelist and Reuben can only describe perceptions of events. As Eadweard Muybridge, the English photographer, whose books Reuben studies, always tried in vain to capture the essence, the "secrets" (*R*, 63) of motion and change beyond words in his sequential photographs of "animal motion," motion always "escaping [his] net," as Muybridge puts it in one of the imaginary conversations

Reuben has with him, Reuben realizes that he can never reach certainty, that he can never fully represent "the flow of time," "motion," "the truth" of the process of life. As a lawyer (or someone practicing law) he wants to "break down the process into discrete, manageable units. Then he could prevent it, stop it from happening " (*R*, 17). But as the law is itself a "fiction of motion, [a] metaphysical passage from disorder to equilibrium, unfair to fair, chaos to order, by establishing a series of steps—a due process," he can only create a "counterillusion," "freezing things into unnatural frames" (*R*, 16–17).

In this situation of the failure to catch the "secrets" of life, of the unreliability as well as the manipulative and oppressive use of language by a racist society, blacks in Homewood are deeply alienated from themselves, feel victimized, or, like Reuben's friend, the former basketball star and current basketball recruiter Wally Carter, always act and think from a distance, seeing their lives as a movie: "He'd learned to treat what was happening as a memory, a film he watched on a screen. But if he could see himself that way, if the only life he knew was not his own, then whose was it?" (*R*, 111). Or watching and "editing" his life as a videocassette: "[S]ince his life was a memory, he could change it next time he played it. He could tell any lie he needed to get by. It's all in your mind. A dream made up as you go along. But if you're not there, living smack-dab in the middle of your life, then where the fuck are you? Every once in a while the question stings Wally. If your life's not a memory or a tale you concoct at will, playing it fast-forward or reverse, stopping and starting in the middle or end, if your life's more than this mix of yes no and maybe and skipping and losing and somebody else working the dials, then who are you?" (*R*, 102). Whereas Wally does not know how to deal with this loss of a stable identity and fails to turn his theory of "abstract hate" into something positive, being harassed by fantasies of violence and murder (did he really kill the white man in a Chicago restroom?), Reuben finds the resources to transform his awareness into a project productive for the black community. If the use of language is "arbitrary," if discourses are socially and culturally constructed, not absolutes or universals, you can deconstruct and, to some degree, dismantle the power of white dominant discourses, try to turn them against themselves. But Reuben fully knows that this is only part of what he has to do. He also sets out to reconstruct non-Western traditions, alternative ways of thinking and constructing the world, such as Egyptian mythology or Kongo or Dogon cosmology, as well as the diasporic African American tradition that still exists even in the devastated black urban communities in the United States. Wideman links Reuben with Thoth, "patron of scribes," the Egyptian god of time, writing, learning, wisdom, and magic whom Reuben asks for help with his business for the community, making a charm according to African cosmology, summoning the "life-sustaining flash of the spirit" (*R*, 61, 67–68). Yet it is not simply a question of rediscovering and learning Egyptian mythology or West African or Kongo cosmology and of combining them in a syncretistic ritual with their African American transformations. The ancient myths, such as the Osiris myth, function as underlying patterns but are deconstructed in the novel as well. Before the charm can work, however, Reuben has to confront his own story, has to acknowledge—as every black person has to—his "Philadelphia," the horrible experience of white racism that destroyed his sole moment of love as well as the attack by white authorities and the white press accusing him of being a charlatan and impostor (*R*, 91, 93, 112, 114).

Reuben knows that "his sense of things, the notes he'd accumulated over the years, added up to nothing" (*R*, 22). He knows that he can never be sure that he can "change" his client's life, or life story, that he can never reach truth or spiritual unity and perfection by his intellectual efforts alone, but that he has to *act*, to *do* his "work" in the black community (*R*, 47, 63). At the end of the novel he succeeds in finding the son of one of his clients; the boy, the young woman Kwansa's child, had been kidnapped by his father, who had abandoned him and her even before the child was born. Yet again, Reuben cannot be sure of his success, of the "truth" of the story. The final chapter of the novel is called "And," indicating that the story will go on, opening it up again, asking us to continue to "Imagine," the last word of the book. It is up to the reader to make sense, or suspend the meaning, of what Wideman has tried to tell in his novel.

Wideman's *Reuben* is an experimental novel that can be called a work of *black*, or *African American, postmodernism*, even though Coleman's use of the term in his interpretation of *Reuben* is exceedingly vague (*BAM*, 115–35). In many of its literary strategies and the questions of identities, histories, and writing raised by Reuben and Wally, it is a work of self-reflexive metafiction, employing cinematic techniques, disruptions of narrative, multiple discourses and genres, and an unstable "floating" narrator (*R*, 35–41, 195–202). It is a novel representing the awareness of the omnipresence—that is, the illusory as well as the productive inevitability—of "fiction" and "fictions" that draws on the tradition of Western modernism and postmodernism that Wideman had become acquainted with after his years as a student at Oxford and in the United

States. But it equally is a work of black, African American "word magic," of African and African American mythology and cosmology, realized in the idioms and the rituals of folklore, music, language, and literature, as he had rediscovered them in his in-depth studies of the black tradition since the 1970s, which had taught him—as the novels of his Homewood trilogy show—that he could "talk about the most complicated and sophisticated and intense moments and understandings and characters in the Afro-American idiom," as he put it in an interview in 1988 (*BAM*, 150). *Reuben* is a work of a black postmodernism that rearticulates the theoretical underpinnings and strategies of writing of a white aestheticist postmodernism and resituates it in the political awareness and the deconstructions of African American history and culture as "American culture." For Wideman, *Reuben* is "a kind of collage . . . you find in something like an Eliot, but that you also find in traditional African art. In masks or dance, you have that eclectic combination" (*BAM*, 159). In Wideman's literary world the writer is a mythmaker, a "power figure," a "lawyer" as a "shaman or a priest" (*BAM*, 151). If the writer is a "storyteller" who teaches us, his readers, to "tell our own stories" "in our own words," "in spite of the madness, the chaos around us, and in spite of the pressure around us not to tell [them]," and if this storytelling is "crucial to survival, individual survival, community survival," storytellers, Wideman continues, "are always inside and outside the story by definition" (*BAM*, 156). There is no pretension of (re)constructing a unified nourishing black tradition, of claiming the essential "truth" of a story, or of ever achieving something like a stable "black identity" (*R*, 44–45). There is no memory that could reclaim a cultural myth that has the authority of "making sense," but only a plurality of myths, of fictions, of stories that compete and intermingle and set the writer and reader free to move beyond pluralist "diversity" and construct his or her own stories, a "fragmentary" and "discontinuous" "identity" as part of the experience of impermanent communities of memory (*BAM*, 158).

Early in the novel Wideman writes: "Reuben had once thought of his memory as a voice, a voice like God's, sure of itself, alone, unimpeachable. It spoke to him and he listened. Then for a time, as he examined his past, trying to capture and understand its meaning, the form of memory was conversation. . . . Lately, his memory had become more like those all-night, call-in, radio talk shows, an unpredictable mix of voices, coming from everywhere and nowhere, . . . voices unspeakably lonely, voices full of themselves or full of that profound emptiness apparent only when people come together in numbers to quell it. . . . Yet no one was in charge.

No host, no writer, no master of ceremonies. No shared notion of style or propriety among the callers. . . . Each voice supreme, aggressive, irreconcilable. Reuben's memory of his past was just this bizarre, urgent competition for air time, disembodied souls calling in from the four corners of the universe" (*R*, 14–15). Reuben is a figure who lives on different levels and in different spheres and "is set above and away from the community," so that "tensions remain, that whole process of moving toward reengagement and I suppose moving away, but the distance, or some distance, is probably always there" (*BAM*, 156). Near the end of *Reuben*, the narrator of the chapter "Toodles" accounts for the multiplicity, but also the dialogics, the storytelling, but also the silences, the distances of memories, but also their living presences, the reflections and reflexions of the imaginings of fictions of truths: "From a great distance, longer than the time it's taken all the voices that have ever told stories to tell their stories, in the welcome silence after so much lying, so much wasted breath, the women's voices reach us. Where we sit. Imagining ourselves imagining them" (*R*, 207–208). In his essay "The Architectonics of Fiction" (1990), Wideman continues these reflections about the writer's medium of voice and language, the enabling power of the "counter-integrative model" of black music, and the writer's stance producing "bodies of enabling legislation, a grammar of nuanced tensions, incompatibilities, doors and windows that not only dramatize the stance itself but implicate the medium. A reciprocal unravelling below whose surface is always the unquiet recognition that this language we're using constantly pulls in many directions at once and unless we keep alert, keep fighting the undertow, acknowledge the currents going our way and every other damn way, that we are not alone but not separate either, that any voice we accomplish is really many voices, that any voice is always steeped in unutterable silences, that the role of speaker, listener, narrator and narrative, the form and direction of the tale may seem to be fixed, but we hold some keys" ("*AF*," 46).

What the black writer sets out to do is dramatize that tension as an intercultural, dialogical process of constant transformation, translation, and reappropriation of black diasporic cultures, a process that, however, never fulfills itself in a continuous life story, but remains full of gaps, ruptures, and contradictions that readers are asked to respond to in their own "fictions." If the African American writer tries to speak to and for the black community, he or she cannot even be sure that the "black community" of the rundown urban neighborhood of sections such as Philadelphia's Homewood still exists or in what ways it exists. And like

Wideman's characters in *Reuben*, the writer like the narrator of the novel has to give up the dream of ever achieving something like a unified (black) identity (or community): "He'd been something different before and would be something else tomorrow" (*R*, 177). As Wideman put it: "My own sense of identity, or the sense of identity which I am evolving as I write my books, has a lot to do with . . . what is fragmentary, what is discontinuous all the time. I probably believe . . . more than most people that the notion of a stable, underpinning personality is itself a fiction" (*BAM*, 158).

The last novel by an African American writer I want to discuss is a novel of the black diaspora and of multiple, cross-cultural, migratory identities that addresses the interrelations of African American, West Indian, and white American cultures, Paule Marshall's *Daughters*, published in 1991.[25] Marshall grew up in Brooklyn as the daughter of parents who had migrated to the United States from Barbados. In her fiction Marshall has explored and reappropriated her Caribbean background and its links to black Africa and their interrelations to African American life in the United States. *Daughters* "is the story of a family, a marriage, and of the young woman, Ursa Beatrice Mackenzie, who is the sole issue of this marriage," as Marshall describes it in an interview. "Ursa is of dual heritage, American through her mother, a schoolteacher from Connecticut, and West Indian through her father, a leading politician on one of the islands, a man known all his life as 'the PM,' the Prime Minister. *Daughters* is, in part, the story of Ursa's struggle to come to terms not only with her family, especially her father, but with the two worlds she inhabits—America, where she lives, and the island where she spent her childhood."[26] In *Daughters*, Marshall reclaims the history of resistance to slavery in the Caribbean as one of both men and women (the statue of Congo Jane and Will Cudjoe in the novel as a *lieu de mémoire* in Pierre Nora's sense), Ursa's topic for her unwritten PhD thesis (*D*, 11, 29, 94, 376), the U.S. Civil Rights and Black Power Movements (*D*, 212–13, 217–18, 223–24), as well as the contemporary fight for independence in the Caribbean countries against the overpowering imperial influence of the United States (*D*, 222, 308). But the novel is also a critique of the male-dominated politics, of black Caribbean politicians, including Ursa's father, Primus Mackenzie ("P.M."), who stands for reelection, politicians who, even if they are not corrupt, are defeated, in the end, by white political pressure and succumb to the temptation of accommodating white U.S. American political structures and interest groups and betraying the interests of the black community on the island. Only (some) black women succeed in keeping their integrity and taking up the political fight for black people and drawing on the resources, the generations and networks of "daughters," black women "in the community of slaves," to use a reference early in the novel to Angela Davis's essay mentioned earlier (*D*, 12). But Marshall does not offer a simple celebration of female bonding as revolutionary action (the daughters' involvement in P.M.'s final defeat in his bid for reelection), but dramatizes the complexities of male–female relationships in the world of the black diaspora, expressing her hope, as she put it in the interview, "for reconciliation, cooperation, love, unity between black women and men. It's a plea for dialogue, for a willingness to reach out and support and save each other" ("*IPM*," 4).

Paule Marshall's novels of the black diaspora focus on the transnational experience of African Americans in the United States who, at the same time, belong to the hybrid cultures of the Caribbean with their black African roots. In "the multiplicity of [their] voices and languages," in their intertextuality, in their creation of interspaces between "genders, races, nations, and hemispheres" they articulate the multicultural and postcolonial reality of the New World, particularly of black people in the Americas.[27] They map the geographic and historical patterns and cultural and psychological repercussions of multidirectional migrations, of recurrent relocations, "disruptions," and redefinitions of "home," "re-engendering" identity politics by focusing in their narrative voices on dimensions and directions of sexual politics in the experiences of different Afro-Caribbean/American women of several generations (cf. *D*, 148–49, 170, 198, 223, 306, 381 for Estelle; 256, 292, 405 for Ursa). Marshall thinks of her work as "a kind of bridge that joins the two great wings of the black diaspora in this part of the world," and she continues, "my way of seeing the world has been so profoundly shaped by my dual experience, those two communities, West Indian and African-American. Those two great traditions—they nurtured me, they inspired me, they formed me. I am fascinated by the interactions of the two cultures, which is really, as I see it, one tradition, one culture" ("*IPM*," 14, 16). In defining her "dual experience" Marshall takes up and revises W. E. B. DuBois's notion of the double-consciousness of black Americans living in the United States and reaffirms the "self-difference" of African cultures in the Americas, the conflicting intercultural constellations that are, however, as Marshall insists, also one culture. In this sense, Marshall's novels interrogate the complexities of African American double-consciousness by inquiring into the contradictions and the interactions of the dimensions and modes of American, African American, and Caribbean multiple identities and communities. One should add that this Caribbean dimension of cultural identity is in itself multiply divided, not just between blacks and whites, but also among the competing influences of the three major colonial powers, the English, the French, and the Spanish, which had at some time colonized the paradigmatic island Triunion of *Daughters* before the U.S. Americans took over. As Carole Boyce Davies writes in her excellent study *Black Women, Writing and Identity: Migrations of the Subject* (1994), "Ursa journeys in different directions across class, race, sexuality and gender identities as she does physically between the Caribbean and the US."[28]

The writer is situated in a web of interacting cultures, traditions, and locations. Paule Marshall is seen by Carole Boyce Davies as a representative example of Afro-Caribbean women writers in the United States: "[A]ll of these writers tend, for varying reasons and to different degrees, to exist marginally in all the literary traditions to which they belong: namely, African-American literature, Caribbean literature, Caribbean women's writing, African-American women's writing, women's writing, Black writing" (*BW*, 116). Quite convincingly, she reads their works as contributions to a revisionary understanding of postmodernism: "I am asserting consistently that all the postmodernist questions of redefinition of the meaning of identity, of home, of linear history, the metanarratives of the self and identity are destabilized in the writing of Black women's experiences" (*BW*, 116). It is the multiple "marginality" of these writers or, better, their articulations of multiple intercultural border crossings, past and present, that turn their works into challenging examples of what I call *multicultural postmodernism*. Their novels do not pursue the idle dream of "returning home," home as a "haven in a heartless world." There is no reintegration into a new (or old) kind of "wholeness." Ursa returns to the United States: "My life is in the United States, for better or for worse" (*D*, 405). But in negotiating—and writing—multiple cultural identities and creolized languages, performing cultural hybridity and creolization, and transforming migratory subjectivities in an explicitly diasporic, inter-American as well as African American frame, these novels respond to the question of a multicultural postmodernism as the project of mutually interrogating and translating the critical discourses of postmodernism, poststructuralism, feminism, multiculturalism, and postcolonialism.

Postmodern Multiculturalism: African American Literary and Cultural Theory

Since the 1970s, African American writers have explored in their novels and critical reflections the complexities and multiple tensions of hybrid, migrant cultural identities and communities, dramatized in their literary strategies the recuperations and renegotiations of histories and modes and representations of cultural memory, created new visions and modes of a dialogic intertextuality, rearticulated the critique and enabling visions of feminist reconstructions of the African American experience, and remapped the vicissitudes and cultural power of transnational, cross-cultural diasporas. The novels discussed in this essay can be seen as fictions of an African American multicultural postmodernism, and they can also be read as a call by writers whom African American literary and cultural theorists have responded to in their studies since the late 1980s. Overcoming their skeptical rejection of the concepts of postmodernism and multiculturalism, some of these critics have transculturated these critical discourses and reinscribed African American cultural practices into contemporary cultural critique. They have redefined African American literature and culture and, finally, American literatures and cultures as articulations of a transnational *postmodern multiculturalism*, if I may switch the words for this purpose.

In her essay "Postmodern Blackness" (1990), the black feminist critic bell hooks criticizes the limitations of most writings on postmodernism, as they are constructed against white "high modernism" and ignore the literatures and cultures of blacks and other minority groups, but she still argues for the "relevance" of a "radical postmodernism" for African Americans: "Radical postmodernist practice, most powerfully conceptualized as a 'politics of difference,' should incorporate the voices of displaced, marginalized, exploited, and oppressed people."[29] She accepts the postmodern critique of notions of stable, authentic identities and community and explores its repercussions for a critique of black "essentialism," but she turns the critique into the productive work of the construction of *multiple* black identities and of *new* and *varied* forms of community ("bonding"). Hooks strongly emphasizes the political implications of her reflections on "postmodern blackness" for the affirmation of "agency" in relation to "racial difference and racial domination." But her explicitly "postmodern oppositional sensibility" also leads her to open up postmodern blackness to the wider context of a multicultural society and the possibility of forging in the process of "decolonization" new coalitions among other groups sharing with black Americans a "sense of deep alienation, despair, uncertainty, loss of sense of grounding": "Radical postmodernism calls attention to those shared sensibilities which cross the boundaries of class, gender, race, etc., that could be fertile ground for the construction of empathy—ties that would promote recognition of common commitments, and serve as a base for solidarity and coalition" (Y, 27).

Bell hooks's reflections find confirmation in Wahneema Lubiano's essay "Shuckin' Off the African-American Other: What's 'Po-Mo' Got to Do with It?" (1991).[30] In spite of the unquestionable shortcomings, the fashionable superficiality, and the ideological slant of some of the postmodernist theory Lubiano uses, she is able to *resituate* and *reinscribe* the specific "otherness" of historical experiences and cultural productions of difference in the "political African-American postmodernist project" into the contemporary debate and political fights about cultural differences and social conflicts ("*SO*," 153). "We can consider African-American postmodernism as not simply a historical moment when modernism's intellectual and cultural hegemony is at least being questioned, but as a general epistemological standpoint for engaging/foregrounding what has been left out of larger discourses, a consideration of certain kinds of difference and the reasons for their historical absences" ("*SO*," 158). This postmodern African American cultural and political project, however, has to find its "internal critique" in the articulation of gender difference, in an "African-American feminist postmodernism" ("*SO*," 160).

In her essay Lubiano refers to the studies of Gayatri Spivak, Bruce Robbins, Dick Hebdige, David Harvey, Fredric Jameson, Craig Owens, Hal Foster, Stuart Hall, and Hortense Spillers on postmodernism theory, but her crucial references are to the work of Cornel West on the "dilemma of the Black intellectual" and "new cultural politics of difference." Philosopher Cornel West has again and again rejected common liberal versions of multiculturalism as well as their essentialist, separatist counterparts. Yet his own project of defining black postmodernism and a "new cultural politics of difference" in the postmodern age is deeply informed by the crucial dimensions and concepts of the discourse of a radical multiculturalism, such as difference, heterogeneity, hybridity, and diaspora. "Why the term 'postmodern'? The term postmodern becomes useful—though in many ways it does obscure and obfuscate—precisely because it helps us situate a new kind of culture being created in the midst of the restructuring of the capitalist international order."[31] In his numerous essays West "historicize[s] and pluralize[s] and contextualize[s] the postmodernism debate."[32] West offers a genealogy of three "historical coordinates for radical cultural criticism today: the "Age of Europe," from 1492 to 1945 (the dialectics of the Enlightenment, the "idea of Europe," with "race" as a constitutive issue, Europe as "always already multicultural" and "multinational"); the emergence of the United States as *the* world power after 1945 ("which sets the immediate context for the emergence of the problematic of postmodernism, of difference, of heterogeneity and so forth"); and the decolonization of the Third World during the twentieth century, particularly since World War II, that has brought the "American Century" to its end and has shattered the liberal consensus and fueled the Civil Rights Movement and protest movements by other minorities and disadvantaged groups, challenging the dominance of a white male Anglo-Saxon culture (*BEM*, 1: 129, 136–37, 140; 2: 121).

The interplay of these "ambiguous legacies" and "hybrid cultures in history" (*BEM*, 1: 4) during the past decades has defined culture and society in the United States and produced postmodernism as a "profoundly American phenomenon": "Because in fact it is the response to the degree to which modernism became part of the ideological arsenal used in the cold war against the Soviets, and the attempt of younger artists, painters, architects, and others to revolt against the modernisms whose own transgressive power was seemingly highly circumscribed, diluted, absorbed, co-opted and so on" (*BEM*, 1: 124). Postmodern culture is neither simply a "set of styles, forms, and figures," nor Lyotard's philosophical notion of the demise of "grand narratives," nor Baudrillard's reflections on the "saturation of simulacra and simulation in consumer-driven America," nor Foucault's or Derrida's poststructuralism (*BEM*, 2: 38). Instead, the postmodern moment in the United States is characterized by a constellation of several intermingling processes, namely the appropriation, the "Americanization" of traveling theories from postwar Europe, from the Frankfurt school to French postmetaphysical philosophy (*qua* poststructuralism), the revisions of American history by the recovery of those formerly excluded, "the workers, the women, African Americans, Native Americans, Latino/a Americans, gays and lesbians, and so forth," and the impact of forms of popular culture (film, television, music) on what used to be called and revered after the European fashion as high culture (cf. *BEM*, 1: 138; 2: 38).

It is this postmodern context of cultural heterogeneity, plurality, dehierarchization, and dissensus that has made us aware that all cultures are hybrid, processes of cross-cultural interaction and translation, are always cultures of difference, multicultures in historically changing constellations.

It is the task of black intellectuals to situate their critiques of postmodern American culture in the specific social and political contexts of the United States and their ambiguous and hybrid critical discourses and to foster, as West writes, "credible sensibilities for an active critical citizenry," for "cultural" and "democratic" citizenship, radical democratic practices West finds most powerfully conceptualized in John Dewey's version of American pragmatism (cf. *BEM*, 1: 19; 2: 123, 129–30, 140–42). But this focus on the specific context of the United States must immediately raise the question of intercultural difference. For American Cultural Studies "in the postmodern crisis," West asks for a *critical* reception of traveling British Cultural Studies, which completely dominated the well-known 1990 Cultural Studies Conference at the University of Illinois at Urbana-Champaign. He insists on a "transculturation" that recognizes the achievements and the blindnesses of European theories in the different U.S. American context *and* on a reappropriation of the "tradition of very important left cultural reflections" in the United States in American Studies, in American Marxism, and Women's Studies ("*PC*," 693).

For his *new* "cultural politics of difference" this means that West grounds it in the "decolonized sensibilities [that] fanned and fueled the Civil Rights and Black Power movements, as well as the student antiwar, feminist, gray, brown, gay, and lesbian movements"[33] and in the rich diversity as well as the ravages of the black experience, committed to the "quest for identity" and "quest for community" in a time threatened by "black nihilism" (*BEM*, 2: 122). Yet in reclaiming specific black American alternative traditions and forms of cultural representation in postmodern times, West articulates their *hybrid*, *intercultural*, *cross-cultural*, *transnational* dimensions. The black intellectual—and writer—is always already positioned not only in a complex, interrelated, contested force field of other cultures and discourses in the heterogeneous multiculture of the United States, but also in a transnational "black diaspora" in a quest for validation and recognition. Confronting the full implications of the "black diaspora" concept, elaborated in the black British critic Paul Gilroy's challenging study *The Black Atlantic: Modernity and Double Consciousness* (1993), means for Cornel West to reject the notions of an "essential Black subject" or community, to recognize "blackness" as a "politically and culturally *constructed* category" (Stuart Hall).[34] It also means to encounter the "politics of representation" in a new cultural politics of difference as it has been explored by radical black diaspora intellectuals, particularly by the Black Women's Movement, by "the powerful critiques and constructive explorations of Black diaspora women (i.e., Toni Morrison)": "Following the model of the Black diaspora traditions of music, athletics, and rhetoric, Black cultural workers must constitute and sustain discursive and institutional networks that deconstruct earlier modern Black strategies for identity formation, demystify power relations that incorporate class, patriarchal, and homophobic biases, and construct more multivalent and multidimensional responses that articulate the complexity and diversity of Black practices in the modern and postmodern world" ("*NCPD*," 104–105). In deconstructing and demystifying traditional binary oppositions such as blackness/whiteness and showing how "Whiteness" is a "politically constructed category parasitic on 'Blackness,'" the postmodern black diaspora intellectual reveals in what West calls "prophetic criticism" the "powerfully hybrid character of what we mean by 'race,' 'ethnicity,' and 'nationality'" *and* discloses options and alternatives for transformative political and cultural praxis ("*NCPD*," 105).

If bell hooks, Wahneema Lubiano, and Cornel West have redefined and resituated the concept of postmodernism for African American literary and cultural critique, Henry Louis Gates, Jr., has done something similar for multiculturalism. His widely influential books *Figures in Black: Words, Signs, and the "Racial" Self* (1987) and *The Signifying Monkey: A Theory of Afro-American Literary Criticism* (1988) account for his own development as a critical theorist in relation to the development of African American literary criticism.[35] Gates acknowledges the historical reasons for the "resistance to theory among critics of black literature" (*FIB*, xix), a resistance to Western "logocentrism" and ethnological appropriation, but counters the skepticism by arguing for the existence of a rich black tradition that has powerfully "theorized about itself" and has produced works of literature that stand up to the most sophisticated and self-reflexive literary theory (*SM*, ix). For Gates, the major task of African American literary theory is to combine a critical engagement with "advanced" Western literary theory and a reclaiming of the indigenous theory of the African American vernacular tradition in order to work out a "double-voiced" theory of reading for the inescapable "double-voicedness" of black literary texts: "The challenge of black literary criticism is to derive principles of literary criticism from the black tradition itself, as defined in the idiom of critical theory but also in the idiom that constitutes the language of blackness, the Signifyin(g) difference that makes the black tradition our very own" (*FIB*, 54; cf. *SM*, xxiii). This specifically black literary theory takes shape as a theory of "reading" that is generated from the "extraordinarily self-reflexive" African and African American vernacular traditions of "signifying," a theory of "textual revisions," of intertextuality that also explores the relations of the black *oral* tradition to the African American *literary* tradition: "This process of intertextual relations I call Signifyin(g), the trope of revision and difference, which I take from the Afro-American idiom" (*FIB*, xxx; cf. *SM*, xx–xxv). Gates did not try to reaffirm anything like an "essential blackness" of African American literature, but to expound and rearticulate the specific historical dynamics of a tradition of African American literature in the con-*textual* force field of African, European, white American, and African American literatures. Black literary theory "defamiliarizes" the texts of the black tradition, creating a distance between readers and texts that reveals their specific double-voiced formal dynamics that is "comparatist, by definition" and that is reconstructive, as, "because of the experience of diaspora, the fragments that contain the traces of a coherent system of order must be reassembled" (*SM*, xxiv; cf. *FIB*, xxiv).

Henry Louis Gates, Jr., has applied his theory of African American literary criticism to the whole tradition of black literature in the United States since its beginnings, but in its most advanced form it was generated by and found its most challenging expression in his analysis of the works of Ishmael Reed. Gates uses different versions of his essay "The Blackness of Blackness: A Critique of the Sign and the Signifying Monkey," which culminates in a subtle analysis of Reed's novel *Mumbo Jumbo*, an essay originally published in *Critical Inquiry* in 1983, as the final chapter in the programmatic collections of essays he edited as *Black Literature and Literary Theory* (1984), and in his own *Figures in Black*.[36] He uses it again in his book *The Signifying Monkey*, where it shares the most prominent position with a penetrating interpretation of Alice Walker's "(re)writing of the speakerly text" of Zora Neale Hurston's novel *Their Eyes Were Watching God* in her own novel *The Color Purple*. It is in this essay on Reed that he takes up the term "postmodernism" to describe the complex, highly self-reflexive formal features of Reed's novels in their revisionary relationship to the black oral and literary traditions, to different lines in black and white literary history, to conflicting philosophical and religious traditions on several continents, to the interplay of different artistic genres and media of communication, and to the multicultural matrix that generated his fiction: "I intend here to discuss the relationship of Ishmael Reed's Signifyin(g) postmodernism to Richard Wright's realism and Ralph Ellison's modernism" (*SM*, 111, cf. *FIB*, 247; *BLLT*, 294). Reed's work is seen as the highly self-reflexive, double-voiced, signifyin(g), multiply parodic "fusion" of a complex, mutually revisionary African American literary tradition defined, in different ways, by Jean Toomer, Ralph Ellison, Sterling Brown, Richard Wright, and Zora Neale Hurston (see *FIB*, 248; *BLLT*, 295), a genealogical chart that Gates extends in *The Signifying Monkey* to complement the contemporary scene of African American writing by adding Amiri Baraka, Toni Morrison, and, more pronouncedly, Alice Walker. *Mumbo Jumbo*, Gates writes, is "a novel about writing itself—not only in the figurative sense of the postmodern, self-reflexive text but also in the literal sense: 'So Jes Grew is seeking its words. Its text. For what good is a liturgy without a text?' Mumbo Jumbo is both a book about texts and a book of texts, a composite narrative composed of subtexts, pretexts, posttexts, and narratives-within-narratives. It is both a definition of Afro-American culture and its deflation" (*SM*, 220; cf. *FIB*, 252; *BLLT*, 298). Gates uses Reed's intermedia literary performance of the deconstruction of both the Western tradition and black modernist writing of blackness as a negative essence *and* of its (historically crucial) reversal in the Black Arts Movement's revisionary gesture of blackness as a trope of presence in his argument in order to resituate postmodern self-reflexivity in a historically specific hybrid, con-textual matrix and to turn his analysis of the *indeterminacy* of the text of blackness, of its inherent double-voicedness and its processes of signifyin(g) into a *dialogic*, productive act of reading (cf. *SM*, 237; *FIB*, 275; *BLLT*, 316).

Gates's "indigenous" black literary theory is, by definition, "impure," is characterized by concepts such as formal revision, double-voicedness, signifyin(g) difference, indeterminacy, repetition with a difference, self-reflexivity, pastiche, parody, hidden polemic, inner dialogization (Bakhtin), discontinuity, fragmentary, hybridity, intertextuality, and diaspora, and in this sense a version of black postmodernist theory. Since the beginning of the 1990s Gates has expanded and refocused his theoretical work, explicitly engaging with feminist theory, postcolonial theory, British (Black) Cultural Studies, and other projects of contemporary theories of culture in various disciplines.[37] In the United States, he rearticulates his vision of an indigenous, double-voiced, black postmodernist literary theory in the public context of the debate on multiculturalism and the concomitant "border discourses" of hybridity, creolization, and diaspora. In the introduction to *Loose Canons: Notes on the Culture Wars* (1992), he writes, "Debates about multiculturalism have given to literary studies a renewed urgency."[38] His commitment to elaborating the cultural, political, civic implications and repercussions of the notion and the program of a multicultural society could, in some (ironic) way, be read as a revisionary "repetition with a difference" of, or a critical act of signifyin(g) on, his most celebrated writer Ishmael Reed's turn from Neo-HooDooism to the literary program of multiculturalism during the second half of the 1970s.

Gates's explorations of the potential of multiculturalism fully acknowledges the critique of the liberal multiculturalism of "cultural diversity," of its "culturalist" reductionism by the displacement of the differential of "power" by "cultural difference" and of "race" by "ethnicity," and of the "obfuscating," ideological use it invites or entails, as Hazel Carby has convincingly shown in her essay "The Multicultural Wars" (1992).[39] Obviously, he also rejects any kind of ethnic fundamentalism and essentialist interest-group politics posing as "multiculturalism." But Gates does not simply dismiss multiculturalism as another capitalist ploy; rather, he tries to work out its dialectics, its limitations, as well as its critical potential in dealing with the very different dimensions and forms of cultural difference in contemporary (postmodern, post-Fordist) societies. In engaging in a critical dialogue with the culturalist version of multiculturalism and its critique by black and postcolonial critics and philosophers, Gates unfolds the inherent "paradoxes" of the social construction of cultural differences, of a new culture concept defined as the outcome of "intercultural relations of forces," of a revisionary notion of cultural identities in process and in dialogue. In his essay "Notes on the Culture Wars: Identities in Dialogue" (1993), he projects a new kind of "liberation politics" beyond pregiven, unified "emancipatory" identities and identitarian politics, a vision of the "modern polity [as] a dynamic space in which citizenship is always being contested rather than the fixed space of the premodern ideal of a republic."[40] For Gates, multiculturalism cannot be an affirmative, revolutionary utopian program in culture and politics, nor is it "relativistic" in the sense of the denial of any "inter-personal criteria of rationality," which would make cross-cultural understanding impossible. Instead, multiculturalism is a "radically anti-utopian" kind of pluralism that rejects all sorts of final solutions, primordial cultural authenticity or purity, or enforced consensus, but accepts its limitations and delves into the "messy affair of cultural variegation" ("*NCW*," 11), the dynamics of identities in dialogue, cultures as sites of contest, process, and negotiations. As Gates writes in another essay, the pluralism of his notion of multiculturalism is not based on a concept of culture that sees it as the fixed property of particular ethnic groups or as based on homogeneity and consensus, but on one that sees it as "porous, dynamic, and interactive."[41] This understanding of multiculturalism also deconstructs the common notion of a monolithic, homogeneous "West" that has to be rejected wholesale and opens up the debate to a study of the "hybrid and variegated nature of our modernity (*LC*, xvi)," even more of post-modernity: "[T]he world we live in is multicultural already. Mixing and hybridity is the rule, not the exception" ("*PID*," 75).

The notion of American culture as hybrid and multicultural, as process, contest, dialogue, and negotiation leads Gates to take up Lionel Trilling's idea of culture as a "struggle, or at least a debate—it is nothing if not a dialectic," outlined in the essay "Reality in America" in *The Liberal Imagination* (1950).[42] Even though Trilling's critique of modernism and his moral commitment as a "man of letters" have been more favorably reassessed by Gates and West in recent years, as against the usual dismissal of his work as a prime example of the shortcomings of 1950s "liberalism," Gates's suggestion that we "should try to think of American culture as a conversation among different voices" is a "repetition with a difference," for he adds"—even if it's a conversation that some of us weren't able to join until recently."[43] Therefore, *if* there is a need for a "common culture," it is *not* something that has to be defended against the impact, the assaults of minorities and adherents of multiculturalism demanding a piece of the cake, but it is a *project of the future*, the *quest* for a "truly common public culture, one responsive to the long-silenced cultures of color" (*LC*, 176; "*GBC*," 713). In the introduction to *Loose Canons*, Gates writes: "Ours is a late twentieth-century world profoundly fissured by nationality, ethnicity, race, class, and gender. And the only way to transcend those divisions—to forge, for once, a civic culture that respects both differences and commonalities—is through education that seeks to comprehend the diversity of human culture" (*LC*, xv). Characterizing his own critical position as one of a "reformed/pluralist liberalism," but one that is inextricably linked and fused with "radical/left politics," in his essay "Trading on the Margins: Notes on the Culture of Criticism" Gates adds: "So it's only when we're free to *explore* the complexities of our hyphenated American culture that we can *discover* what a genuinely common American culture *might* look like" (*LC*, 175–76, my emphasis).

Obviously, Gates's vision of transcending "those divisions" and building up a "genuinely common American culture" through education has to be articulated in a much more radical engagement with the critical potential of the border discourses and of the discourses of transculturation and cultural translation he had explored and elaborated in his most advanced literary theory and criticism. Indeed, his essays on multiculturalism and the "culture wars" situate this critical project in the context of a postcolonial, transnational perspective and of the move toward internationalizing American (Culture) Studies. For Gates, the struggle to realize a genuinely multicultural public or civic culture in the United States manifests itself in the debate over the "politics of representation" (in the double sense) and over revising the canon in literary and cultural studies. These culture wars also show that the conventional way of discussing these issues has become totally inadequate. The hybrid and diasporic quality of the American multiculture asks cultural critics to transcend the limits of parochial "minority" cultures as well as the abstractions of generalizing (or totalizing) high theory from Marxism to postcolonialism and insist on the particularity and the case-specific reach of cultural theories. This also means that multicultural critique in the United States not only has to explode the narrow frame of national boundaries and explore the meaning of "America" in its complex cross-cultural interrelationships, but also has to reconceive the explanatory model for understanding the role of the United States in a global context. Gates draws on the reflections on the consequences of the demise of Eastern bloc Communism and the globalization processes in the economy, in communication, and in the circulation of U.S. American mass culture by the historian David Brion Davis and the anthropologist Arjun Appadurai, who point out how fatuous it would be to see these developments basically as the final "Americanization" of the world. In spite of the tremendous, worldwide power of the United States, it would be seriously mistaken and wrongheaded to identify "globalization" with "Americanization." The old center–periphery model in international political analysis and its concomitant notion of American cultural imperialism is seriously reductive and arrogant, even in versions that "'might account for multiple centers and peripheries'" (Appadurai, quoted in *LC*, 191), as it fails to do justice to the specificities of the complex and contested interactions of cultures, the processes of transculturation in the encounters of cultures, *including* radical changes in U.S. American culture, and the alternative articulations of other cultures of difference all over the world. The working out of a multicultural "common" political or civic culture in and of the United States in an era of "transnational capital, transnational labor, and transnational culture" (*LC*, 190) has to be situated in the force field of the multiple dialogical interrelationships of a new global cultural economy that is, as Appadurai elaborates, a "'complex, overlapping, disjunctive order'" (Appadurai, quoted in *LC*, 191).

Gates briefly suggests that "American studies is surely the proper site to begin a study of both the globalization of America and the Americanization of the globe—and, equally, the resistance bred by both of these trends" (*LC*, 192). This new agenda for (U.S.) American Studies returns us to the genealogy and the crucial role African American Studies can play in pursuing this project. Gates's claim that "what is often referred to loosely as the 'multicultural' movement traces its origins in the academy to the birth of Afro-American Studies in the late 1960s" (*LC*, xii) certainly is fully justified only if we read it to include Ishmael Reed's move toward a less "cultural nationalist" concept and project of multiculturalism during the 1970s. But Gates is right when he argues that for a student of African American culture the insight that American culture is multicultural, mixed, hybrid, a palimpsest has always been taken for granted by black writers, artists, and critics. "African-American culture, then, has been a model of multiculturalism and plurality. And it is this cultural impulse, I believe, that represents the very best hope for us, collectively, to forge a new, and vital, common American culture in the twenty-first century" (*LC*, xvii). In a later interview he elaborates this observation: "I mean, if you're black American, the idea of hybridity and creolization which Todorov and all these people are just discovering is part and parcel of your everyday historical experience. The African-American culture is a hybrid, but so is American culture. It's just that America's been in denial about that hybridity, that cross-pollination, that creolization for centuries. My understanding of multiculturalism depends on bringing these subterranean cultures—that which has been buried, that which has been denied, that which has been repressed—to the surface and redefining our common public culture, because our common public culture has always been hybrid."[44]

This crucial and formative role of African American Cultural Studies for understanding or, better, for creating a fully multicultural and cosmopolitan public or civic "American" culture, for reconceiving American Studies at large, gives Gates's project of an anti-utopian, pragmatist, pluralist multiculturalism its radical substance. It demands, however, that the new African American Studies seriously explore "the hyphen in African-American, on both sides of the Atlantic," chart "both the moments of continuity and discontinuity between African cultures and African American cultures" (*LC*, 125). It also demands a more radical investigation of the transnational perspectives of the black diaspora beyond the old claims of a "heritage" and "home territory" of one's own, as it has been pursued so incisively in British Black Cultural Studies by scholars like Paul Gilroy, Stuart Hall, and Kobena Mercer.[45] Also, the interrelations among African Americans and other minority cultures have to be given more attention. Some more recent remarks by Gates about the current and future stages of African American literary criticism may be taken to point in this direction (*BLLT*, 21; cf. *LC*, 102–103). Gates himself adds an additional dimension when he writes in another version of his essay "African American Studies in the 21st Century" about the mutually enriching interrelationships between humanistic scholarship in the West and "in Asian and African cultures" (*LC*, 6). But for Gates this whole agenda for the next century has *two* crucial and urgent interconnected objectives, "an emphasis upon cultural studies *and* public policy, as two broad and fruitful rubrics under which to organize our discipline" (*LC*, 124, my emphasis). Gates's commitment to public policy, his project for working as a public intellectual is based on his dialogic, anti-utopian multiculturalism and shares with Cornel West a critical indebtedness to the tradition of American pragmatist thought, particularly to John Dewey (*LC*, 118–20).

American Literature(s) and Culture(s) as Multicultural Postmodernisms

The critical analysis of contemporary African American novels and literary and cultural critique in terms of cultural hybridity and diasporic discourses has shown that the very term "African American" is used in a manner too restrictive and in some cases misleading if it defines the scope and horizon of "black writing" exclusively from the perspective of the United States. This is not so much a question of terminology, of looking for *the* exact term, as the term "black," obviously, also has serious shortcomings and drawbacks, as a question of explicitly decentering the critical discourse of hybridity and diaspora in understanding African American/black writings by exposing the multiple, conflicting, and multidirectional intercultural relations that provide the dynamics of these texts and approaching them from different locations in a dialogic manner. The fictions of an African American multicultural postmodernism have explored and dramatized some of these dimensions and transgressive modes of the wider scope of African American literatures, especially the African and Afro-Caribbean interconnections. African American critics have elaborated these intercultural genealogies as well as the current cross-cultural, intertextual interrelations in their projects of a vernacular, indigenous theory of African American literature (Henry Louis Gates, Jr., Houston A. Baker, Jr.) and reinscribed these vernacular literary theories in a challenging theory of postmodern American culture. In this theory of a postmodern multiculturalism, African American critics have succeeded in elaborating, from a postcolonial and/or feminist position, the intercultural dynamics of the hybridity of African American cultures in the United States *and* the transnational, cross-cultural contact zones (Mary Louise Pratt) of the black diaspora on different continents, an awareness that has begun to decenter African American cultural critique and to include the specific cultures of difference of the Black Atlantic and of diasporic cultures of "black" people in Great Britain and other countries.

Of course, the analysis of contemporary African American fiction and literary and cultural theory in its emphasis on the dimensions and repercussions of cultural hybridity and diasporic discourses is only one, though undoubtedly a very important case study in the analysis of multicultural postmodernism in the United States. If we want to get a fuller vision and grasp of the wide range of literary voices of a multicultural postmodernism and of the different projects of literary and cultural theorizing, we have to complement, and correct, this exemplary discussion by looking at texts written by members of other minority groups and cultures of difference. The very concepts of cultural hybridity and diaspora are, of course, not exclusive to African American culture, but have been articulated in very heterogeneous historical and geographical contexts. Homi Bhabha's highly influential theory of hybridity was developed in contexts of British colonialism and the postcolonial world of the newly independent states, and it cannot be applied to the U.S. American experience without considerable qualifications. Also, hybridity as a concept has played a crucial role in recent Latin American critical debates on the contacts and conflicts of cultures that have characterized the history of those countries. It has been further extended in Néstor García Canclini's postmodern notion of *culturas híbridas*, which tries to explain the recent cultural processes of migration, exile, the globalization of mass culture, the transformation and derealization of social space, and the instability of meanings and flow of discontinuous images in the fragmented world of today.[46] Or the diaspora concept refers back to the Jewish experience and had to be redefined in its application to the black diaspora, the Black Atlantic, as Paul Gilroy has done in his magisterial study *The Black Atlantic.* The critical notion of diasporic discourses takes on even more strikingly different forms when it refers to the diasporic experiences of "Asian American" communities and cultures that are constituted transnationally by different legal, political, and racial positionings. Moreover, the other key concepts of border discourses mentioned earlier, such as creolization, border cultures/crossings, and *mestizaje*, have been employed and redefined according to their specific historical, political, social, and cultural situations by other U.S. American groups of "minority cultures" or "cultures of difference." Let me only refer to the crucially formative role of physical and cultural border crossings, creolizing languages, and "mestiza consciousness" in Gloria Anzaldúa's powerful book *Borderlands / La Frontera* (1987) or the specific historical modes of the creolization or hybridization of cultures in Louise Erdrich's novels that dramatize, through conflicting voices and often hybrid strategies of writing, the intercultural struggles as well as the creative agency that define Native American culture today (that inform the most challenging discussions of these issues and their implications for reconceiving American Studies).[47]

In characterizing what I have called multicultural postmodernism I have talked about multiple identities and unstable communities, and taken up terms such as transculturation, border cultures/crossings, cultural hybridity, *mestizaje*, creolization, and diaspora in order to grasp the achievements, the challenges, and the specific forms of articulation in the writings of history, rememory, and interculturality by members of minority groups in the United States. Unquestionably, writers and critics of these differently constituted "minority cultures" have explored much more penetratingly than in the past not just the diverse conflicts and interactions between their own group and the (white) dominant majority culture, but particularly the multiple fault lines of cultural difference within their own group culture as well as the inherent differences in what had been seen before as a monolithic white dominant culture. What still has to be done more persistently is the exploration, in fiction and in theory, of the interplay and the negotiations between *several different* minority cultures or border cultures themselves, as the common notion of more or less clearly defined cultural groups, including ethnic groups, has been superseded in social reality by cultural mixing and hybridity in terms of race, ethnicity, and other dimensions of multiculturality. Minority and feminist discourses have made crucial and energizing contributions to the theory of postmodernism and multiculturalism in the United States. It is here that a concept at crucial points referred to in this essay, the concept of cultural translation, as it has been suggested by Homi Bhabha, or of cultural translatability, as theorized, in a different manner, by Wolfgang Iser, promises to offer discursive strategies that can explore the interplay of the critical terms of border discourses and articulate these complex and contested processes of transculturation in a globalizing world, but only if they remain conscious of the inescapable ambivalence and indeterminacy of acts of "cultural translation," renounce the notion of "a space between cultures," and are conceived and performed in an explicitly dialogical manner.[48]

The focus on minority cultures and cultures of difference in this essay does not mean, however, that the notions of multicultural identities and communities, of multiple subject positions and locations in space and time, of what can be called border discourses apply only to texts written by authors from minorities or marginalized groups. What the discussion of the selected texts in the essay has shown, it seems to me, is that they must be seen as characteristic, in different ways of course, of all Americans, of American culture, or American cultures, in the plural, at large. "American," in this sense, is not limited to the United States, but even if we direct our critical attention explicitly to the United States, we find that in the postmodern U.S. American multiculture everybody is a "mixed blood"; cultural identities and communities are always unstable, changing, and intercultural and have always to be negotiated in new ways. A closer study of the "experimental" fiction of "white" American writers will show that some of them have increasingly realized that their own writings are to be part of the project of a multicultural postmodernism. For American Culture Studies today and in the future, therefore, the discourses of postmodernism and multiculturalism are in complex ways interrelated and qualify and define each other. Postmodernism has always to be seen as inherently multicultural and multiculturalism as radically postmodern.

APPENDIX: PUBLICATIONS OF PROFESSOR DR. GÜNTER H. LENZ (1940–2012)

Books

1970 *Die Dichtungstheorie S. T. Coleridges: Die Imagination als Paradigma der romantischen Poetologie*, Neue Beiträge zur Anglistik und Amerikanistik, Band 9 (Frankfurt: Athenäum), 334 pp. Summary: "S. T. Coleridge's Theory of Poetry: The Paradigmatic Role of the Concept of the Imagination in Romantic Poetics," in Werner Habicht, ed., *English and American Studies in German, 1971* (Tübingen: M. Niemeyer, 1972), 100–102.

1977 *Amerikastudien: Theorie, Geschichte, interpretatorische Praxis*, Sonderband, Amerikastudien /American Studies (Stuttgart: Reclam), 287 pp. (coedited with Martin Christadler).

1984 *History and Tradition in Afro-American Culture* (Frankfurt: Campus), 334 pp. (edited). Summary: Werner Habicht, ed., *English and American Studies in German, 1984* (Tübingen: M. Niemeyer, 1985), 149–51.

1986 *The Crisis of Modernity: Recent Critical Theories of Culture and Society in the United States and West Germany* (Frankfurt: Campus; Boulder, CO: Westview Press), 374 pp. (coedited with Kurt L. Shell). Summary: Horst Weinstock, ed., *English and American Studies in German, 1986* (Tübingen: M. Niemeyer, 1987), 155–58.

1990 *Reconstructing American Literary and Historical Studies* (Frankfurt: Campus; New York: St. Martin's Press), 435 pp. (coedited with Hartmut Keil and Sabine Bröck-Sallah). Summary: Horst Weinstock, ed., *English and American Studies in Germany, 1990* (Tübingen: M. Niemeyer, 1991), 112–15.

1993 *Afro-Amerika im amerikanischen Dokumentarfilm* (Trier: Wissenschaftlicher Verlag Trier), 242 pp. (edited, essays in English or German).

1994 *Der amerikanische Dokumentarfilm: Herausforderungen für die Didaktik* (Tübingen: Gunter Narr), 232 pp. (coedited with Lothar Bredella).

1995 *American Studies in Germany: European Contexts and Intercultural Relations* (Frankfurt: Campus; New York: St. Martin's Press), 280 pp. (coedited with Klaus J. Milich).

1998 *Amerikanische Kurzgeschichten im 20. Jahrhundert* (Stuttgart: Reclam), 670 pp. (edited).

2000 *TransAtlantic Encounters: Multiculturalism, National Identity, and the Uses of the Past* (Amsterdam: VU University Press), 198 pp. (coedited with Peter J. Ling).

2003 *Postmodern New York City: Transfiguring Spaces—Raum-Transfigurationen* (Heidelberg: Universitätsverlag Winter), 357 pp. (coedited with Utz Riese).

2006 *CinematoGraphies: Fictional Strategies and Visual Discourses in 1990s New York City* (Heidelberg: Universitätsverlag Winter), 360 pp. (coedited with Dorothea Löbbermann and Karl-Heinz Magister).

2006 *Toward a New Metropolitanism: Reconstituting Public Culture, Urban Citizenship, and the Multicultural Imaginary in New York and Berlin* (Heidelberg: Universitätsverlag Winter), 496 pp. (coedited with Friedrich Ulfers and Antje Dallmann).

Essays

1972 "Von der Erkenntnis der literarischen Struktur zur Struktur der literarischen Erkenntnis: Metakritische Bemerkungen zu R. S. Crane und Northrop Frye," *Jahrbuch für Amerikastudien* 17: 100–27.

1973 "James Baldwin," in Martin Christadler, ed., *Amerikanische Literatur der Gegenwart in Einzeldarstellungen* (Stuttgart: Kröner), 155–89.

1974 "Der Einspruch der Geschichte: Idealistische Ästhetik und klassizistische Praxis im Hinblick auf Hölderlins Empedokles-Projekt," in Kuno Schuhmann, Wilhelm Hortmann, and Armin Paul Frank, eds., *Miscellanea Anglo-Americana: Festschrift für Helmut Viebrock* (Munich: Karl Pressler), 231–78 (with Klaus Hofmann).

1977 "American Studies—Wissenschaftskritik und Wissenschaftsgeschichte: Bemerkungen zur neueren Theoriediskussion um die American Studies in den USA," in Martin Christadler and Günter H. Lenz, eds., *Amerikastudien: Theorie, Geschichte, interpretatorische Praxis*, Sonderband, Amerikastudien / American Studies (Stuttgart: Reclam), 29–103.

1981 "Southern Exposures: The Urban Experience and the Re-Construction of Black Folk Culture and Community in the Works of Richard Wright and Zora Neale Hurston," *New York Folklore* 7 (Summer): 3–39. Revised version also in Günter H. Lenz, ed., *History and Tradition in Afro-American Culture* (Frankfurt: Campus, 1984) , 84–117.

1982 "American Studies: Beyond the Crisis? Recent Redefinitions and the Meaning of Theory, History, and Practical Criticism," in Jack Salzman, ed., *Prospects 7: An Annual of American Cultural Studies* (Cambridge: Cambridge University Press), 53–113.

1983 "Gettoerfahrung, Gettokultur, Gettoliteratur: Zur afroamerikanischen Literatur zwischen den Weltkriegen (1914–1945)," in Berndt Ostendorf, ed., *Amerikanische Gettoliteratur: Zur Literatur ethnischer, marginaler und unterdrückter Gruppen in den USA* (Darmstadt: Wissenschaftliche Buchgesellschaft), 149–233.

1984 "American Studies—Amerikastudien—Landeskunde: Probleme einer Didaktik der Amerikastudien," in Lothar Bredella, ed., *Die USA in Unterricht und Forschung* (Bochum: Kamp), 22–39.

1984 "Black Poetry and Black Music—History and Tradition: Michael Harper and John Coltrane," in Günter H. Lenz, ed., *History and Tradition in Afro-American Culture* (Frankfurt: Campus), 277–326.

1985 "Urban Ghetto, Symbolic Space, and Communal Rituals: Zur literarischen

Verarbeitung Harlems in der Harlem Renaissance," in Lothar Bredella, ed., *Das Verstehen einer paradoxen Epoche in Schule und Hochschule: The American 1920s* (Bochum: Kamp), 78–113.

1986 "Ishmael Reed," in Hedwig Bock and Albert Wertheim, eds., *Essays on the Contemporary American Novel* (Munich: Hueber), 305–34.

1986 "Tradition, Discontinuity, and Counterdiscourse: Some Problems in American Radical Cultural Criticism Since the 1960s," in Günter H. Lenz and Kurt L. Shell, eds., *The Crisis of Modernity* (Frankfurt: Campus; Boulder, CO: Westview Press), 191–249.

1986 "'Making Our Own Future Text': Neo-HooDooism, Postmodernism, and the Novels of Ishmael Reed," in Winfried Herget, K. P. Jochum, and Ingeborg Weber, eds., *Theorie und Praxis im Erzählen des 19. und 20. Jahrhunderts: Studien zur englischen und amerikanischen Literatur zu Ehren von Willi Erzgräber* (Tübingen: Narr), 323–44.

1986 "The Politics of Black Music and the Tradition of Poetry: Amiri Baraka and John Coltrane," *Jazzforschung / Jazz Research* 18 (Hochschule für Musik und Darstellende Kunst Graz): 193–231.

1987 "American Studies and the Radical Tradition: From the 1930s to the 1960s," in Jack Salzman, ed., *Prospects 12: An Annual of American Cultural Studies* (Cambridge: Cambridge University Press), 21–58.

1987 "History, Folk Tradition, and Fictional Voice: Die schwarze Südstaatenliteratur seit dem Civil Rights Movement," *Gulliver: Deutsch-Englische Jahrbücher* 21: 93–113.

1988 "The Politics of Traveling Theory: Revisions of Deconstruction, Postmodernism, and Neo-Marxism in Recent American Literary Criticism," in Lothar Bredella and Dietmar Haack, eds., *Perceptions and Misperceptions: The U.S.A. and Germany—Studies in Intercultural Understanding* (Tübingen: Narr), 209–40.

1988 "Symbolic Space, Communal Rituals, and the Surreality of the Urban Ghetto: Harlem in Black Literature from the 1920s to the 1960s," *Callaloo* 11 (Spring): 309–45.

1990 "Reconstructing American Literary Studies: History, Difference, and Synthesis," in Günter H. Lenz, Hartmut Keil, and Sabine Bröck-Sallah, eds., *Reconstructing American Literary and Historical Studies* (Frankfurt: Campus; New York: St. Martin's Press), 21–50.

1990 "The Politics of American Culture: Kulturelles Selbstverständnis und öffentlicher Diskurs im Amerika der achtziger Jahre," in Franz Greß and Hans Vorländer, eds., *Liberale Demokratie in Europa und den USA, Festschrift für Kurt L. Shell* (Frankfurt: Campus), 49–70.

1990 "The Radical Imagination: Revisionary Modes of Radical Cultural Criticism in Thirties America," in Steve Ickringill, ed., *Looking Inward—Looking Outward: From the 1930s through the 1940s* (Amsterdam: VU University Press), 94–126.

1991 "Dokumentarischer Appell und kultureller Gegendiskurs in David Loeb Weiss' *No Vietnamese Ever Called Me Nigger*," in Mo Beyerle and Christine

Noll Brinckmann, eds., *Der amerikanische Dokumentarfilm der sechziger Jahre: Direct Cinema und Radical Cinema* (Frankfurt: Campus), 412–25.

1991 "'Ethnographies': American Culture Studies and Postmodern Anthropology," in Jack Salzman, ed., *Prospects 16: An Annual of American Cultural Studies* (Cambridge: Cambridge University Press), 1–40.

1991 "Edward W. Said," in Hartmut Heuermann and Bernd-Peter Lange, eds., *Contemporaries in Cultural Criticism* (Frankfurt: Peter Lang), 443–70.

1993 "Multicultural Critique and the New American Studies," in Hans Bak, ed., *Multiculturalism and the Canon of American Culture* (Amsterdam: VU University Press), 27–56.

1993 "Black Politics, Community, and Culture: Afro-Amerika im amerikanischen Dokumentarfilm. Eine Einleitung," in Günter H. Lenz, ed., *Afro-Amerika im amerikanischen Dokumentarfilm* (Trier: Wissenschaftlicher Verlag Trier), 7–21.

1993 "Ethnographic (Re-)Visions and Southern Blues Culture: William Ferris, Jr., *Delta Blues Singer: James 'Sonny Ford' Thomas* (1970) and *Give My Poor Heart Ease: Mississippi Delta Blues Men* (1975)," in Günter H. Lenz, ed., *Afro-Amerika im amerikanischen Dokumentarfilm* (Trier: Wissenschaftlicher Verlag Trier), 189–216.

1994 "After Poststructuralism and Deconstruction: A New American Exceptionalism?," in Gerhard Hoffmann and Alfred Hornung, eds., *Affirmation and Negation in Contemporary American Culture* (Heidelberg: Carl Winter), 177–94 (with Heinz Ickstadt).

1994 "American Studies: Multikulturalität und Postmoderne," in Berndt Ostendorf, ed., *Multikulturelle Gesellschaft: Modell Amerika?* (Munich: Wilhelm Fink), 167–88.

1994 "American Studies as Multicultural Critique: Postmodern Culture, Interdisciplinarity, and Intercultural Identities," in Günther Blaicher and Brigitte Glaser, eds., *Anglistentag 1993 Eichstätt: Proceedings* (Tübingen: Max Niemeyer), 269–86.

1995 "Introduction," in Günter H. Lenz and Klaus J. Milich, eds., *American Studies in Germany: European Contexts and Intercultural Relations* (Frankfurt: Campus; New York: St. Martin's Press), 9–25 (with Klaus J. Milich).

1995 "American Studies" and "New German Critique," in Rüdiger B. Wersich, ed., *USA Lexikon: Schlüsselbegriffe zu Politik, Wirtschaft, Gesellschaft, Kultur, Geschichte und zu den deutsch-amerikanischen Beziehungen* (Berlin: Erich Schmidt), 70–73, 527–28.

1996 "Transcultural American Studies: Conceptualizing Multicultural Identities and Communities—Some Notes," in Herbert Christ and Michael K. Legutke, eds., *Fremde Texte Verstehen: Festschrift für Lothar Bredella* (Tübingen: Gunter Narr), 191–202.

1996 "Refractions of Modernity—Reconstituting Modernism in West Germany after World War II: Jackson Pollock, Ezra Pound, and Charlie Parker," in Olaf Hansen and Thomas Liesemann, eds., *Demokratie und Kunst in Amerika—Democracy and the Arts in the U.S.A.: Festschrift zu Ehren von Martin*

Christadler (Trieste: Edizioni Parnoaso), 183–208. Revised and extended version in Cristina Giorcelli and Rob Kroes, eds., *Living with America: 1946–1996* (Amsterdam: VU University Press, 1997), 129–70.

1997 "La poetica della Black Music e della poesia nera: Michael Harper, Amiri Baraka, John Coltrane," in Franco Minganti, ed., *Jazztoldtales: Jazz e Fiction, letteratura e jazz* (Imola: Bacchilega Editore), 96–134.

1998 "Transnational American Studies: Negotiating Cultures of Difference, Multicultural Identities, Communities, and Border Discourses," in Klaus J. Milich and Jeffrey Peck, eds., *Multiculturalism in Transit: A German–American Exchange* (Providence, RI: Berghahn Books), 129–66. Slightly different version as "Transnational American Studies: Negotiating Multicultural Identities, Communities, and Border Discourses in Cultures of Difference," in "Americas Abroad," ed. Donald Pease, special issue, *Annals of Scholarship* 12, nos. 3–4 (1998): 139–67.

1998 "Bebop und die Suche nach säkularer Transzendenz in der nord- und südamerikanischen Literatur der frühe Postmoderne: Jack Kerouacs *On the Road* und Julio Cortázars *El Perseguidor*," in Claudius Armbruster and Karin Hopfe, eds., *Horizont-Verschiebungen—Interkulturelles Verstehen und Heterogenität in der Romania: Festschrift für Karsten Garscha* (Tübingen: Gunter Narr), 279–303.

1999 "Toward a Dialogics of International American Culture Studies: Transnationality, Border Discourses, and Public Culture(s)," *Amerikastudien / American Studies* 44, no. 1: 5–23.

1999 "Internationalizing American Studies: Predecessors, Paradigms, and Dialogical Cultural Critique—A View from Germany," in Rob Kroes, ed., *Predecessors: Intellectual Lineages in American Studies* (Amsterdam: VU University Press), 226–55.

2000 "Border Cultures, Creolization, and Diaspora: Negotiating Cultures of Difference in America," in Roland Hagenbüchle and Joseph Raab, eds., *Negotiations of America's National Identity*, 2 vols. (Tübingen: Stauffenberg), 2: 362–86.

2000 "Historians, Histories, and Public Cultures: Multicultural Discourses in the United States and Germany," in Günter H. Lenz and Peter J. Ling, eds., *TransAtlantic Encounters: Multiculturalism, National Identity, and the Uses of the Past* (Amsterdam: VU University Press), 63–103.

2000 "Introduction," in Günter H. Lenz and Peter J. Ling, eds., *TransAtlantic Encounters: Multiculturalism, National Identity, and the Uses of the Past* (Amsterdam: VU University Press), 1–14 (with Peter J. Ling).

2000 "Multicultural Postmodernism: Cultural Hybridity and Diaspora in Contemporary African American Literary and Cultural Theory," in Susanne Rohr, Peter Schneck, and Sabine Sielke, eds., *Making America: The Cultural Work of Literature* (Heidelberg: Carl Winter), 235–51.

2000 "Die kulturelle Dynamik der afroamerikanischen Musik: Duke Ellingtons Kulturbegriff und seine Bedeutung in der afroamerikanischen Literatur und Kritik," in Wolfram Knauer, ed., *Duke Ellington und die Folgen*, Darmstädter Beiträge zur Jazzforschung (Hofheim: Wolke), 157–205.

2000 "Cultural Hybridity and Diaspora in African American Literature and Criticism: Fictions of a Postmodern Multiculturalism," in Utz Riese, ed., *Kontakzone Amerika: Literarische Verkehrsformen kultureller Übersetzung* (Heidelberg: Carl Winter), 73–108.

2001 "The Politics of African American Literary and Cultural Critique: From the Black Arts/Black Aesthetic Movement to a Black Postmodern Multiculturalism," in Fritz Gysin and Christopher Mulvey, eds., *Black Liberation in the Americas* (Hamburg: LIT), 203–18.

2001 "Teaching Cultural Difference: Multiculturalism and the Internationalization of American Studies," in Frank Trommler and Elliott Shore, eds., *The German–American Encounter: Conflict and Cooperation Between Two Cultures, 1800–2000* (New York: Berghahn Books), 305–24 (with John Carlos Rowe).

2001 "Die Vermittlung kultureller Differenz: Multikulturalismus und die Internationalisierung der Amerikastudien," in Frank Trommler and Elliott Shore, eds., *Deutsch-amerikanische Beziehungen: Konflikt und Kooperation im 19 und 20. Jahrhundert* (Stuttgart: Deutsche Verlags-Anstalt), 379–401, 446–48 (with John Carlos Rowe).

2001 "Periodization and American Studies," in George T. Kurian et al., eds., *Encyclopedia of American Studies*, vol. 3 (New York: Grolier International), 293–96.

2002 "Middle Passages: Histories, Re-Memories, and Black Diasporas in Novels by Toni Morrison, Charles Johnson, and Caryl Phillips," in Gordon Collier and Frank Schulze-Engler, eds., *Crabtracks: Progress and Process in Teaching the New Literatures in English* (Amsterdam: Rodopi), 235–52.

2002 "Toward a Dialogics of International American Culture Studies: Transnationality, Border Discourses, and Public Culture(s)," in Donald E. Pease and Robyn Wiegman, eds., *The Futures of American Studies* (Durham, NC: Duke University Press), 461–85.

2002 "Transculturations: American Studies in a Globalizing World—The Globalizing World in American Studies," ed. Günter H. Lenz, *Amerikastudien / American Studies* 47: 99–119, "Introduction," 97–98.

2003 "'The riffs, runs, breaks, and distortions of the music of a community in transition'—Redefining African American Modernism and the Jazz Aesthetic in Langston Hughes' *Montage of a Dream Deferred* and *Ask Your Mama*," A Gathering in Honor of Jules Chametzky, *Massachusetts Review* 44, nos. 1 and 2: 269–82.

2003 "Mapping Postmodern New York City: Reconfiguring Space, Metropolitan Culture, and Urban Fiction—An Introduction," in Günter H. Lenz and Utz Riese, eds., *Postmodern New York City: Transfiguring Spaces—Raum-Transformationen* (Heidelberg: Universitätsverlag Winter), 11–32.

2004 "The Transfiguring Imagination of a Black Urban Modernism: Recodifying Public Space and Cultural Rituals in the Literature, Music, and Art of the Harlem Renaissance," in William Boelhower and Anna Scacchi, eds., *Public Space, Private Lives: Race, Gender, Class, and Citizenship in New York, 1890–1929* (Amsterdam: VU Press), 67–96.

2004 "Irreconcilabilities and Transgressions: Edward W. Said's Idea of a Worldly Criticism—An Introduction," *Zeitschrift für Anglistik und Amerikanistik* 52: 317–29.

2005 "The Distinguished W. E. B. Du Bois Lectures: On Public Culture in a Transatlantic Perspective—Introduction," in Daniel R. Coats, Richard Sennett, Hayden White, and Mark Poster, *On Public Culture in a Transatlantic Perspective, Distinguished W. E. B. Du Bois Lectures, 2002/2003*, Öffentliche Vorlesungen (Berlin: Humboldt-Universität), 5–9 (with Antje Dallmann).

2006 "New EthniCities: Recodifying Urban Spaces and Intercultural Translation in New York Fictions of the 1990s," in Günter H. Lenz, Dorothea Löbbermann, and Karl-Heinz Magister, eds., *CinematoGraphies: Fictional Strategies and Visual Discourses in 1990s New York City* (Heidelberg: Universitätsverlag Winter), 241–70.

2006 "Literary Transfigurations of Intercultural Translations: New EthniCities and Migratory Topographies in New York Fictions of the 1990s," in Günter H. Lenz, Friedrich Ulfers, and Antje Dallmann, eds., *Toward a New Metropolitanism: Reconstituting Public Culture, Urban Citizenship, and the Multicultural Imaginary in New York and Berlin* (Heidelberg: Universitätsverlag Winter), 399–449.

2006 "Introduction," in Günter H. Lenz, Friedrich Ulfers, and Antje Dallmann, eds., *Toward a New Metropolitanism: Reconstituting Public Culture, Urban Citizenship, and the Multicultural Imaginary in New York and Berlin* (Heidelberg: Universitätsverlag Winter), 11–33.

2007 "Justice, Governance, Cosmopolitanism, and the Politics of Difference: Reconfigurations in a Transnational World—Introduction," in Kwame Anthony Appiah, Seyla Benhabib, Iris Marion Young, and Nancy Fraser, *Justice, Governance, Cosmopolitanism, and the Politics of Difference—Reconfigurations in a Transnational World, Distinguished W. E. B. Du Bois Lectures, 2004/2005*, Öffentliche Vorlesungen (Berlin: Humboldt-Universität), 5–13 (with Antje Dallmann).

2009 "Radical Cosmopolitanism: W. E. B. Du Bois, Germany, and African American Pragmatist Visions for 21st Century Europe," in Alfred Hornung and Rüdiger Kunow, eds., *Representation and Decoration in a Postmodern Age* (Heidelberg: Universitätsverlag Winter), 65–96.

2011 "Introduction" and "Redefinitions of Citizenship and Revisions of Cosmopolitanism: Challenges of Transnational Perspectives," *Journal of Transnational American Studies* (e-journal) 3, no. 1, article 17; http://escholarship.org/uc/item/8n55g7q6.

2011 "Toward a Politics of American Transcultural Studies: Discourses of Diaspora and Cosmopolitanism," in Winfried Fluck, Donald E. Pease, Jr., and John Carlos Rowe, eds., *Re-Framing the Transnational Turn in American Studies* (Hanover, NH: Dartmouth College Press), 391–425.

NOTES

Series Editor's Preface

1. Lenz recommends in particular that international scholars who accuse the United States of cultural imperialism "pursue the question of how far their own American studies programs, often founded as 'area studies programs' in the period of the Cold War, have been implicated in, and actively supportive of these imperial politics." Günter Lenz, "Toward a Dialogics of International American Culture Studies: Transnationality, Border Discourses, and Public Culture(s)," in Donald E. Pease and Robyn Wiegman, eds., *The Futures of American Studies* (Durham, NC: Duke University Press, 2002), 461–85, 481.

Among the books on this topic that Günter Lenz has written or edited, I recommend the following: *American Studies in Germany: European Contexts and Intercultural Relations* (Frankfurt: Campus; New York: St. Martin's Press, 1995) (coedited with Klaus J. Milich); *TransAtlantic Encounters: Multiculturalism, National Identity, and the Uses of the Past* (Amsterdam: VU University Press, 2000) (coedited with Peter J. Ling); *History and Tradition in Afro-American Culture* (Frankfurt: Campus, 1984); and *The Crisis of Modernity: Recent Critical Theories of Culture and Society in the United States and West Germany* (Frankfurt: Campus; Boulder, CO: Westview Press, 1986) (coedited with Kurt L. Shell). Among the essays on this topic, I would select the following as especially pertinent: "The Politics of American Culture: Kulturelles Selbstverständnis und öffentlicher Diskurs im Amerika der achtziger Jahre," in Franz Greß and Hans Vorländer, eds., *Liberale Demokratie in Europa und den USA, Festschrift für Kurt L. Shell* (Frankfurt: Campus, 1990), 49–70; "Reconstructing American Literary Studies: History, Difference, and Synthesis," in Günter H. Lenz, Hartmut Keil, and Sabine Bröck-Sallah, eds., *Reconstructing American Literary and Historical Studies* (Frankfurt: Campus; New York, St. Martin's Press, 1990), 21–50; "Multicultural Critique and the New American Studies," in Hans Bak, ed., *Multiculturalism and the Canon of American Culture* (Amsterdam: VU University Press, 1993), 27–56; "After Poststructuralism and Deconstruction: A New American Exceptionalism?," in Gerhard Hoffmann and Alfred Hornung, eds., *Affirmation and Negation in Contemporary American Culture* (Heidelberg: Carl Winter, 1994), 177–94 (with Heinz Ickstadt); "American Studies as Multicultural Critique: Postmodern Culture, Interdisciplinarity, and Intercultural Identities," in Günther Blaicher and Brigitte Glaser, eds., *Anglistentag 1993 Eichstaett: Proceedings* (Tübingen: Max Niemeyer, 1994), 269–86; "Transnational American Studies: Conceptualizing Multicultural Identities and Communities—Some Notes," in Herbert Christ and Michael K. Legutke, eds., *Fremde Texte Verstehen: Festschrift für Lothar Bredella* (Tübingen: Gunter Narr,

1996), 191–202; "Transnational American Studies: Negotiating Multicultural Identities, Communities, and Border Discourses in Cultures of Difference," in "Americas Abroad," ed. Donald Pease, special issue, *Annals of Scholarship* 12, nos. 3–4 (1998): 139–67; "Internationalizing American Studies: Predecessors, Paradigms, and Dialogical Cultural Critique—A View from Germany," in Rob Kroes, ed., *Predecessors: Intellectual Lineages in American Studies* (Amsterdam: VU University Press, 1999), 226–55; "Border Cultures, Creolization, and Diaspora: Negotiating Cultures of Difference in America," in Roland Hagenbüchle and Joseph Raab, eds., *Negotiations of America's National Identity*, 2 vols. (Tübingen: Stauffenberg, 2000), 2: 362–86; "Multicultural Postmodernism: Cultural Hybridity and Diaspora in Contemporary African American Literary and Cultural Theory," in Susanne Rohr, Peter Schneck, and Sabine Sielke, eds., *Making America: The Cultural Work of Literature* (Heidelberg: Carl Winter, 2000), 235–51; "Historians, Histories, and Public Cultures: Multicultural Discourses in the United States and Germany," in Günter H. Lenz and Peter J. Ling, eds., *TransAtlantic Encounters: Multiculturalism, National Identity, and the Uses of the Past* (Amsterdam: VU University Press, 2000), 63–103; "Teaching Cultural Difference: Multiculturalism and the Internationalization of American Studies," in Frank Trommler and Elliott Shore, eds., *The German–American Encounter: Conflict and Cooperation Between Two Cultures, 1800–2000* (New York: Berghahn Books, 2001), 305–24 (with John Carlos Rowe); "Toward a Dialogics of International American Culture Studies: Transnationality, Border Discourses, and Public Culture(s)," in Donald E. Pease and Robyn Wiegman, eds., *The Futures of American Studies* (Durham, NC: Duke University Press, 2002), 461–85; "Transculturations: American Studies in a Globalizing World—The Globalizing World in American Studies" (ed. Günter H. Lenz), *Amerikastudien /American Studies* 47 (2002): 99–119, "Introduction," 97–98.

2. Philip Fisher, "Introduction: The New American Studies," in Philip Fisher, ed., *The New American Studies: Essays from "Representation"* (Berkeley: University of California Press, 1991), i–xxxiii.

3. Ibid., xxii.

4. Lenz, "Transnational American Studies," "Toward a Dialogics of International American Culture Studies," and "Toward a Politics of American Transcultural Studies: Discourses of Diaspora and Cosmopolitanism," in Winfried Fluck, Donald E. Pease, and John Carlos Rowe, eds., *Re-Framing the Transnational Turn in American Studies* (Hanover, NH: Dartmouth College Press, 2011), 391–425.

5. For a discussion of transculturation that is important to Lenz's argument, see Mary Louise Pratt, *Imperial Eyes: Travel Writing and Transculturation* (New York: Routledge, 1992), 6. Lenz elaborates upon this discussion in "Border Cultures, Creolization, and Diaspora" and "Multicultural Postmodernism."

6. The relevance of discourses of the border to the East Berlin–West Berlin divide has been a preoccupation of Lenz's since German reunification. In addition to "Toward a Dialogics of International American Culture Studies," see Lenz's "'Ethnographies': American Culture Studies and Postmodern Anthropology," *Prospects* 16 (1991): 1–40; and "Transnational American Studies."

7. See David A. Hollinger, *Postethnic America: Beyond Multiculturalism* (New York: Basic Books, 1995), and Lenz, "American Studies as Multicultural Critique."

8. Lenz analyzes this process in a slightly different, earlier version: "Transnational American Studies: Negotiating Multicultural Identities, Communities, and Border Discourses in Cultures of Difference," *Annals of Scholarship* 12, nos. 3–4 (1998): 139–43.

9. After World War II, the relationship between German and U.S. scholars in American Studies was marked by a transferential structure that involved dual critiques—the critique of German authoritarianism by American popular culture and the critique of the standardization of American mass culture by German critical theory. But the temptation to turn exchanges between scholars in the United States and in Germany into an occasion to reaffirm the nationalist traits in both cultures has informed U.S.–German relationships throughout the Cold War. Lenz supplies a fine analysis of "radical recontextualization" in "Toward a Dialogics of International American Culture Studies," 464.

10. Lenz explicitly discusses the role American Studies played in these democratic re-education programs in "Refractions of Modernity—Reconstituting Modernism in West Germany after World War II: Jackson Pollock, Ezra Pound, and Charlie Parker," in Olaf Hansen and Thomas Liesemann, eds., *Demokratie und Kunst in Amerika—Democracy and the Arts in the U.S.A.: Festschrift zu Ehren von Martin Christadler* (Trieste: Edizioni Parnoaso, 1996), 183–208; revised and extended version in Cristina Giorcelli and Rob Kroes, eds., *Living with America: 1946–1996* (Amsterdam: VU University Press, 1997), 129–70.

11. Lenz presents a more robust version of his notion of American Culture Studies in his critique of U.S. multiculturalist discourse, "American Studies as Multicultural Critique," but Lenz's engagement with the radical political implications of U.S. American Studies has been a signature aspect of his project from the outset. For representative examples of such scholarship, see "American Studies: Beyond the Crisis? Recent Redefinitions and the Meaning of Theory, History, and Practical Criticism," *Prospects* 7 (1982): 53–111; "Tradition, Discontinuity, and Counterdiscourse: Some Problems in American Radical Cultural Criticism Since the 1960s," in Lenz and Shell, eds., *The Crisis of Modernity*, 191–249; and "American Studies as Multicultural Critique."

12. Ulf Hannerz, "The World in Creolization," *Africa* 57 (1987): 546.

13. For a sustained elaboration of global localisms' transformation of Americanization see "Internationalizing American Studies."

14. "Toward a Dialogics of International American Culture Studies," 479. The essays Lenz critiques in arriving at this formulation are Donald E. Pease, "New Americanists, Revisionist Interventions into the Canon," *boundary 2* 17, no. 1 (1990); Pease, "National Identities, Postmodern Artifacts, and Postnational Narratives," *boundary 2* 19, no. 1 (1992); and Pease, "New Perspectives on US Cultures and Imperialism," in Amy Kaplan and Donald E. Pease, eds., *Cultures of United States Imperialism* (Durham, NC: Duke University Press, 1993).

15. "Toward a Dialogics of International American Culture Studies," 468.

Introduction

Acknowledgments: Donald Pease was a good friend of Günter and the entire Lenz family. It was Don's idea that we edit and publish posthumously Günter's manuscript. I am very grateful to Don and Richard Pult of the University Press of New England for the publication of this work. Klaus Milich, Günter's PhD student and dear friend, made available Günter's plan and all of the extant manuscripts for the chapters, which he uploaded to a Google.docs site. Reinhard Isensee, Günter's friend and colleague at the Humboldt University (Berlin), produced the list of publications in the appendix to this volume. Reinhard also arranged for Leon Fritz, a candidate in the masters of arts program in American Studies at the Humboldt University, to identify many of the missing citations in the manuscript. Finally, we all express our deep gratitude and friendship to Professor Friedrich Ulfers of New York University, whose generosity has made possible the publication of this book. Fred's friendship with Günter and his family is profound and abiding. For all of us, work on this manuscript was a labor of love.

1. Lenz's publications are listed at the end of this volume.

2. Max Horkheimer and Theodor W. Adorno, *Dialectic of Enlightenment: Philosophical Fragments*, ed. Gunzelin Schmid Nörr, trans. Edmund Jephcott (Stanford, CA: Stanford University Press, 2002). *Dialectic of Enlightenment* was first printed in Amsterdam in 1947.

3. By 1957, the membership of the CPUSA was a mere 10,000, and 1,500 members were probably government informants.

4. Michael Denning, *The Cultural Front: The Laboring of American Culture in the Twentieth Century* (New York: Verso Books, 1996).

5. Ferdinand de Saussure, *Course in General Linguistics*, ed. Charles Bally and Albert Sechehaye, with Albert Reidlinger; trans. Wade Baskin (New York: McGraw-Hill, 1966), 120.

6. Sacvan Bercovitch, *The Rites of Assent: Transformations in the Symbolic Construction of America* (New York: Routledge, 1993), 353.

7. See Molefi Kete Asante, *Afrocentricity: The Theory of Social Change*, rev. ed. (New York: African American Images, 2003), first published in 1980; Chela Sandoval, *Methodology of the Oppressed* (Minneapolis: University of Minnesota Press, 2000).

8. Henry Nash Smith, Leo Marx, and Richard Slotkin, "Reassessments," in Sacvan Bercovitch and Myra Jehlen, eds., *Ideology and Classic American Literature* (New York: Cambridge University Press, 1986), 21–90.

9. Richard Poirier, *The Renewal of Literature: Emersonian Reflections* (New York: Random House, 1987).

10. John Carlos Rowe, "Edward Said and American Studies," *American Quarterly* 56, no. 1 (2004): 33–47.

1. After Deconstruction: Reconstructing American Literary and Cultural Studies in the 1980s

1. Tzvetan Todorov, "All Against Humanity," *Times Literary Supplement*, October 4, 1985, 1093–94, further references in the text as "AAH."

2. Ihab Hassan, "'Making Sense': The Trials of Postmodern Discourse," *New Literary History* 18 (Winter 1987): 437–59, and "Pluralism in Postmodern Perspective," *Critical Inquiry* 12 (Spring 1986): 503–20.

3. Samuel Weber, "After Eight: Remarking Glyph," *Glyph* 8 (1981): 234, further references in the text as "AE"; Rodolphe Gasché, "Deconstruction as Criticism," *Glyph* 6 (1979): 180. Cf. Gasché's more recent book, *The Tain of the Mirror: Derrida and the Philosophy of Reflection* (Cambridge, MA: Harvard University Press, 1986).

4. Gasché, "Deconstruction as Criticism," 178.

5. Maria Ruegg, "The End(s) of French Style: Structuralism and Post Structuralism in the American Context," *Criticism* 21 (1979): 192, 206.

6. Frank Lentricchia, *After the New Criticism* (Chicago: University of Chicago Press, 1980), ch. 5. Cf. the critical remarks in Andrew Parker, "'Taking Sides' (on History): Derrida Re-Marx," *Diacritics* 11 (Fall 1981): 63ff.

7. Edward W. Said, *The World, the Text, and the Critic* (Cambridge, MA: Harvard University Press, 1983), 3f., etc., further references in the text as *WTC*. Cf. my essay "Tradition, Discontinuity, and Counterdiscourse: Some Problems in American Radical Cultural Criticism Since the 1960s," in Gunter H. Lenz and Kurt L. Shell, eds., *The Crisis of Modernity: Recent Critical Theories of Culture and Society in the United States and West Germany* (Frankfurt: Campus; Boulder, CO: Westview Press, 1986), 192–97 (on Graff), 218–29 (on Said).

8. Terry Eagleton, "The Idealism of American Criticism," *New Left Review*, no. 127 (May–June, 1981): 53–65: Cornel West, "Fredric Jameson's Marxist Hermeneutics," *Boundary 2* 11, nos. 1–2 (Fall 1982–Winter 1983): 177–200.

9. Jacques Derrida, *Of Grammatology*, trans. Gayatri Spivak (Baltimore: Johns Hopkins University Press, 1976), 11, 22ff., 103f.; Lentricchia, *After the New Criticism*, 179ff.; Gayatri Spivak, "French Feminism in an International Frame," *Yale French Studies*, no. 62 (1981): 174f., and "Marx after Derrida," in William E. Cain, ed., *Philosophical Approaches to Literature* (Lewisburg, PA: Bucknell University Press, 1984), 227. Cf. Derrida's own commentary in Harold Bloom et al., *Deconstruction and Criticism* (New York: Continuum, 1979), 83f.

10. Fredric Jameson, *Marxism and Form: Twentieth-Century Dialectical Theories of Literature* (Princeton, NJ: Princeton University Press, 1971), 10.

11. Leo Marx, "Pastoralism in America," in Sacvan Bercovitch and Myra Jehlen, eds., *Ideology and Classic American Literature* (Cambridge: Cambridge University Press, 1986), 36–69. Cf. Marx, "Susan Sontag's 'New Left' Pastoral: Notes on Revolutionary Pastoralism in America," *Tri-Quarterly* 23–24 (1972): 552–75, "American Institutions and Ecological Ideals," *Science* 170 (November 27, 1970): 945–52, and *The Machine in the Garden: Technology and the Pastoral Ideal in America* (New York: Oxford University Press, 1964).

12. Samuel Weber, "Capitalizing History: Notes on the Political Unconscious," *Diacritics* 13 (Summer 1983): 14–28.

13. Cf. my essay "Tradition, Discontinuity, and Counterdiscourse."

14. Fredric Jameson, "Postmodernism, or The Cultural Logic of Capitalism," *New Left Review*, no. 146 (July–August 1984): 53–92.

15. Jonathan Arac, "Introduction," *Boundary 2* 11, nos. 1–2 (Fall 1982–Winter 1983): 2; John Springer and Elizabeth McLemore, "Marxism and Deconstruction," *Genre* 17 (Spring–Summer 1984): 76.

16. Michael Ryan, *Marxism and Deconstruction: A Critical Articulation* (Baltimore: Johns Hopkins University Press, 1982), further references in the text as *MD*.

17. Cf. Barbara Foley's attack in "The Politics of Deconstruction," *Genre* 17 (Spring–Summer 1984): 113–34.

18. Paul de Man, "The Resistance to Theory," *Yale French Studies*, no. 63 (1982):

11. Cf. Christopher Norris, *The Deconstructive Turn: Essays in the Rhetoric of Philosophy* (London: Methuen, 1983), and, particularly, *The Contest of Faculties: Philosophy and Theory after Deconstruction* (London: Methuen, 1985), 8–11, 74–77, 80–96; and Frank Lentricchia, *Criticism and Social Change* (Chicago: University of Chicago Press, 1985), part 1.

19. For the debate on de Man's war writings and their implications for a critical understanding of his deconstructionist work see, e.g., Lindsay Waters and Wlad Godzich, eds., *Reading de Man Reading* (Minneapolis: University of Minnesota Press, 1989).

20. Andreas Huyssen, "Mapping the Postmodern," *New German Critique*, no. 33 (Fall 1984): 5–52 (also in Lenz and Shell, eds., *The Crisis of Modernity*, 253–99), further references in the text as "MTP."

21. Paul A. Bové, "The Ineluctability of Difference: Scientific Pluralism and the Critical Intelligence," *Boundary* 2, 11, nos. 1–2 (Fall 1982–Winter 1983): 155–176, esp. pp. 156f. Cf. I. Hassan.

22. Cf. Hal Foster, ed., *The Anti-Aesthetic: Essays on Postmodern Culture* (Port Townsend, WA: Bay Press, 1983); Huyssen, "Mapping the Postmodern."

23. Cf. Bové's "appropriation" of Stanley Aronowitz's work in "The Ineluctability of Difference."

24. Jacques Derrida, "Speculations—on Freud," *Oxford Literary Review*, 3, no. 2 (1978): 82, quoted in Spivak, "Marx after Derrida," 228.

25. Andrew Parker, "Between Dialectics and Deconstruction: Derrida and the Reading of Marx," in Gregory S. Jay and David L. Miller, eds., *After Strange Texts: The Role of Theory in the Study of Literature* (Tuscaloosa: University of Alabama Press, 1985), 147.

26. Rainer Nägele, "The Scene of the Other: Theodor W. Adorno's Negative Dialectic in the Context of Poststructuralism," *Boundary* 2 11, nos. 1–2 (Fall 1982–Winter 1983): 62, 77.

27. Cf. Jacques Derrida, *Positions* (Chicago: University of Chicago Press, 1981), 37–96 (interview with Jean-Louis Houdebine and Guy Scarpetta).

28. Parker, "Between Dialectics and Deconstruction," 147, 167f.

29. John Brenkman, "Deconstruction and the Social Text," *Social Text* 1 (Winter 1979): 187, further references in the text as "DST."

30. Jonathan Arac, Wlad Godzich, and Wallace Martin, eds., *The Yale Critics: Deconstruction in America* (Minneapolis: University of Minnesota Press, 1983), x, xxxiv, and passim.

31. Jacques Derrida, *Memoires for Paul de Man*, trans. Cecile Lindsay, Jonathan Culler, and Eduardo Cadava (New York: Columbia University Press, 1986), 18.

32. Kenneth Dauber, "Criticism of American Literature," *Diacritics* 7 (March 1977): 55f., and "American Culture as Genre," *Criticism* 22 (1980): 100.

33. Sohnya Sayres et al., eds., *The 60s Without Apology* (Minneapolis: University of Minnesota Press, 1984), 8, passim.

34. West, "Fredric Jameson's Marxist Hermeneutics."

35. Sacvan Bercovitch, "The Rites of Assent: Rhetoric, Ritual, and the Ideology of American Consensus," in Sam B. Girgus, ed., *The American Self: Myth, Ideology and*

Popular Culture (Albuquerque: University of New Mexico Press, 1981), 29. Cf. my essay "Tradition, Discontinuity, and Counterdiscourse," 208–13.

36. Fredric Jameson, "The Symbolic Inference; or, Kenneth Burke and Ideological Analysis," *Critical Inquiry* 4 (Spring 1978): 507–32. Cf. also Lentricchia's extensive treatment of Burke's work in his *Criticism and Social Change.*

37. Cf. Sacvan Bercovitch, ed., *Reconstructing American Literary History* (Cambridge, MA: Harvard University Press, 1986).

38. Walter Benn Michaels and Donald E. Pease, eds., *The American Renaissance Reconsidered* (Cambridge, MA: Harvard University Press, 1986): 90–112 (J. Arac) and 113–55 (D. Pease). Cf. my discussion of Matthiessen's work in my essay "American Studies and the Radical Tradition: From the 1930s to the 1960s," *Prospects* 12 (1987): 21–58.

39. Cf. my essay "Tradition, Discontinuity, and Counterdiscourse," 213–18.

40. Ihab Hassan, *The Right Promethean Fire: Imagination, Science, and Cultural Change* (Urbana-Champaign: University of Illinois Press, 1980), 24.

41. Cf. Ihab Hassan, "Desire and Dissent in the Postmodern Age," *Kenyon Review*, new. ser., 5 (Winter 1983): esp. 11ff.

42. Ihab Hassan, *Paracriticisms: Seven Speculations of the Times* (Urbana-Champaign: University of Illinois Press, 1975), xv, 165ff.

43. Gilles Deleuze and Félix Guattari, "What Is Minor Literature?" *Mississippi Review* 22 (Spring 1983): 13–33. For a general discussion of the topic, cf. Louis A. Renza, *"A White Heron" and the Question of Minor Literature* (Madison: University of Wisconsin Press, 1984).

44. John Carlos Rowe, "'To Live Outside the Law, You Must Be Honest': The Authority of the Margin in Contemporary Theory," *Cultural Critique*, no. 2 (1985): 37, further references in the text as "TLOL."

45. Barbara Johnson, *A World of Difference* (Baltimore: Johns Hopkins University Press, 1987), 2, further references in the text as *WOD*.

46. Barbara Johnson, "Gender Theory and the Yale School," in Robert Con Davis and Ronald Schleifer, eds., *Rhetoric and Form: Deconstruction at Yale* (Oklahoma City: University of Oklahoma Press, 1985), 78.

47. Werner Sollors, "A Critique of Pure Pluralism," in Bercovitch, ed., *Reconstructing American Literary History*, 251–52.

48. W. J. T. Mitchell, "Pluralism as Dogmatism," *Critical Inquiry* 12 (Spring 1986): 498, 502; Philip Gleason, "American Identity and Americanization," in Stephan Thernstrom et al., eds., *Harvard Encyclopedia of American Ethnic Groups* (Cambridge: Cambridge University Press, 1980), 44–45; Sollors, "Critique of Pure Pluralism," 274; Bercovitch, "Afterword," in Bercovitch and Jehlen, eds., *Ideology and Classic American Literature*, 437f.; cf. his essay "The Problem of Ideology in American Literary History," *Critical Inquiry* 12 (Summer 1986): 649.

49. Werner Sollors, *Beyond Ethnicity: Consent and Descent in American Culture* (New York: Oxford University Press, 1986), 14–15.

50. Herbert G. Gutman, "The Missing Synthesis: Whatever Happened to History?" *Nation* 233 (November 21, 1981), 521, 553–54, further references in the text as "TMS"; Thomas Bender, "Making History Whole Again," *New York Times Book*

Review, October 6, 1985, 1, 42–43, further references in the text as "MHWA"; Bender, "Wholes and Parts: The Need for Synthesis in American History," *Journal of American History* 73 (June 1986): 120–36, further references in text as "WAP."

51. Sollors, *Beyond Ethnicity*, 6–10, 15, 27, 36–39, 57, 59, cf. 176.

52. W. J. T. Mitchell, "*Critical Inquiry* and the Ideology of Pluralism," *Critical Inquiry* 8 (Summer 1982): 613, cf. 614–18.

53. Hayden White, "Historical Pluralism," *Critical Inquiry* 12 (Spring 1986): 482, 484, 486–89, 490f., 493.

54. Hassan, "Pluralism in Postmodern Perspective," 503, 506, 508f., 514, 516.

55. Emory Elliott, "New Literary History: Past and Present," *American Literature* 57 (December 1985): 617, cf. 614; cf. also his later essay "The Politics of Literary History," *American Literature* 59 (May 1987): 268–76.

56. Elliott, "New Literary History," 617; Annette Kolodny, "The Integrity of Memory: Creating a New Literary History of the United States," *American Literature* 57 (May 1985): 292, 294–96, 304.

57. Kolodny, "The Integrity of Memory," 306f.; Sacvan Bercovitch, "America as Canon and Context: Literary History in a Time of Dissensus," *American Literature* 58 (March 1986): 101, cf. "The Problem of Ideology," 635.

58. Bercovitch, "The Problem of Ideology," 635–37, 640, 648; "Afterword," 423, 424–25, 427, 432, 435. See also Myra Jehlen, "Introduction: Beyond Transcendence," in Bercovitch and Jehlen, eds., *Ideology and Classic American Literature*, 1–18.

59. Emory Elliott, ed., *The Columbia Literary History of the United States* (New York: Columbia University Press, 1988), Introduction.

60. Bercovitch, "America as Canon and Context," 101; "The Problem of Ideology," 634, 636, 639ff., 650; "Afterword," 427, 431, 436.

61. Bercovitch, "The Problem of Ideology," 642; see 641–651 for the general reassessment of the "radicalism" of the American Renaissance, and "Afterword," 428–37.

62. Sacvan Bercovitch, "Preface," *Reconstructing American Literary History*, viii.

63. Bercovitch, "The Problem of Ideology," 650.

2. *New Historicism, New American Exceptionalism, and New American Studies: Versions of a New Synthesis*

1. Elizabeth Fox-Genovese, "Between Individualism and Fragmentation: American Culture and the New Literary Studies of Race and Gender," *American Quarterly* 42 (1990): 9, further references in text as "BIF."

2. Robert F. Berkhofer, Jr., "A New Context for a New American Studies?," *American Quarterly* 41 (1989): 591, further references in the text as "NC."

3. Richard Rorty, "Habermas and Lyotard on Postmodernism," *Praxis International* 4 (April 1984): 32–44.

4. Richard Rorty, *Consequences of Pragmatism (Essays: 1972—1980)* (Minneapolis: University of Minnesota Press, 1982), xviii.

5. Cornel West, "Afterword," in John Rajchman and Cornel West, eds., *Post-Analytic Philosophy* (New York: 1985), 267, cf. 269.

6. Christopher Norris, "Philosophy as a Kind of Narrative: Rorty on Postmodern Liberal Culture," *enclitic* 7 (Fall 1983): 157f.

7. Cf. John Rajchman, "Philosophy in America," in Rajchman and West, eds., *Post-Analytic Philosophy*, xxiii–xxvii.

8. Even though the term "New Historicism" now is often used to characterize all the very heterogeneous new programs of "rehistoricizing" literary criticism, I find it more helpful to apply the term only to the old *Representations* group (which by no means agrees on all relevant issues), if we want to develop a coherent critical argument.

9. Stephen Greenblatt, "Toward a Poetics of Culture," in H. Aram Veeser, ed., *The New Historicism* (New York: Routledge, 1989), 1–2.

10. Steven Knapp and Walter Benn Michaels, "Against Theory," in W. J. T. Mitchell, ed., *Against Theory: Literary Studies and the New Pragmatism* (Chicago: University of Chicago Press, 1985), 12, 26.

11. Steven Knapp and Walter Benn Michaels, "A Reply to Our Critics," in Mitchell, ed., *Against Theory*, 101, 104, 105, further references in the text as "RC."

12. Steven Knapp and Walter Benn Michaels, "A Reply to Richard Rorty: What Is Pragmatism?" in Mitchell, ed., *Against Theory*, 140, 142, 145, cf. 28.

13. Cf. Walter Benn Michaels, *The Gold Standard and the Logic of Naturalism: American Literature at the Turn of the Century* (Berkeley: University of California Press, 1987), 178, further references in the text as *GS*.

14. See my essay "Tradition, Discontinuity, and Counterdiscourse: Some Problems in American Radical Cultural Criticism Since the 1960s," in Günter H. Lenz and Kurt L. Shell, eds., *The Crisis of Modernity: Recent Critical Theories of Culture and Society in the United States and West Germany* (Frankfurt: Campus,1986), 191–249.

15. George Kateb, "Thinking about Human Extinction: (I) Nietzsche and Heidegger," *Raritan* 6 (Fall 1986): 1–28; "Thinking about Human Extinction (II): Emerson and Whitman," *Raritan* 6 (Winter 1986): 1–22, further references in the text as "EW"; and "Walt Whitman and the Culture of Democracy," *Political Theory* 18 (November 1990), 545–71, further references in the text as "WCD." Rosenblum's quote is from "A Response to George Kateb," in the same issue of *Political Theory*, 576.

16. For a full exposition of this argument see Kateb, "Thinking about Human Extinction: (I) Nietzsche and Heidegger."

17. Rosenblum, "A Response," 584–85.

18. See Leo Marx, "A Response to George Kateb," *Political Theory* 18 (November 1990): 597.

19. Stanley Cavell, *The Senses of Walden*, expanded ed. (San Francisco: North Point Press, 1981), 33, further references in the text as *SW*. Cavell's works are quoted as follows: *The Claim of Reason: Wittgenstein, Skepticism, Morality, and Tragedy* (New York: Oxford University Press, 1979), as *CR*; *Themes Out of School: Effects and Causes* (Chicago: University of Chicago Press, 1984), as *TOS*; *In Quest of the Ordinary: Lines of Skepticism and Romanticism* (Chicago: University of Chicago Press, 1988), as *IQO*; *This New Yet Unapproachable America: Lectures after Emerson after Wittgenstein* (Albuquerque, NM: Living Batch Press, 1989), as *TN*; *Conditions Handsome and Unhandsome: The Constitution of Emersonian Perfectionism* (LaSalle, IL: Open Court, 1990), as *CHU*.

20. For a general exposition of Cavell's notion of skepticism see his *The Claims of*

Reason and Michael Fischer's *Stanley Cavell and Literary Skepticism* (Chicago: University of Chicago Press, 1989).

21. Richard Poirier, *The Renewal of Literature: Emersonian Reflections* (New York: Random House, 1987).

22. Cornel West, *The American Evasion of Philosophy: A Genealogy of Pragmatism* (Madison: University of Wisconsin Press, 1989); Sacvan Bercovitch, "The A-Politics of Ambiguity in *The Scarlet Letter*," *New Literary History* 19 (1988): 629–54, "Hawthorne's A-Morality of Compromise," *Representations*, no. 24 (Fall 1988): 1–27, and "Emerson, Individualism, and the Ambiguities of Dissent," *South Atlantic Quarterly* 89 (Summer 1990): 623–62. Parts of the preceding three essays have been included in Bercovitch's *The Office of "The Scarlet Letter"* (Baltimore: Johns Hopkins University Press, 1991).

23. Philip Fisher, ed., "Introduction," *The New American Studies: Essays from "Representations"* (Berkeley: University of California Press, 1991), further references in the text as "Intro."

24. See also Fisher's essay, reprinted in *The New American Studies*, "Democratic Social Space: Whitman, Melville, and the Promise of American Transparency," *Representations*, no. 24 (Fall 1988): 60–101.

3. American Studies and Literary and Cultural Critique: The Question of Radical Traditions [in the 1980s]

1. See, e.g., Gene Wise, *American Historical Explanations: A Strategy for Grounded Inquiry* (Homewood, IL: Dorsey, 1973; rev. ed. Minneapolis: University of Minnesota Press, 1980); Wise, "Some Elementary Axioms for an American Culture Studies," *Prospects* 4 (1979): 517–47; Jay Mechling, "In Search of an American Ethnophysics," in Luther S. Luedtke, ed., *The Study of American Culture: Contemporary Conflicts* (Deland, FL: Everett/Edwards, 1977), 241–77; Mechling, "If They Can Build a Square Tomato: Notes Toward a Holistic Approach to Regional Studies," *Prospects* 4 (1979): 59–77; and the essays by Wise, Mechling, Karen Lystra, and R. Gordon Kelly in the "On the Shoulders of Giants" section, *Prospects* 8 (1983): 1–58.

2. See Cecil F. Tate, *The Search for a Method in American Studies* (Minneapolis: University of Minnesota Press, 1973); Gene Wise, " 'Paradigm Dramas' in American Studies: A Cultural and Institutional History of the Movement," *American Quarterly* 31, no. 3 (1979): 293–337; and two excellent review essays, Burton J. Bledstein, "American Studies: A Life and Times," *Michigan Quarterly Review 19* (Summer 1980): 410–20, and Giles Gunn, "American Studies as Cultural Criticism," *Yale Review* 72 (Winter 1983): 296–305.

3. Kenneth S. Lynn, "The Regressive Historians," *American Scholar* 47 (Autumn 1978): 471–500 (on Leo Marx, 480–89); "Looking Backward" (rev. of T. Jackson Lears, *No Place of Grace*), *New York Times Book Review*, January 10, 1982.

4. See my essay "American Studies—Beyond the Crisis? Recent Redefinitions and the Meaning of Theory, History, and Practical Criticism," *Prospects* 7 (1982): 53–113.

5. Cf. Daniel Bell, *The Cultural Contradictions of Capitalism* (New York: Basic Books, 1976); Gerald Graff, *Literature against Itself: Literary Ideas in Modern Society* (Chicago: University of Chicago Press, 1979); Eugene Goodheart, *Culture and*

the Radical Conscience (Cambridge, MA: Harvard University Press, 1973), and *The Failure of Criticism* (Cambridge, MA: Harvard University Press, 1978); and Christopher Lasch, *The Culture of Narcissism* (New York: Norton, 1978). See, e.g., Richard H. Pells, *Radical Visions and American Dreams: Culture and Social Thought in the Depression Years* (New York: Harper & Row, 1973), and Melvyn Dubofsky, "Not So 'Turbulent Years': Another Look at the American 1930's," *Amerikastudien /American Studies* 24, no. 1 (1979): 5–20.

6. See chapter 1, under Situating Theory: Political Criticism and America.

7. Sacvan Bercovitch, "The Problem of Ideology in American Literary History," *Critical Inquiry* 12 (Summer 1986): 639–40. For a critical assessment of the current "rehistoricization" in American literary and cultural studies see my essay "Reconstructing American Literary Studies: History, Difference, and Synthesis," in Günter H. Lenz, Hartmut Keil, and Sabine Broeck-Sallah, eds., *Reconstructing American Literary and Historical Studies* (Frankfurt: Campus; New York: St. Martin's Press, 1990), 21–50.

8. The importance of the World War II years is emphasized in Philip Gleason's review essay, "World War II and the Development of American Studies," *American Quarterly* 36 (1984): 343–58.

9. Richard H. Pells, *Radical Visions and American Dreams* (New York: Harper Torchbooks, 1974, orig. 1973).

10. Terry A. Cooney, *The Rise of the New York Intellectuals: "Partisan Review" and Its Circle, 1933–1945* (Madison: University of Wisconsin Press, 1986); Alexander Bloom, *Prodigal Sons: The New York Intellectuals and Their World* (New York: Oxford University Press, 1986); Alan M. Wald, *The New York Intellectuals: The Rise and Decline of the Anti-Stalinist Left from the 1930s to the 1980s* (Chapel Hill: University of North Carolina Press, 1987).

11. Richard H. Pells, *The Liberal Mind in a Conservative Age: American Intellectuals in the 1940s and 1950s* (New York: Harper & Row, 1985), 149f.

12. Gerald Graff, *Literature against Itself: Literary Ideas in Modern Society* (Chicago: University of Chicago Press, 1979), 85, further references in the text as *LAI*.

13. Gerald Graff, "Textual Leftism," *Partisan Review* 49 (Fall 1982): 558–76.

14. Gerald Graff, "The Pseudo-Politics of Interpretation," *Critical Inquiry* 9, no. 3 (March 1983): 597–610.

15. Gerald Graff, "An Ideological Map of American Literary Criticism," *Revue française d'études américaines* 16 (February 1983): 101.

16. Jane P. Tompkins, "Graff against Himself," *MLN* 96, no. 5 (December 1981): 1094.

17. Graff, "An Ideological Map," 105.

18. Christopher Lasch, *The Culture of Narcissism: American Life in an Age of Diminishing Expectations* (New York: W. W. Norton, 1991), 29, further references in the text as *CN*.

19. Christopher Lasch, "Politics and Social Theory: A Reply to the Critics," *Salmagundi* 46 (Fall 1979): 194, 195, 196, further references in the text as "PST."

20. Christopher Lasch, "Mass Culture Reconsidered," *Democracy* 1, no. 4 (1981): 7–22, further references in the text as "MCR."

21. Christopher Lasch, *The Minimal Self: Psychic Survival in Troubled Times* (New York: W. W. Norton, 1984), further references in the text as *MS*.

22. Christopher Lasch, "The Cultural Cold War: A Short History of the Congress for Cultural Freedom," in Barton Bernstein, ed., *Towards a New Past: Dissenting Essays in American History* (New York: Random House, 1968), 323, further references in the test as "CCW."

23. Christopher Lasch, *The New Radicalism in America, 1889–1963* (New York: W. W. Norton, 1965), and *The Agony of the American Left* (New York: Alfred A. Knopf, 1969).

24. Wise, "'Paradigm Dramas,'" 293.

25. Burton J. Bledstein, "American Studies: A Life and Times," *Michigan Quarterly Review* 19 (Summer 1980): 410–20, further references in the text as "AS."

26. Sacvan Bercovitch, *The American Jeremiad* (Madison: University of Wisconsin Press, 1978), 3, further references in the text as *AJ*.

27. Sacvan Bercovitch, *The Puritan Origins of the American Self* (New Haven, CT: Yale University Press, 1975).

28. Sacvan Bercovitch, "The Rites of Assent: Rhetoric, Ritual, and Ideology of American Consensus," in Sam B. Girgus, ed., *The American Self: Myth, Ideology, and Popular Culture* (Albuquerque: University of New Mexico Press, 1980), 5, further references in the text as "RA."

29. Sacvan Bercovitch, "New England's Errand Reprised," in John Higham and Paul Conkin, eds., *New Directions in American Intellectual History* (Baltimore: Johns Hopkins University Press, 1979), 100.

30. Alan Trachtenberg, *The Incorporation of America: Culture and Society in the Gilded Age* (New York: Hill & Wang, 1982), further references in the text as *IA*.

4. *American Cultural Critique: Toward a Politics of Postmodernism and Postcolonial Discourse [1970–1990]*

1. Fredric Jameson, *Marxism and Form: Twentieth-Century Dialectical Theories of Literature* (Princeton, NJ: Princeton University Press, 1974), ix, further references in the text as *MF*.

2. Fredric Jameson, *The Prison-House of Language: A Critical Account of Structuralism and Russian Formalism* (Princeton, NJ: Princeton University Press, 1974), 101–216.

3. Fredric Jameson, *The Political Unconscious: Narrative as a Socially Symbolic Act* (Ithaca, NY: Cornell University Press, 1994), 251, 286, further references in the text as *PU*; Jameson, *Marxism and Form*, 346.

4. Fredric Jameson, "Reification and Utopia in Mass Culture," *Social Text* 1 (Winter 1979): 140.

5. Stanley Aronowitz, as quoted in Frederick G. Hunter, "Commitment and Autonomy in Art: Antinomies of Frankfurt Esthetic Theory," *Berkeley Journal of Sociology* 30 (1985): 51.

6. Craig Owens, "The Discourse of Others: Feminists and Postmodernism," in Hal Foster, ed., *Postmodern Culture* (London: Pluto Press, 1985), 62.

7. Gayatri Spivak, "The Politics of Interpretations," *Critical Inquiry* 9 (September 1982): 277, further references in the text as "*PI*."

8. Victor Turner, *The Ritual Process: Structure and Anti-Structure* (New York: De Gruyter, 1995): xi, 96.

9. Hayden White, *The Content of the Form: Narrative Discourse and Historical Representation* (Baltimore: Johns Hopkins University Press, 1987), 204.

10. Fredric Jameson, "Periodizing the 60s," in Sohnya Sayres et al., eds., *The 60s Without Apology* (Minneapolis: University of Minnesota Press, 1984), further references in the text as "*PS*"; Jameson, "Foreword," Jean-François Lyotard, *The Postmodern Condition*, trans. Brian Massumi (Minneapolis: University of Minnesota Press, 1979); Jameson, *Postmodernism, Or the Logic of Late Capitalism* (Durham, NC: Duke University Press, 1991).

11. Frederic Jameson, "Marxism and Historicism," in *Syntax of History, The Ideologies of Theory: Essays, 1971–1986*, vol. 2 (Minneapolis: University of Minnesota Press, 1988), 150.

12. Fredric Jameson, "Criticism in History," in Norman Rudich, ed., *Weapons in Criticism: Marxism in America and the Literary Tradition* (Palo Alto, CA: Ramparts Press, 1976), 33, further references in the text as "*CH*."

13. Fredric Jameson, "Marxism and Teaching," *New Political Science* 1, nos. 2 and 3 (1979–80): 33.

14. Paul A. Bové, *Intellectuals in Power: A Genealogy of Critical Humanism* (New York: Columbia University Press, 1986), further references in the text as *IP*.

15. Paul A. Bové, "Closing up the Ranks: Xerxes' Hordes Are at the Pass," *Contemporary Literature* 26, no. 1 (Spring 1985): 91–106, and *Intellectuals in Power.*

16. Jim Merod, *The Political Responsibility of the Critic* (Ithaca, NY: Cornell University Press, 1987), 180–95.

17. Edward W. Said, *The World, the Text, and the Critic* (Cambridge, MA: Harvard University Press, 1983), 166, further references in the text as *WTC*.

18. Edward W. Said, "An Ethics of Language," review of Foucault's *The Archaeology of Knowledge and the Discourse on Language*, *Diacritics* 4, no. 2 (Summer 1974): 28–37, 29, further references in the text as "Ethics"; Said, *Beginnings: Intention and Method* (New York: Basic Books, 1975), 296–97, further references in the text as *B*.

19. Michel Foucault, *Power/Knowledge: Selected Interviews and Other Writings, 1972–1977*, ed. Colin Gordon (New York: Pantheon, 1980), 117, further references in the text as *P/K*.

20. Edward W. Said, *Orientalism* (New York: Random House, 1978), 31–72, further references in the text as *O*.

21. John Carlos Rowe, "'To Live outside the Law, You Must Be Honest': The Authority of the Margin in Contemporary Theory," *Cultural Critique* 1 (Winter 1985–86): 62.

22. Edward W. Said, *The Question of Palestine* (New York: Times Books, 1979), ix, x, further references in the text as *QP*.

23. Edward W. Said, *Covering Islam: How the Media and Experts Determine How We See the Rest of the World* (New York: Random House, 1981), further references in the text as *CI*.

24. James Clifford, "On Orientalism," *History and* Theory 19, no. 3 (October 1980): 212–14.

25. Edward W. Said, "Opponents, Audiences, Constituencies, and Community," *Critical Inquiry* 9, no. 1 (September 1982): 1, further references in the text as "Opp."

26. Frank Lentricchia, *Criticism and Social Change* (Chicago: University of Chicago Press, 1983), 11.

27. Edward W. Said, "Orientalism Reconsidered," *Cultural Critique* 1 (Fall 1985): 89–107, further references in the text as "*OR*."

28. Edward W. Said, "Representing the Colonized: Anthropology's Interlocutors," *Critical Inquiry* 15, no. 2 (Winter 1989): 205–25, further references in the text as "*RC*."

29. Gayatri Spivak, "Can the Subaltern Speak?" in Cary Nelson and Lawrence Grossberg, eds., *Marxism and the Interpretation of Culture* (Urbana-Champaign: University of Illinois Press, 1988), 271–315.

30. Edward Said, "Intellectuals in the Post-Colonial World," *Salmagundi* (Skidmore College), no. 70–71, "Intellectuals" (Spring–Summer 1986), 54f.

31. Michael M. J. Fischer and Mehdi Abadi, Debating Muslims: Cultural Dialogues in Postmodernity and Tradition (Madison: University of Wisconsin Press, 1990).

32. Edward W. Said, After the Last Sky: Palestinian Lives, photographs by Jean Mohr (New York: Pantheon Books, 1986), 6, further references in the text as *LS*.

5. *Postmodern Anthropology, Multicultural Critique, and American Culture Studies*

1. For a discussion of Matthiessen's and Ware's work and the early context of American Studies see my essay "American Studies and the Radical Tradition: From the 1930s to the 1960s," *Prospects* 12 (1987): 21–58, as well as Caroline Ware, ed., *The Cultural Approach to History* (New York: Columbia University Press, 1940).

2. A. L. Kroeber and Talcott Parsons, "The Concepts of Culture and of Social System," *American Sociological Review* 23 (October 1958): 582–83.

3. John William Ward, *Red, White, and Blue: Men, Books, and Ideas in American Culture* (New York: Oxford University Press, 1969), 5f., 9.

4. See my essay "American Studies—Beyond the Crisis? Recent Redefinitions and the Meaning of Theory, History, and Practical Criticism," *Prospects* 7 (1982): 53–113.

5. Dell Hymes, ed., *Reinventing Anthropology* (New York: Pantheon Books, 1972).

6. Jay Mechling, "In Search of an American Ethnophysics," in Luther Luedtke, ed., *The Study of American Culture: Contemporary Conflicts* (Deland, FL: Everett/Edwards, 1977), 241–77; John L. Caughey, "The Ethnography of Everyday Life: Theories and Methods for American Culture Studies," *American Quarterly* 34 (1982): 222–43, and "Ethnography, Introspection, and Reflexive Culture Studies," *Prospects* 7 (1982): 115–39.

7. See, e.g., Victor Turner, "Process, System, and Symbol: A New Anthropological Synthesis," *Daedalus* 1106, no. 3 (1977): 61–80, and *From Ritual to Theatre: The Human Seriousness of Play* (New York: Performing Arts Journal Publications, 1982); Clifford Geertz, *The Interpretation of Cultures* (New York: Basic Books, 1973), and *Local Knowledge: Further Essays in Interpretive Anthropology* (New York: Basic Books, 1983). Geertz's work is most pertinently discussed in Karen Lystra's essay "Clifford Geertz and the Concept of Culture," *Prospects* 8 (1983): 31–48, in Giles Gunn, *The Culture of Criticism and the Criticism of Culture* (New York: Oxford University Press, 1987), ch. 5, and in Vincent Pecora, "The Limits of Local Knowledge,"

in H. Aram Veeser, ed., *The New Historicism* (New York: Routledge, 1989), 243–76. Turner's influence can be seen, e.g., in Richard Beeman, "The New Social History and the Search for 'Community' in Colonial America," *American Quarterly* 29 (1977): 422–43, Robert B. Stepto's *From Behind the Veil: A Study of Afro-American Narrative* (Urbana-Champaign, IL: University of Illinois Press, 1979), Sacvan Bercovitch, *The American Jeremiad* (Madison: University of Wisconsin Press, 1978), esp. xii, 153, 188, 204f., and Michael Cowan, "Boundary as Center: Inventing an American Culture," *Prospects*12 (1987): 1–20. For an effort to combine in a study of mass culture ethnographic work Geertz's semiotic theory of culture, reader-response criticism, and Jameson's dialectic of ideology and utopia see Janice Radway's *Reading the Romance: Women, Patriarchy, and Popular Literature* (Chapel Hill: University of North Carolina Press, 1984). For a critical discussion of the "symbolic anthropology" of Geertz and Turner see Sherry B. Ortner, "Theory in Anthropology since the Sixties," *Comparative Studies in Society and History* 26 (January 1984): 127–32.

8. James Clifford and George E. Marcus, eds., *Writing Culture: The Poetics and Politics of Ethnography* (Berkeley: University of California Press, 1986), 120, further references in the text as *WC*; Stephen A. Tyler, "Ethnography, Intertextuality and the End of Description," *American Journal of Semiotics* 3, no. 4 (1985): 83–84. See also Vincent Crapanzano, "On the Writing of Ethnography," *Dialectical Anthropology* 2, no. 1 (1977): 69–73, and Clifford Geertz's critical look at these recent developments in his book *Works and Lives: The Anthropologist as Author* (Stanford, CA: Stanford University Press, 1988).

9. Talal Asad, ed., *Anthropology and the Colonial Encounter* (London: Ithaca Press, 1973); Diane Lewis, "Anthropology and Colonialism," *Current Anthropology* 14 (1973): 581–602 (with comments and reply); Michel Leiris, "L'Ethnographie devant le colonialisme (1950)," *Brisées* (Paris: Mercure de France, 1960), 125–45.

10. See also Stephen A. Tyler, "Postmodern Ethnography: From Document of the Occult to Occult Document," in Clifford and Marcus, eds., *Writing Culture*, esp. 123–24; and Paul Rabinow, "Representations Are Social Facts: Modernity and Postmodernity in Anthropology," in ibid., 234–41.

11. James Clifford, "On Ethnographic Authority," *Representations* 1 (Spring 1983): 133, reprinted in his *The Predicament of Culture: Twentieth Century Ethnography, Literature, and Art* (Cambridge, MA: Harvard University Press, 1988), 21–54. A recent example is the volume *Debating Muslims: Cultural Dialogues in Postmodernity and Tradition* by Michael M. J. Fischer and Mehdi Abedi (Madison: University of Wisconsin Press, 1990), which in its ambiguous title plays upon the dialogues, multiple discursive positionings, contestations, and polyphony among Muslims, between Muslims and non-Muslims, and between the two authors, one a Muslim insider and one a non-Muslim outsider.

12. Cf. Hayden White, "Critical Pluralism," *Critical Inquiry* 12 (Spring 1986): 488ff.

13. George E. Marcus and Michael M. J. Fischer, *Anthropology as Cultural Critique: An Experimental Moment in the Human Sciences* (Chicago: University of Chicago Press, 1986), 1f., 113ff., further references in the text as *ACC*.

14. The relation of surrealism and anthropology is discussed in James Clifford, "On Ethnographic Surrealism," *Comparative Studies in Society and History* 23 (1981), 539–64, reprinted in *The Predicament of Culture*, 117–51.

15. Gisela Welz, Unpublished paper on the problem of "going/staying native" in anthropological research and practice (1986). For a critical, wide-ranging discussion of the problem of "auto-ethnography" see David M. Hayano, "Auto-Ethnography: Paradigms, Problems, and Prospects," *Human Organization* 38 (Spring 1979): 99–104.

16. Paul Rabinow, *Reflections on Fieldwork in Morocco* (Berkeley: University of California Press, 1977), 6, 151–55, 162.

17. Roy Wagner, *The Invention of Culture*, rev. ed. (Chicago: University of Chicago Press, 1981), 4, further references in the text as *IC*.

18. As to the dialogic mode cf. Kevin Dwyer's essays "The Dialogic of Ethnology," *Dialectical Anthropology* 4, no. 3 (1979): 205–24, and "On the Dialogic of Fieldwork," *Dialectical Anthropology* 2, no. 2 (1977): 143–51.

19. George E. Marcus and Dick Cushman, "Ethnographies as Texts," *Annual Review of Anthropology* 11 (1982): 44, and Tyler, "Ethnography, Intertextuality," 91–93 (for a critique of the "ethnography of speaking" and "dialogic anthropology") and 95 (quote). See also Tyler's "Postmodern Ethnography," 126f., 129f., 138.

20. Rabinow, *Reflections*, 5–6. Cf. Vincent Crapanzano's experimental study *Tuhami: Portrait of a Moroccan* (Chicago: University of Chicago Press, 1980), esp. ch. 4. The critics of *Writing Culture* often focus on Stephen Tyler's highly evocative and dense contribution and base their polemic on an understanding of postmodernism as an "anything goes" playful arbitrariness that has nothing to do with the notion of postmodernity developed in the work of Clifford, Marcus, Rabinow, et al. This also applies to some of the feminist critiques discussed later.

21. Henrietta L. Moore, *Feminism and Anthropology* (Minneapolis: University of Minnesota Press, 1988), 190, cf. 194–95. Cf. Paul Rabinow's discussion of Foucault in "Representations Are Social Facts," 239–41, his critique of Clifford on 241–47, and his essay "Discourse and Power: On the Limits of Ethnographic Texts," *Dialectical Anthropology* 10 (1985): 1–13.

22. Cf. also Pecora's critique of Geertz's semiotic approach to other cultures, in "The Limits of Local Knowledge," 264–65; ibid., 223; Edward W. Said, "Representing the Colonized: Anthropology's Interlocutors," *Critical Inquiry* 15 (Winter 1989): 217. Marcus and Fischer emphasize the importance of "world historical political economy" in chapter 4 of *Writing Culture*; see also the essay by Marcus in *Writing Culture*, 165–93.

23. Said, "Representing the Colonized," 223; Gayatri Chakravorty Spivak, *In Other Worlds: Essays in Cultural Politics* (New York: Methuen, 1987), 207, 209–10, and "Can the Subaltern Speak?," in Cary Nelson and Lawrence Grossberg, eds., *Marxism and the Interpretation of Culture* (Urbana-Champaign: University of Illinois Press, 1988), 271–315.

24. See Marc Poster, *Foucault, Marxism, and History: Mode of Production versus Mode of Information* (Cambridge: Polity Press, 1984), and *Critical Theory and Poststructuralism: In Search of a Context* (Ithaca, NY: Cornell University Press, 1989); John Carlos Rowe, "Metavideo: Fictionality and Mass Culture in a Postmodern Economy,"

in Patrick O'Donnell and Robert Con Davis, eds., *Intertextuality and Contemporary American Fiction* (Baltimore: Johns Hopkins University Press, 1989), 214–35, and "Surplus Economies: Deconstruction, Ideology, and the Humanities," in Murray Krieger, ed., *The Aims of Representation: Subject/Text/History* (New York: Columbia University Press, 1987), 131–58.

25. Moore, *Feminism and Anthropology*, vi, 6, 193–94.

26. Marilyn Strathern, "An Awkward Relationship: The Case of Feminism and Anthropology," *Signs* 12 (1987): 277, 289–90. See also M. Z. Rosaldo, "The Use and Abuse of Anthropology: Reflections on Feminism and Cross-Cultural Understanding," *Signs* 5 (1980): 389–417, and Rabinow, "Representations Are Social Facts," 254–56.

27. Marilyn Strathern, "Out of Context: The Persuasive Fictions of Anthropology," *Current Anthropology* 28 (June 1987): 265, 267, 268–69, 289–90; cf. the critical discussion following the article (270–79).

28. Frances E. Mascia-Lees, Patricia Sharpe, and Colleen Ballerino Cohen, "The Postmodern Turn in Anthropology: Cautions from a Feminist Perspective," *Signs* 15 (1989): 9, 14, 16, 22, 27, 31–33.

29. Marcus and Cushman, "Ethnographies as Texts," 54–58. See also Michael M. J. Fischer's explicit use of an ethnography of literary and film productions to explore class-contested yet philosophically and emotionally similar strands of Iranian culture in his "Towards a Third-World Poetics: Seeing Through Short Stories and Films in the Iranian Culture Area," *Knowledge and Society* 5 (1984): 171–241.

30. Clifford, *The Predicament of Culture*, 12. See also Rabinow, "Representations Are Social Facts," 242.

31. Compare with footnote 34 in the original text.

32. Sacvan Bercovitch, "The Problem of Ideology in American Literary History," *Critical Inquiry* 12 (Summer 1986): 639; cf. his "America as Canon and Context: Literary History in a Time of Dissensus," *American Literature* 58 (1986): 99–107, and his "Afterword," in Sacvan Bercovitch and Myra Jehlen, eds., *Ideology and Classic American Literature* (Cambridge: Cambridge University Press, 1986), 418–46. See also Annette Kolodny, "The Integrity of Memory: Creating a New Literary History of the United States," *American Literature* 57 (1985): 291–307.

33. For a critical analysis of the dangers and the potential of the "new pluralism" see Bercovitch, "Afterword," 437–39. Cf. my essay "Reconstructing American Literary Studies: History, Difference, and Synthesis," in Günter H. Lenz, Hartmut Keil, and Sabine Broeck-Sallah, eds., *Reconstructing American Literary and Historical Studies* (Frankfurt: Campus; New York: St. Martin's Press, 1990), part 5.

34. David Harvey, *The Condition of Postmodernity: An Enquiry into the Origins of Cultural Change* (New York: Wiley, 1992), further references in the text as *CP*; Fredric Jameson, *Postmodernism, Or, The Cultural Logic of Late Capitalism* (Durham, NC: Duke University Press, 1991), further references in the text as *P*; Mark Poster, *The Mode of Information: Poststructuralism and Social Context* (Chicago: University of Chicago Press, 1990).

35. John Carlos Rowe, "The Writing Class," in Mark Poster, ed., *Politics, Theory, and Contemporary Culture* (New York: Columbia University Press, 1993), 41–82.

36. Andreas Huyssen, "Mapping the Postmodern," *New German Critique*, no. 33, "Modernity and Postmodernity" (1984): 5–52.

37. Tania Modleski, *Feminism Without Women: Culture and Criticism in a "Post-feminist" Age* (London: Routledge, 1991), 56.

38. Elizabeth Meese, *Crossing the Double Cross: The Practice of Feminist Criticism* (Chapel Hill: University of North Carolina Press, 1986); Modleski, *Feminism Without Women*, 41.

39. Hazel V. Carby, *Cultures in Babylon: Black Britain and African American* (London: Verso, 1999), 15.

40. Modleski, *Feminism Without Women*, 55; Homi Bhabha, *The Location of Culture* (New York: Routledge, 1994), 18–28.

41. Henry Louis Gates, Jr., *The Signifying Monkey: A Theory of African Literary Criticism* (New York: Oxford University Press, 1988), xxi.

42. Homi K. Bhabha, "The Other Question," *Screen* 24 (November–December 1983): 18–36; Bhabha, "Of Mimicry and Man: The Ambivalence of Colonial Discourse," *October*, no. 28 (Spring 1984): 125–33; Bhabha, "Representation and the Colonial Text: A Critical Exploration of Some Forms of Mimeticism," in Frank Gloversmith, ed., *The Theory of Reading* (Brighton: Harvester; Totowa, NJ: Barnes & Noble, 1984); Bhabha, "Signs Taken for Wonders: Questions of Ambivalence and Authority under a Tree Outside Delhi, May 1817," *Critical Inquiry* 12 (Autumn 1985), 144–65; and especially Bhabha, "The Commitment to Theory," *New Formations* 5 (Summer 1988): 5–23; Abdul R. JanMohamed, "The Economy of Manichean Allegory: The Function of Racial Difference in Colonialist Literature," *Critical Inquiry* 12 (Autumn 1985): 59–87; Abdul JanMohamed and David Lloyd, "Introduction: Toward a Theory of Minority Discourse," *Cultural Critique*, no. 6 (Spring 1987): 5–12, cf. no. 7 (Fall 1987): 5–17. For recent contributions to problems of "postcolonial discourse" cf., e.g., Stephen Slemon, "Monuments of Empire: Allegory/Counter-Discourse/Post-Colonial Writing," *Kunapipi* 9, no. 3 (1987): 1–16; "Post-Colonial Allegory and the Transformation of History," *Journal of Commonwealth Literature* 23, no. 1 (1988): 157–68; Helen Tiffin, "Post-Colonial Literatures and Counter-Discourse," *Kunapipi* 9, no. 3 (1987): 17–34; Tiffin, "Post-Colonialism, Post-Modernism and the Rehabilitation of Post-Colonial History," *Journal of Commonwealth Literature* 23, no. 1 (1988): 169–81; and the contributions to the Spring 1990 issue of *Research in African Literatures*, vol. 21. (I thank my colleague Dieter Riemenschneider for bringing these essays to my attention.)

43. Among the most challenging publications about the political, social, and educational implications of multiculturalism in the United States are Milton M. Gordon, ed., "America as a Multicultural Society," special issue, *Annals of the American Academy of Political and Social Sciences* 454 (March 1981); Diane Ravitch, "Multiculturalism: E Pluribus Plures," *American Scholar* 59 (Summer 1990): 337–54; Rosalie Pedalino Porter, *Forked Tongues: The Politics of Bilingual Education* (New York: Basic Books, 1990); Cornel West, "The New Cultural Politics of Difference," *October*, no. 53 (Summer 1990): 93–109; Dinesh D'Souza, *Illiberal Education: The Politics of Race and Sex on Campus* (New York: Free Press, 1991); and Arthur Schlesinger, Jr., *The Disuniting of America: Reflections on a Multicultural Society* (Knoxville, TN: Whittle Direct Books, 1991).

6. Cultural Hybridity and Diaspora in African American Literature and Criticism: Fictions of a Postmodern Multiculturalism

1. Günter H. Lenz, "American Studies as Multicultural Critique: Postmodern Culture, Interdisciplinarity, and Intercultural Identities," in Günter Blaicher and Brigitte Glaser, eds., *Anglistentag 1993 Eichstätt: Proceedings* (Tübingen: Max Niemeyer, 1994), 269–86.

2. For an outstanding discussion of the theoretical implications of a dialectics/dialogics of identity and difference in the intertextuality of black women writings, see Mae G. Henderson, "Speaking in Tongues: Dialogics, Dialectics, and the Black Woman Writer's Literary Tradition," in Cheryl A. Wall, ed., *Changing Our Own Words: Essays on Criticism, Theory, and Writing by Black Women* (New Brunswick, NJ: Rutgers University Press, 1989), 16–37, 215–21.

3. Günter H. Lenz, "Transnational American Studies: Negotiating Cultures of Difference—Multicultural Identities, Communities and Border Discourses," in Klaus J. Milich and Jeffrey Peck, eds., *Multiculturalism in Transit: A German–American Exchange* (Providence, RI: Berghahn), 129–66.

4. Ishmael Reed, *Shrovetide in Old New Orleans* (Garden City, NY: Doubleday, 1978), 252–57, cf. 37–43, 219–36, further references in the text as *SONO*.

5. See Günter Lenz, "'Ethnographies': American Culture Studies and Postmodern Anthropology," *Prospects* 16 (1991): 29–32.

6. Alice Walker, *The Temple of My Familiar* (New York: Harcourt Brace Jovanovich,1989), 83.

7. Alice Walker, "The Writer at Work," in Claudia Tate, ed., *Black Women Writers at Work* (New York: Continuum, 1983), 176, 184.

8. Bonnie Braendlin, "Alice Walker's *The Temple of My Familiar* as Pastiche," *American Literature* 68 (March 1996): 47–67.

9. Henry Louis Gates, Jr., *The Signifying Monkey: A Theory of Afro-American Literary Criticism* (New York: Oxford University Press, 1988), xxvi–xxvii, 103–7, 124.

10. Toni Morrison, "The Site of Memory," in Russell Ferguson, Martha Gever, Trinh T. Minh-ha, Cornel West, eds., *Out There: Marginalization and Contemporary Culture* (Cambridge, MA: MIT Press, 1990), 303, further references in the text as "*SOM*."

11. Gloria Naylor and Toni Morrison, "A Conversation," *Southern Review* 21 (1985): 583–85.

12. Toni Morrison, "Rootedness: The Ancestor as Foundation," in Mari Evans, ed., *Black Women Writers (1950–1980): A Critical Evaluation* (Garden City, NY: Doubleday Anchor, 1984), 339–45, further references in the text as "*R*."

13. Toni Morrison, *Beloved* (New York: Alfred A. Knopf, 1987), 274, further references in the text as *B*.

14. Toni Morrison, *Playing in the Dark: Whiteness and the Literary Imagination* (Cambridge, MA: Harvard University Press, 1992), 44, further references in the text as *PID*.

15. Sherley Ann Williams, *Dessa Rose* (New York: William Morrow, 1986), further references in the text as *DR*. See also Herbert Aptheker, *American Negro Slaves Revolts* (New York: International, 1974), and Angela Davis, "Reflections on the Black Woman's Role in the Community of Slaves," *Massachusetts Review* 13, no. 1–2, "Women: An Issue" (1972): 81–100.

16. Henderson, "Speaking in Tongues."

17. Gloria Naylor, *Mama Day* (New York: Random House, 1988), 175, further references in the text as *MD*.

18. Charles Johnson, *Being and Race: Black Writing since 1970* (Bloomington: Indiana University Press, 1990), 10, further references in the text as *BAR*.

19. Charles Johnson, *Middle Passage* (New York, Atheneum, 1990), 29, 27, further references in the text as *MP*.

20. Ashraf H. A. Rushdy, "The Phenomenology of the Allmuseri: Charles Johnson and the Subject of the Narrative of Slavery," *African American Review* 26, no. 3 (Fall 1991): 393.

21. Brian Fagel, "Passages from the Middle: Coloniality and Postcoloniality in Charles Johnson's *Middle Passage*," *African American Review* 30, no. 4 (1996): 632.

22. John Edgar Wideman, "The Architectonics of Fiction," *Callaloo* 13 (Winter 1990): 42–46, further references in the text as "*AF*."

23. John Edgar Wideman, *Reuben* (New York: Henry Holt, 1987), further references in the text as *R*.

24. John Edgar Wideman, quoted in James W. Coleman, *Blackness and Modernism: The Literary Career of John Edgar Wideman* (Jackson: University Press of Mississippi, 1989), 116, further references in the text as *BAM*.

25. Paule Marshall, *Daughters* (New York: Atheneum, 1991), further references in the text as *D*.

26. Daryl Cumber Dance, "An Interview with Paule Marshall," *Southern Review* 28 (January1992): 2, further references in the text as "*IPM*."

27. Stelamaris Coser, *Bridging the Americas: The Literature of Paule Marshall, Toni Morrison and Gayl Jones* (Philadelphia: Temple University Press, 1995), 2, 9, 169–73.

28. Carole Boyce Davies, *Black Women, Writing and Identity: Migrations of the Subject* (New York: Routledge, 1994), 119, further references in the text as *BW*.

29. bell hooks, *Yearning: Race, Gender, and Cultural Politics* (Boston, MA: South End Press, 1990), 25, further references in the text as *Y*.

30. Wahneema Lubiano, "Shuckin' Off the African-American Native Other: What's 'Po-Mo' Got to Do with It?" *Cultural Critique* 18:4 (Spring 1991): 149–86, further references in the text as "*SO*."

31. Cornel West, "The Postmodern Crisis of Black Intellectuals," in Lawrence Grossberg, Cary Nelson, ande Paul Treichler, eds., *Cultural Studies* (New York: Routledge, 1992), 690, further references in the text as "*PC*."

32. Cornel West, *Beyond Eurocentrism and Multiculturalism: Prophetic Thought in Postmodern Times*, vol. 1 (Monroe, ME: Common Courage Press, 1993), 121, and *Beyond Eurocentrism and Multiculturalism: Prophetic Reflections—Notes on Race and Power in America*, vol. 2 (Monroe, ME: Common Courage Press, 1993), 38, further references in the text as *BEM* 1 and *BEM* 2, respectively.

33. Cornel West, "The New Cultural Politics of Difference," *Columbia University Academic Commons* 53 (1990), 101, further references in the text as "*NCPD*."

34. Paul Gilroy, *The Black Atlantic: Modernity and Double Consciousness* (Cambridge, MA: Harvard University Press, 1993).

35. Henry Louis Gates, Jr., *Figures in Black: Words, Signs, and the Racial Self*

(New York: Oxford University Press, 1987), and *The Signifying Monkey: A Theory of Afro-American Literary Criticism* (New York: Oxford University Press, 1988), further references in the text as *FIB* and *SM*, respectively.

36. Henry Louis Gates, Jr., "The Blackness of Blackness: A Critique of the Sign and the Signifying Monkey," *Critical Inquiry* 9, no. 4 (June 1983): 685–723; Gates, ed., *Black Literature and Literary Theory* (New York: Methuen, 1984), further references in the text as *BLLT*.

37. Charles Rowell, "An Interview with Henry Louis Gates, Jr.," *Callaloo* 14, no. 2 (1991): 444–63.

38. Henry Louis Gates, Jr., *Loose Canons: Notes on the Culture Wars* (New York: Oxford University Press, 1992), xiii, further references in the text as *LC*.

39. Hazel V. Carby, "The Multicultural Wars," in Gina Dent, ed., *Black Popular Culture* (Seattle: Bay Press, 1992), 187–99.

40. Henry Louis Gates, Jr., "Notes on the Culture Wars: Identities in Dialogue," *Profession 93* (1993): 10, further references in the text as "*NCW*."

41. Gates, Henry Louis, Jr., "Pluralism and Its Discontents," *Contention* 2 (Fall 1992): 74–75, further references in the text as "*PID*."

42. Lionel Trilling, *The Liberal Imagination: Essays in Literature and Society* (New York: Viking Press, 1950).

43. Henry Louis Gates, Jr., "Good-Bye Columbus? Notes on the Culture of Criticism," *American Literary History* 3, no. 4 (1991), 712, further references in the text as "*GBC*."

44. Teodros Kiros, "The Colors of Multiculturalism: An Interview with Henry Louis Gates," *New Political Science* 38–39 (Winter–Spring 1996–97): 181.

45. Paul Gilroy, *Small Acts: Thoughts on the Politics of Black Cultures* (London: Serpent's Tail, 1993); Stuart Hall, "Cultural Identity and Diaspora," in Jonathan Rutherford, ed., *Identity: Community,Culture, Difference* (London: Lawrence & Wishart, 1990), 222–37; Kobena Mercer, *Welcome to the Jungle: New Positions in Black Cultural Studies* (New York: Routledge, 1993).

46. Néstor García Canclini, *Hybrid Cultures: Strategies for Entering and Leaving Modernity* (Minneapolis: University of Minnesota Press, 1995), xxi.

47. See, in Chicano/Chicana/Latin American Studies, José David Saldívar, *The Dialectics of Our America: Genealogy, Cultural Critique, and Literary History* (Durham, NC: Duke University Press, 1991), and *Border Matters: Remapping American Cultural Studies* (Berkeley: University of California Press, 1997); in Native American Studies, Arnold Krupat, *Ethnocriticism: Ethnography, History, Literature* (Berkeley: University of California Press, 1992).

48. See Homi K. Bhabha, *The Location of Culture* (New York: Routledge, 1994); Wolfgang Iser, "On Translatability: Variables of Interpretation," in Wolfgang Riehle and Hugo Keiper, eds., *Anglistentag 1994 Graz, Proceeding* (Tübingen: Max Niemeyer, 1994), 299–310; Utz Riese, "Cultural Translation? Möglichkeiten und Unmöglichkeit der Übersetzung von Kulturen im postkolonialen Raum," *Weimarer Beiträge* 44 (1988): 74–91.